JAUNTING ON THE SCORIAC TEMPESTS

Borgo Press Books by BRIAN STABLEFORD

Algebraic Fantasies and Realistic Romances: More Masters of Science Fiction
Beyond the Colors of Darkness and Other Exotica
Changelings and Other Metamorphic Tales
A Clash of Symbols: The Triumph of James Blish
The Cosmic Perspective and Other Black Comedies
The Cure for Love and Other Tales of the Biotech Revolution
The Devil's Party: A Brief History of Satanic Abuse
The Dragon Man: A Novel of the Future
Firefly: A Novel of the Far Future
The Gardens of Tantalus and Other Delusions
Glorious Perversity: The Decline and Fall of Literary Decadence
Gothic Grotesques: Essays on Fantastic Literature
The Haunted Bookshop and Other Apparitions
Heterocosms: Science Fiction in Context and Practice
In the Flesh and Other Tales of the Biotech Revolution
The Innsmouth Heritage and Other Sequels
Jaunting on the Scoriac Tempests and Other Essays on Fantastic Literature
The Moment of Truth: A Novel of the Future
News of the Black Feast and Other Random Reviews
An Oasis of Horror: Decadent Tales and Contes Cruels
Opening Minds: Essays on Fantastic Literature
Outside the Human Aquarium: Masters of Science Fiction, Second Edition
The Path of Progress and Other Black Melodramas
Slaves of the Death Spiders and Other Essays on Fantastic Literature
The Sociology of Science Fiction
Space, Time, and Infinity: Essays on Fantastic Literature
The Tree of Life and Other Tales of the Biotech Revolution
Yesterday's Bestsellers: A Voyage Through Literary History

JAUNTING ON THE SCORIAC TEMPESTS

AND OTHER ESSAYS ON FANTASTIC LITERATURE

by

Brian Stableford

THE BORGO PRESS

An Imprint of Wildside Press LLC

MMIX

I.O. Evans Studies in the Philosophy and Criticism of Literature
ISSN 0271-9061

Number Forty-Four

Copyright © 1996, 1999, 2000, 2001, 2002, 2004, 2006, 2009 by Brian Stableford

All rights reserved.
No part of this book may be reproduced in any form without the expressed written consent of the publisher.

www.wildsidepress.com

FIRST EDITION

CONTENTS

About the Author 6
Introduction 7

PART ONE: INTRODUCTIONS TO THE EARLY WORKS OF M. P. SHIEL

Jaunting on the Scoriac Tempests and Reeling Bullions of Hell:
    Shapes in the Fire 13
The Decadent Detective: *Prince Zaleski* 22
The Black and White Mystery of *The Purple Cloud* 32
The Durance of Decadence: *The Pale Ape and Other Pulses* 42

PART TWO: NINETEENTH-CENTURY WRITERS

Edward Lytton Bulwer and the Gothic Lifestyle 51
Humphry Davy's Dream 64
Resisting Panthea's Siren Song; Robert Hunt and the Poetry
    of Science 80
Haunted by the Pagan Past: Vernon Lee 108

PART THREE: TWENTIETH-CENTURY WRITERS

J. G. Ballard 123
Lord, What Fools These Mortals Be! Confrontation with Death
    in James Morrow's *The Eternal Footman* 152
Dean R. Koontz 166
Terry Pratchett 182

Bibliography 198
Index 207

ABOUT THE AUTHOR

BRIAN STABLEFORD was born in Yorkshire in 1948. He taught at the University of Reading for several years, but is now a full-time writer. He has written many science fiction and fantasy novels, including *The Empire of Fear*, *The Werewolves of London*, *Year Zero*, *The Curse of the Coral Bride*, and *The Stones of Camelot*. Collections of his short stories include *Sexual Chemistry: Sardonic Tales of the Genetic Revolution*, *Designer Genes: Tales of the Biotech Revolution*, and *Sheena and Other Gothic Tales*. He has written numerous nonfiction books, including *Scientific Romance in Britain, 1890-1950*, *Glorious Perversity: The Decline and Fall of Literary Decadence*, and *Science Fact and Science Fiction: An Encyclopedia*. He has contributed hundreds of biographical and critical entries to reference books, including both editions of *The Encyclopedia of Science Fiction* and several editions of the library guide, *Anatomy of Wonder*. He has also translated numerous novels from the French language, including several by the feuilletonist Paul Féval.

Jaunting on the Scoriac Tempests, by Brian Stableford

INTRODUCTION

The first four essays in this book all featured as introductions to a series of new editions of the works of M. P. Shiel, issued by Tartarus Press. The first one had originated as a relatively brief essay in a Salem Press reference book before being expanded to serve as a "Centenary Essay on *Shapes in the Fire*" in the third issue of the *Redondan Cultural Foundation Newsletter* (November 1996). Ray Russell of Tartarus Press asked to reprint the longer version in the Tartarus Press edition of *Shapes in the Fire* in 2000, and I revised it again to serve that purpose.

In order to conserve a uniformity of outlook and build up a consistent critical account of Shiel's early work, Ray Russell subsequently asked me to introduce his editions of *Prince Zaleski* (2002), *The Purple Cloud* (2004) and *The Pale Ape and Other Pulses* (2006). The series may well continue in future, and it is possible that I might be invited to extend the set further, but the four items reprinted here form a coherent unit, by virtue of examining the four Shiel books that feature his most flamboyant exercises in "Decadent style". (Because they were designed to stand alone as introductions to separate volumes, there is a certain amount of repetition in the four articles that is redundant here but whose removal would have caused dire problems of continuity; I apologize for any irritation this may cause.)

As the essays explain, the English Decadent Movement inspired by the example of the French Movement that flourished between 1884 and 1900 was short-lived, its brief fashionability being rudely slain by the trial and conviction of its most prominent figurehead, Oscar Wilde. Decadent prose fiction flourished in England for a few years in the early 1890s, and was then put aside and largely forgotten, but while it lasted Shiel was by far its most adventurous exponent. His work in this vein has always fascinated me, because of my keen interest in the mechanics of Decadent style and the manner in which it extrapolated the various aspects of its typical subject matter. More than any other writer, Shiel had a thorough understanding of what Edgar Allan Poe had been attempting to do in his own pioneering experiments in the methodology of short fiction and prose poetry, and attempted to carry those experiments forward in all three of the key genres originated by Poe: psychological horror fiction, scientific romance and detective fiction.

* * * * * * *

The Decadent Movements of the nineteenth-century *fin-de-siècle* involved scholarly fantasies and lifestyle fantasies as well as literary fantasies, and in that regard their ultimate precursors had historical roots that extended back through Charles Baudelaire and Edgar Allan Poe to English models connected with the Gothic elements of the English Romantic movement, especially to the literary work and lifestyle of Lord Byron. In England, those exemplars inspired a different pattern of historical development, carried forward into the Victorian era in a spirit of careful dilution. One of the key figures in that revisionist process was the writer who used various versions of his name before being elevated to the peerage as Baron Lytton of Knebworth.

I wrote a couple of reference-book articles on Lytton in the 1980s and expanded one of them into an essay on *The Last Days of Pompeii* for a series of articles I did for *Million: The Magazine of Popular Fiction*, some of which were reprinted by The Borgo Press as *Yesterday's Bestsellers*. Although there is always a certain risk in writing critical essays on contemporary writers, arising from the possibility of bumping into them in the flesh, one is usually quite safe writing about Victorian authors—but not in this instance. In the course of a Dedalus launch party held at the French Institute in London, I was unexpectedly confronted by a intimidatingly tall man, who looked down at me from a great height and said: "I hear that you've written some articles about Bulwer-Lytton". When I admitted that I had, he said; "He was my ancestor; I'm Henry Cobbold". Fortunately, he was not in search of retribution for any accidental slight, but only wanted to recruit me to the cause of attempting to reignite some contemporary interest in the long-neglected author.

Henry invited me to meet his father, the current tenant of Bulwer's old stately home, Knebworth. Lord Cobbold was kind enough to invite me in his turn to a small gathering of scholars at the House of Lords—a delightful and fascinating experience. With the help of John Sutherland, the Cobbolds organized an academic conference at

University College, London, on 5 July 2000, for which I wrote a paper on "Edward Lytton Bulwer and the Gothic Lifestyle". Alas, the paper proved a trifle too flamboyant for the taste of Alan Christensen, the dour academic charged with the task of editing the conference papers for publication, and he rejected it contemptuously, thus ending my brief association with the Bulwer bandwagon. This is the first time it has appeared in print.

My research into Bulwer's work dovetailed with more widely-ranging research I had long been doing into the interconnections between nineteenth-century science and English literature. Having published a supposedly-definitive study of *Scientific Romance in Britain, 1890-1950* in 1985, I had continued to extrapolate that study back in time, with particular reference to the lingering influence of Romanticism on scientific romance. One writer who seemed crucial in this regard was the Romantic poet-turned-scientist, Humphry Davy, whose *Consolations in Travel* had been a key influence on the French astronomer and writer of visionary fantasies Camille Flammarion. I was subsequently asked to compile a new translation of Flammarion's classic scientific romance *Lumen* for Wesleyan University Press, and was able to offer an account of the inspiration Flammarion had drawn from *Consolations in Travel* more detailed than the essay included here could contain. "Davy's Dream" first appeared in *The New York Review of Science Fiction* 149 (January 2001).

Another Romantic poet-turned-scientist who probably took some inspiration from *Consolations in Travel* was Robert Hunt. "Resisting Panthea's Siren Song", which first appeared in *Foundation* 85 (Summer 2002), was the result of one of the short bursts of scholarly enthusiasm to which I sometimes fall prey. Many years before, in 1975, the book dealer John Eggeling had drawn my attention to a curious book by the minor Scottish poet William Wilson entitled *A Little Earnest Book Upon a Great Old Subject* (1851), in which Wilson had coined the term "science-fiction" seventy-five years before Hugo Gernsback. Although I could not afford to buy the copy of the book that John was offering for sale (he eventually sold it to Sam Moskowitz) I obtained a copy through Inter-Library Loan from the National Library of Scotland, and wrote an article about Wilson's characterization of the then-imaginary genre of "science-fiction". The article was published in *Foundation* in 1976 and reprinted in my Borgo Press collection *Opening Minds*.

The article noted that Wilson claimed to have obtained the idea of "science-fiction" from reading a book he described as "Hunt's

Poetry of Science"—a title that I could not trace at the time, although I did riffle through the many pages of the British Museum catalogue devoted to authors named Hunt (not attentively enough, by the time I reached authors whose first names began with R, to pick up the title as I scanned the pages). In 2000, however, I came across a reference to a book called *Panthea* by Robert Hunt, which prompted me to check the catalogue of the London Library in case they might have a copy. They did—although it was filed in the Theology section rather than the Fiction section—but it was the next item in the catalogue, *The Poetry of Science*, that increased my excitement as it set a bell ringing in my memory.

I borrowed and read both books, realized the significance of Hunt's career and published works to the obscure literary history connecting British Romanticism with scientific romance, and unearthed everything I possibly could in order to explain that relevance at length. I could not have done that without the academic resources I possessed by virtue of holding borrower's cards for the libraries at King's College, Winchester, where I was then doing some part-time teaching, and the University of Reading. Both library cards have now been revoked, so this will presumably be the last authentic academic article I will be able to write.

* * * * * * *

The small group of writers who assisted M. P. Shiel in the development of English Decadent prose also included Vernon Lee, another writer whose works in that vein have long been a source of fascination to me. "Haunted by the Pagan Past" arose from a brief and ill-fated association with Barbara and Christopher Roden's Ash-Tree Press, the Canadian publisher on whom Ray Russell had modelled Tartarus Press.

In the late 1990s I attempted to interest the Rodens in a volume of translations of work by the French Decadent writer Jean Lorrain, about which they seemed rather dubious but which they did not actually reject. Christopher Roden did, however, ask whether I would like to write the introduction to an omnibus of Vernon Lee's supernatural fiction that they were planning to issue. In the hope that they might take the Lorrain collection, I agreed, although I was a little anxious about the fact that Lee's work was not yet in the public domain in Europe. I also photocopied some esoteric items from the London Library collection to augment the contents of the Lee volume, for which I proposed the title *Haunted by the Pagan Past*.

I sent off the introduction and other materials and waited—and waited. When nothing had happened after nine months or so I sent an email enquiring what the state of play was, and when I got no reply I submitted the Lorrain collection to Tartarus and gave the introduction to Keith Brooke, who had asked me for an essay to put on his *Infinity Plus* website; it went up there in 2001. Shortly thereafter I got an email from Christopher Roden (from an address that was not the same as the seemingly-redundant one to which I had sent mine) saying that he was now ready to go ahead with the Lee collection, provided that I would rewrite my introduction, which he thought unsatisfactory. When I explained that I had despaired of hearing from him and given the introduction away to someone else he took offence, and any chance of any future collaboration went out of the window.

(The problem of defunct email addresses—made worse by the fact that most such addresses seem only to be viable for short periods of time before they are drowned in spam—is a curse far worse than the mislaid letters that provided plot levers for so many Victorian novels. I sometimes wonder how much work I might have lost by virtue of the fact that the first email address I acquired had to be abandoned several years ago, although I was unable to inform its users of the change because the computer holding the address book had abruptly given up the ghost. The redundant address still reappears regularly in various directories, and is thus likely to be used by anyone attempting to make contact—no one in the world of publishing will any longer deign to use actual mail for anything other than previously-negotiated contracts.)

* * * * * * *

The four essays on contemporary writers were all commissioned (by email) by various editors. The one on J. G. Ballard was written for the fifth supplement to Scribner's continually-updated survey of *British Writers*, where it appeared in 1999. "Lord, What Fools These Mortals Be! Confrontation with Death in The Eternal Footman" was written for a special issue of the journal *Paradoxa: Studies in World Literary Genres* (vol. 5 no. 12; 1999) devoted to Morrow's works. Jim Morrow was kind enough to provide me with a manuscript copy of the then-unpublished novel to enable me to write the article.

The last two essays, on Dean Koontz and Terry Pratchett, were commissioned by Gale, a prolific publisher of reference books, which became the first to move most of its work into databases available to subscribers on the World Wide Web. Rumor has it that Gale became part of a larger organization shortly thereafter—that is the sort of thing that happens all the time in modern publishing—but whether that was responsible for the lack of subsequent communication I have no idea. At any rate, my log of completed work informs me that I delivered the two essays on 22 March 2004, but I have no idea whether or not they were subsequently published—or, if so, in what form. (Because I no longer have access to an academic library I cannot get into the Gale databases, and my attempts to determine whether the articles exist by ingenious use of Google have proved futile.) My suspicion is that they were never used, having been consigned to the dustbin due to some abrupt change of policy, but they might actually exist somewhere in the gated communities of cyberspace, which humble artisans like me are unable to explore, no matter how many of their building materials we might be hired to supply.

* * * * * * *

Because these essays were written to different publishers' briefs, various styles of referencing were employed therein. Although I have combined all the bibliographies into one, I have not unified the formats of the citations in the text, or inserted specific page references where none were initially included. I have deleted the page references originally included in the Morrow article, which were to the manuscript rather than the published book. Again, I apologize for any irritation that this inconsistency might cause.

—Brian Stableford, Reading
August 2006

JAUNTING ON THE SCORIAC TEMPESTS AND REELING BULLIONS OF HELL

Shapes in the Fire was the second collection of M. P. Shiel's short stories to be published by John Lane, one of the two publishers who played host to the fledgling English Decadent Movement. By the time it was issued, in 1896, that Movement was dead, having been murdered in its cradle by the Marquess of Queensberry; its figurehead and principal theorist, Oscar Wilde, had been despatched to Reading Gaol via Wormwood Scrubs. The word "decadence" subsequently acquired such a terrifying notoriety that Arthur Symons abruptly decided that his history of "The Decadent Movement in Literature" would have to be retitled *The Symbolist Movement in Literature*, and that it would concentrate narrowly on French writers—thus concealing by omission the fact that the aesthetic priorities of literary Decadence had briefly attained a wonderful extreme in a precious handful of collections of vivid English prose.

Of all these collections—others issued from the pens of Wilde, Count Stenbock, Arthur Machen, Vincent O'Sullivan and R. Murray Gilchrist—*Shapes in the Fire* is the boldest and the most flamboyant. As well as two *contes*, three *nouvelles* and a narrative poem, it contains a literary manifesto that extends and elaborates the arguments set out in Wilde's essay on "The Decay of Lying". The essay does not reflect Shiel's final thoughts on such matters—another essay, first used as a preface to *This Knot of Life*, was eventually given pride of place in his collection of essays on *Science, Life and Literature*—but youthful exuberance is not always better tempered by mature reflection and this might be one of the cases in which recklessness may be given preference over caution.

Literary decadence was defined and described by Théophile Gautier in a preface that he added to the third edition of Baudelaire's *Les Fleurs du Mal* after the author's death. According to that prospectus the Decadent style is "no other thing than Art arrived at that point of extreme maturity that determines civilizations which have

13

grown old; ingenious, complicated, clever, full of delicate hints and refinements, gathering all the delicacies of speech, borrowing from technical vocabularies, taking color from every palette, tones from all musical instruments, contours vague and fleeting, listening to translate subtle confidences, confessions of depraved passions and the odd hallucinations of a fixed idea turning to madness".

Gautier goes on to say that "contrary to the classical style, [the Decadent style] admits of backgrounds where the specters of superstition, the haggard phantoms of dreams, the terrors of night, remorse which leaps out and falls back noiselessly, obscure fantasies that astonish the day, and all that the soul in its deepest depths and innermost caverns conceals of darkness, deformity and horror, move together confusedly."

The modest apologia for the doctrine of art for art's sake and the tentative celebration of fantastic embellishment that Wilde subsequently set forth in "The Decay of Lying" is more restrained and far more flirtatious, by virtue of being fitted for an audience of Victorians. It embeds its arguments within a dialogue between two aesthetic amateurs, whose views the unsympathetic reader is politely permitted to discount. Shiel evidently felt this procedure far too effete. *His* dialogue recruits no less a personage than the prime minister of England, Lord X—, to serve as a sounding-board for the outspoken ideas of the dedicated artist "O. O'Malley Phipps". (Phipps was, of course, the second of Shiel's given names; Wilde's given names were Oscar O'Flahertie Wills.)

The prime minister featured in this dialogue is obviously Archibald Philip Primrose, Lord Rosebery, a flamboyant figure by Victorian standards. Rosebery, who had succeeded William Ewart Gladstone as leader of the Liberal party, held the position for only fifteen unhappy months, impotently presiding over a divided cabinet against the steadfast opposition of the House of Lords, before he was succeeded in June 1895 by the dogged Unionist Lord Salisbury. The moral backlash that consumed Oscar Wilde was in part occasioned by distress in high places regarding the allegedly decadent lifestyle of Rosebery, an alleged homosexual who surrounded himself with a coterie of young men. We can only guess as to how close Shiel's acquaintance with Rosebery might have been, but he certainly knew members of Rosebery's circle. It might or might not be significant that Rosebery inherited the Liberal leadership when Gladstone vacillated over the issue of increasing appropriations to the navy; Shiel's first novel, *The Yellow Danger*, serialized in 1898 as "The Empress of the Earth", was a naval romance whose political rhetoric closely echoes Rosebery's unashamed Imperialism.

In the dialogue, Phipps defines fine art as "a self-consciously-wise product of the pure imagination". Following Coleridge, he draws a distinction between fancy ("the adventure-luck of the touring soul") and the imagination ("Euclid grown Orphic...winged Reason...the mathematics of fancy") and suggests that "gross" (*i.e.*, popular) art consists of products of fancy and observation, without the vaulting ambition of authentic imagination. Following Walter Pater, he places music highest among the arts and suggests that all art should aspire to its condition because "in proportion as the other branches of art cease to be observational—that is, to be in close relation with actual 'life'—in that proportion they rise to the height of the highest, or music".

Like Joris-Karl Huysmans' overblown *alter ego* Jean Des Esseintes, Shiel's Phipps is not a man to dabble in half-measures. He seems to agree with Des Esseintes—who opined that the perfect form of Decadent prose is the prose poem—although he makes his own case in reverse, couching it as an assault on the novel. This dismissal is appended to his argument to the effect that women are incapable of true artistic creativity; the fact that they are so accomplished in novel-writing is held up as "an indication to a waking mind that there is something fearfully wrong with the *novel*; that it is not, in fact, a true art-form."

Phipps goes on to argue that no true artist should write for money, and that the novel is primarily a money-making device, in whose toils artistic ambition is inevitably ground down to mere prostitution. Shiel was, of course, to go on to write a great many novels himself, having acquired the habit by writing serials for C. Arthur Pearson's relentlessly middlebrow periodicals. There is no reason for lovers of his work to regret this apparent betrayal of his *alter ego*'s ideals, given that, if he had not first written "The Empress of the Earth", he might not have been able to find a publisher for that undeniable masterpiece *The Purple Cloud*—and, after all, a man must live. It is worth bearing in mind, though, that *Shapes in the Fire* was probably the first and perhaps the last work that Shiel penned *entirely* for art's sake. For this reason, there is perhaps no other work in his extensive canon that better defines what he was, and of what he was capable.

* * * * * * *

Shiel's principal literary influence was Edgar Allan Poe. Poe was not the originator of Gothic lifestyle fantasy—that honor belongs to Lord Byron—but he had become its torch-bearer-in-chief when Victorianism had obliterated Byronism in England. The eponymous hero of Shiel's first John Lane collection, *Prince Zaleski* (1895), is an obvious extrapolation of Poe's amateur detective C. Auguste Dupin. As such, he is one of many, but he is the only one to have taken the lifestyle fantasy element of Dupin's character to a further extreme.

The introductory paragraphs of "The Murders in the Rue Morgue" explain how the relatively well-off narrator discovers a kindred spirit in the eccentric Dupin, and is thus permitted "the expense of renting, and furnishing in a style which suited the rather fantastic gloom of our common temper, a time-eaten and grotesque mansion, long deserted through superstitions into which we did not inquire, and tottering to its fall in a retired and desolate portion of the Faubourg St Germain". There the two men live a secluded life, admitting no visitors and going out only by night. "It was a freak of fancy in my friend," Poe's narrator observes, "to be enamored of the night for her own sake; and into this *bizarrerie*, as into all his others, I quietly fell; giving myself up to his wild whims with a perfect *abandon*. The sable divinity would not herself dwell with us always; but we could counterfeit her presence. At first dawn of the morning we closed all the massy shutters of our old building; lighted a couple of tapers which, strongly perfumed, threw out only the ghastliest and feeblest of rays. By the aid of these we then busied our souls in dreams—reading, writing or conversing until warned by the clock of the advent of the true Darkness."

Dupin's most famous English descendant is, of course, Sherlock Holmes, whose lifestyle as described in *A Study in Scarlet* (1887) had marked Decadent elements. Under the influence of the terminally tedious Dr Watson and the pressure of fame, however, Holmes sacrificed his flamboyant eccentricity by slow but inexorable degrees; his nocturnal habits and drug-addiction were gradually de-emphasized. No such domestication spoiled Prince Zaleski, who easily outdid all his rivals in status and style. His own admiring chronicler describes his home as "a vast tomb of Mausoleums in which lay deep sepulchers how much genius, culture, brilliancy, power!" In Zaleski's own room, "Even in the semi-darkness of the very faint greenish luster radiated from an open censer-like *lampas* of fretted gold in the centre of the domed encausted roof, a certain incongruity of barbaric gorgeousness in the furnishing filled me with amazement. The air was heavy with the scented odor of this light, and the fumes of the narcotic *cannabis sativa*." Whereas Holmes favored the musical distraction of the violin, "One side of [Zaleski's] room was occupied by an organ whose thunder in that circumscribed place must have set all these relics of dead epochs clashing and jingling in fantastic dances." (5)

Shapes in the Fire is equally redolent with exaggerated echoes of Poe, of which "Vaila", seen as a reprise of "The Fall of the House of Usher", is surely the very archetype of an "exaggerated echo". The cry of "Madman!" that resounds through the House of Usher is similarly echoed in "Xélucha", but the setting and manner of the story also pay direct homage to the French sources that nourished the tide of *fin-de-siècle* Decadence. Mérimée is presumably named for Prosper Mérimée, suggesting that the first inspiration of Shiel's story must have been *Carmen*—a *nouvelle* in which the raw power of femininity is doubly "conquered" by the bandit lover who kills the eponymous *femme fatale* and the arid reductionism of the antiquarian who hears and frames the bandit's dispirited account.

The "consumption" that has killed Cosmo in "Xélucha" was presumably syphilis rather than tuberculosis. Syphilis was the inevitable penalty suffered by the great majority of those who elevated Decadent style to the status of a lifestyle fantasy, but its tertiary derangements were ambivalently borne by those who had believed Cesare Lombroso and his French disciple Joseph Moreau de Tours when they proclaimed that genius was a form of madness. Shiel's Mérimée is forced by his brief encounter to recognize that the careful avoidance of such a fate is not without costs of its own.

"Xélucha" is as close to a wholehearted celebration of Decadent lifestyle fantasy as Shiel ever came thereafter. "Premier and Maker" reveals that Shiel had read Max Nordau's *Degeneration*, whose elevation to best-seller status in 1895 followed hot on the heels of the Wilde trials, and that censorious epic might have succeeded in souring his view of the *fin de siècle*. The second story in *Shapes in the Fire*, "Maria in the Rose-Bush", is much more ambivalent in its examination of the doctrine that Beauty is the highest value of all. Here, in contrast to the first tale, Shiel uses an essay-like frame narrative to distance both teller and reader from the substance of the tale, effectively submitting it to the stultifying dominion of history. It is a requiem of sorts, and not the only one in the book.

"Vaila" was later to be rewritten as "The House of Sounds" and some critics agree with Shiel in preferring the later, much sparer, version. "Xélucha" was also toned down for subsequent reprinting, although the original version is similarly preferred by many readers. Whether one agrees with Shiel's modification of these stories or not—I do not—there is no doubt that the earlier and more pyrotechnic version of "Vaila" wears its wildness very well. In purely stylistic terms it is the most extravagantly and most unrepentantly Decadent thing Shiel ever wrote. It is, of course, no mere imitation of Poe. Like Oscar Wilde, Shiel borrowed only in order to expand; his ambition was always to add an extra petal to a glorious corolla, and he set out not to recapitulate but to outdo Poe's dark extravaganza.

More than any other tale in *Shapes in the Fire*, "Vaila" sets out to add a full measure of education to its fancy, to combine the Orphean with the Euclidean; its extremism is carefully underlain with philosophical analysis, in a seamless fashion that Poe never quite contrived. It offers us in the plight of its doomed neurasthenic not merely an adamantine allegory ("For such, this earth—I had almost said this universe—is clearly no fit habitation, but a Machine of Death, a baleful Vast") but a new vision of Creation, in which the supreme Omniscience would not be the vision of an All-Seeing Eye but a marvelously acute aural sensitivity to the least vibration. The fate of Harco Harfager is measured out more carefully and more extensively than that of any of Poe's doomed aristocrats, not merely by the narrator who undertakes the arduous journey to his Stygian and storm-racked abode but by the great and terribly ingenious clock that counts the durance of his heritage. The clock does nothing so conventional as chime; the bells that toll for Harfager, perceptible only to his supernaturally-enhanced hearing, are tiny things strategically placed within his aunt's coffin, awaiting disturbance by her terminal and vermin-assisted decay.

In literary works, of course, the pathetic fallacy is no fallacy at all—author-determined weather has no option but to symbolize feeling—but weather was never such a demonic Stakhanovite as it is while Harco Harfager's doom rushes upon him. It is not surprising, when the crisis comes, that it overwhelms the observer as well as the observed: "No but God, no, no," I cried, "I will no more wander hence, my God! I will even perish with Harfager! Here let me waltzing pass, in this Ball of the Vortices, Anarchie of the Thunders! Did not the great Corot call it translation in a chariot of flame? But this is gaudier than that! redder than that! This is jaunting on the scoriac tempests and reeling bullions of hell! It is baptism in a sun!" Unfortunately, someone has to tell the story, and the narrator is spared; such is the burden of authorship.

JAUNTING ON THE SCORIAC TEMPESTS, BY BRIAN STABLEFORD

Placing the interlude in which "Premier and Maker" is presented after "Vaila" was an excellent decision on Shiel's part; the mood of the book becomes much quieter in its later phases and the essay is far more appropriately placed as a languid retrospective explanation of "Vaila" than a laborious anticipatory introduction to "Xélucha". "Tulsah", the third *femme fatale* story in the book, follows the example of "Xélucha" in taking the form of a madman's manuscript, but here there is no framing device at all. The narrator is the man beguiled and damned by the eponymous lamia, even though he is doomed to perish, prey to the venom of supernatural serpents and the all-consuming fires of Hell. In "Xélucha" the price of passion is disease: a disease that rots the body and mind alike; in "Tulsah" passion itself becomes the consuming fire. In "Vaila" Omniscience is aural but in "Tulsah" it has reverted to the sight of "an Eye that glares and glares for ever!"—an Eye that is given all the familiar names of the One God but is preferably equated with "Saranyû [*i.e.* 'Erinyes', Counteraction]".

In Vedic myth Saranyu was the wife of the sun, who left her husband because she could not bear the brightness of his rays. The rays that he gave up in order to reclaim her were transformed into deadly weapons, employed by other deities to assail the living; Saranyu was also the mother of Yama, the guardian of Hell. The Erinyes of Greek Myth were, of course, the vengeful Furies who harried the living and exacted the tortures to which the least fortunate inhabitants of Hell were condemned. Their invocation in "Tulsah" underlines the notion that fiery passion can provide its own punishment, in the form of a scarifying conscience; the chamber in which the narrator seals himself is his own self-inflicted Hell, which isolates him from everything except that which he desires to keep at bay: the monstrous metamorphosite of his lust.

After the Wilde trial, of course, homosexual and bisexual writers found it politic to conceal their inclinations in their work and their lives alike, and the map of Shiel's own desires is laid out very obliquely indeed in his books—but Decadence was relabeled Symbolism because its practitioners understood the logic of disguised representations very well. The narrator of "Tulsah", explaining the origins of his philosophy, refers to a doctrine whose origins are "deep in the roots of the universe" and adds: "Loosely allied to it is phallic, and—very much more intimately—serpent, worship...and since Flame is torture, so is the Serpent the fit emblem of Hell. Hence the wisdom of the Hebrew serpent-myth of the temptation and fall of man; and hence, too, came it, that the Zabians, worshipping in the first instance the heavenly hosts of fire, were also worshippers of the snaky uncleanness."

Given that it follows "Tulsah", one is inevitably tempted to read a further level of metaphorical significance into "The Serpent-Ship", which is similarly doom-laden, albeit in a strangely jocular fashion. A serpent-ship is a Viking longboat, and the one that bears the hero Hrolf away to meet his fate in the poem is not the first one to have been briefly formed by the flickering of the shapes in the fire; the last phase of the narrator's journey to the remote isle of Vaila requires the recruitment of a modern ship built in that exact image.

"The Serpent-Ship" is the slightest piece in the book, and it is followed by the longest. "Phorfor" is also the least Decadent of the shapes, its climax substituting an almost-conventional sentimentality for the raw nihilism of "Xélucha", "Vaila" and "Tulsah". The imaginary land in which it is set is as far from "Vaila" as symbolic geography will permit, reached by following a "seine of streams, overwaved by that bulbous Nile-lily which the Greeks called 'lotus'". Like Harco Harfager, Numa is returning home, but his home is not naturally storm-tormented; indeed, it is time-lost in a kind of narcoleptic dream, and Numa's eventual fate is to become a lotus-eater himself, bedded on an elaborate bridal couch with his beloved Areta. The couch is overhung by "immortal flowers of amaranth", which spell out the name of APHRODITE PEITHO. Peitho was the personification of persuasion, especially in amatory matters; she is frequently represented as an attendant of Aphrodite and sometimes, as here, identified with her. This destiny is not, of course attained without difficulty. Numa constantly fails to please Areta in the early phases of the story, only partly because she mistakenly thinks him guilty of petty crimes committed against the corpse of the saintly Sergius.

"Phorfor" is, in every significant respect, an inversion of "Tulsah", where love was all-too-easily plucked from the funeral pyre in which Tulsah should have been consumed. Here, everything is prettified; passion is redeemed by piety, its strife driven out into the wilderness in the person of a convenient scapegoat. The pattern of fiery metaphors set out in "Tulsah" is revised in a scrupulously self-conscious manner in "Phorfor" when Numa inherits the key that Sergius had caused to be inlaid on his coffin and conducts a painstaking dissection of its symbolism. That analysis leads him to the "angel-song" that was the artistic essence of Sergius' saintliness—and which, in order to win Areta's sympathies at last, he contrives to transform and glorify.

JAUNTING ON THE SCORIAC TEMPESTS, BY BRIAN STABLEFORD

"Phorfor" could not, of course, provide a *lasting* conclusion to the shifting of those shapes in the fire which (in the words of Sergius' song) perpetually "come and go". In its choice of title, the book defines itself as something transient, without finality. Shiel's retreat from the ambiguous horrors of the Decadent world-view was temporary—but so were his many returns to its tortuous confusions. *Shapes in the Fire* mapped out the quasi-pendular swing of his subsequent returns, and it was the fate of his most sorely bruised characters—Adam Jeffson of *The Purple Cloud* most archetypally—to catch, after long and arduous trials, a glimpse of the magic land of Phorfor and the arms of Aphrodite. On the other hand, Shiel never lost sight of the fact that such endings were intrinsically and fatally *novelistic*, and it is undoubtedly significant that the deity who presides over the final words of "Phorfor" and the entire volume is Aphrodite *Peitho*. Although this has a perfectly straightforward significance it is probable—given Shiel's sensitivity to the sound and music of language—that it also has also another.

Peitho is so insignificant a figure in Greek myth as not even to warrant a mention in the edition of William Smith's *Classical Dictionary* issued in 1891, but *Pytho* is there, being the Latin name of Delphi. Pytho derives from Python, the name that the Delphic oracle inherited from the archetypal serpent slain by Apollo—a serpent whose name was derived from the Greek *pythein*, to decay, on the grounds that after Apollo slew the creature in question its body did indeed decay in a particularly conspicuous fashion. If there is a lesson to be taken from *Shapes in the Fire* it is not that angel-songs will soar in the end above the devil's best tunes, but rather that such conclusions are only fit for lotus-eaters. Peitho surely has to be read as a calculatedly innocuous—but altogether inadequate—substitute for Pytho.

THE DECADENT DETECTIVE: PRINCE ZALESKI

The Cedric Chivers edition of *Prince Zaleski*, issued in 1967, carries a note on the jacket flap informing the reader that "Mrs Gladstone took a great interest in M. P. Shiel's writing, and it was partly through her intervention that *Prince Zaleski* was published, in 1893, with decorations by Aubrey Beardsley". Mrs. Gladstone's husband was, of course, the Grand Old Man of British politics, who served continuously in the House of Commons from 1832 to 1895, having several times refused a promotion to the Lords. In his essay "About Myself" Shiel recalls that he "came into relation" with Mrs. Gladstone through Earl Grey and Sir Alexander Harris of the Colonial Office and that she "profoundly influenced my goings and comings." As well as John Lane, the original publisher of *Prince Zaleski*, Mrs. Gladstone introduced him to the notorious radical editor W. T. Stead, around whose anecdotal plot-outline Shiel was to construct his potboiler *The Rajah's Sapphire*, 1896.

It was presumably while Mrs. Gladstone was influencing his goings and comings that Shiel met Arthur Primrose, Earl of Rosebery, who succeeded Gladstone as prime minister in March 1894. Rosebery featured in Shiel's extravagant homage to the aesthetic dimension of Liberal politics "Premier and Maker", which appeared in his second collection of stories, *Shapes in the Fire* (1896). Along with another acquaintance Shiel made at the time, Oscar Wilde, Rosebery was obsessively pursued and harassed by the dreadful Marquess of Queensberry—who held Rosebery responsible for corrupting his elder son, Lord Drumlanrig, just as he held Wilde responsible for corrupting the younger, Lord Alfred Douglas. Drumlanrig's suicide in 1895 was one of the factors influencing Rosebery's early removal from office, although it was a matter about which little could safely be said in public, especially after Wilde's conviction and sentence to two years' hard labor.

JAUNTING ON THE SCORIAC TEMPESTS, BY BRIAN STABLEFORD

Shiel says in "About Myself" that the idea of writing *Prince Zaleski* came to him one day while he was gazing at the sky, recalling the days when, at the age of seventeen—which is to say, some time between 21 July 1882 and 20 July 1883—he had just discovered the works of Edgar Allan Poe and had "begun to smoke". He does not specify what it was that he was smoking, but observes that the combination of influences transported him to a "Nephelococcugia" (Aristophanes' Cloud-Cuckoo-Land) from which, we may infer, he never entirely returned. The essay adds a supplementary comment that *Prince Zaleski* has "more Poe in it than Job"—a curious combination of the obvious and the elliptical. Why, one is invited to wonder, should it have had any Job in it at all? And if it does, where, exactly, is it to be found?

We know from other sources that Shiel considered Job, or the author of his story, to be "the greatest genius among writers who ever lived" and "the greatest poet who ever lived" but that judgment inevitably invites further interpretation. How did Shiel come to identify himself so strongly with Job, the crux of a conflict between Jehovah and a challenging adversary, that he not only recast his story in his own eventual masterpiece, *The Purple Cloud* (1901), but sought to incorporate him into his work from the very first? Shiel aspired, of course, to be a supreme stylist in much the same vein, but style is, in the final analysis, inseparable from *weltanschauung*. Although his work has appeared to some unsympathetic readers and critics to be more style than substance, the produce of a man periodically addicted to decoration for decoration's sake, this is a woefully untenable thesis. The great majority of Shiel's writings are exceedingly substantial; he is always grappling with ideas, and perpetually preoccupied with those aspects of his ideas which qualify them as afflictions: motive forces of considerable, and sometimes terrible, power. *Prince Zaleski* is by no means the most substantial of his books, but nor is it the least, and its substance is certainly not unproblematic.

Prince Zaleski seems, especially to "connoisseurs" of detective fiction who are so narrowly focused on the puzzle aspect of a plot that matters of style and *weltanschauung* go unheeded, to be the most bizarre of all literary detectives. The mysteries that confront him are no less grotesque than he is, and may therefore seem unsatisfactory to those same connoisseurs. His creator, on the other hand, regarded him—with good reason—as a "legitimate son" of Poe's Dupin, while tacitly damning Sherlock Holmes as a mere bastard. Perhaps Shiel was being a little unkind; the early pages of *A Study in*

Scarlet equip Sherlock Holmes with several conspicuously Decadent traits, of which he never entirely dispossessed himself, even when he had to clean up his act in order to become an *habitué* of that archetypally *arriviste* literary drawing-room *The Strand Magazine*. Even so, there is no doubt that it is Zaleski, not Holmes, who is the truer as well as the bolder extrapolation of C. Auguste Dupin.

"The Murders in the Rue Morgue" explains how the relatively well-off narrator discovers a kindred spirit in the eccentric Dupin, and is thus permitted "the expense of renting, and furnishing in a style which suited the rather fantastic gloom of our common temper, a time-eaten and grotesque mansion, long deserted through superstitions into which we did not inquire, and tottering to its fall in a retired and desolate portion of the Faubourg St Germain". There the two men live a secluded life, admitting no visitors and going out only by night. "It was a freak of fancy in my friend," the narrator observes, "to be enamored of the night for her own sake; and into this *bizarrerie*, as into all his others, I quietly fell; giving myself up to his wild whims with a perfect *abandon*. The sable divinity would not herself dwell with us always; but we could counterfeit her presence. At first dawn of the morning we closed all the massy shutters of our old building; lighted a couple of tapers which, strongly perfumed, threw out only the ghastliest and feeblest of rays. By the aid of these we then busied our souls in dreams—reading, writing or conversing until warned by the clock of the advent of the true Darkness."

There is no doubt that Poe considered Dupin to be a fantastic projection of himself; the third Dupin story, "The Mystery of Marie Roget", details a process of ratiocination that he had developed in respect of an actual case. In real life, of course, poor Edgar Poe never found a benefactor willing to rent a crumbling mansion where he might live in the manner described. Perhaps he would not really have liked to—there is a definite element of parodic humor in his descriptions of Dupin—but his playfulness might be regarded as a mask to protect the self-indulgent sincerity of his fantasy.

Even in America—the least hospitable nation on Earth to Decadent ideas and ideals—a few of Poe's readers found something deeply appealing in the notion: something that touched their own calculated perversity and private self-indulgence. His immediate literary descendants were, however, all European, and almost all French. This was partly attributable to the fact that Poe had a genius for a French translator, but mainly due to the fact that France was situated at a cultural pole precisely opposite to that of America; it was the most hospitable nation on Earth to Decadent ideas and ideals. France was the destination of Victorian England's Decadent exiles, from the pioneer of Dandyism George Brummell to Algernon Swinburne and Shiel's luckless acquaintances Oscar Wilde and Ernest Dowson. Shiel was to follow them himself, for a while, but he could never settle there (true Decadents cannot settle anywhere, because their essential paradoxicality ensured that the find hospitable circumstances almost as unbearable as inhospitable ones) and he kept on coming back until necessity forced him to remain.

It is significant that the "combination of smokes" that showed Shiel the way to Cloud-Cuckoo-Land in the early 1880s did not bear literary fruit for a decade. Although Baudelaire became the presiding spirit of a Parisian Decadent Movement almost as soon as Shiel turned eighteen, the movement was not imported into England until Arthur Symons became its English standard-bearer in 1893. Symons did not carry the colors for long; he threw them away on the day of Oscar Wilde's conviction and proclaimed himself and his movement Symbolist instead—thus, in effect, retaining the style while, however absurdly, disowning the substance. He was not alone in this; Théophile Gautier, introducing a posthumous edition of *Les Fleurs du Mal*, had been careful to stress that Baudelaire's triumph was principally and primarily, if not quite exclusively, a matter of style. It was, in fact, Gautier who first described and defined "the Decadent style" as "ingenious, complicated, clever, full of delicate hints and refinements, gathering all the delicacies of speech, borrowing from technical vocabularies, taking color from every palette, tones from all musical instruments, contours vague and fleeting, listening to translate subtle confidences, confessions of depraved passions and the odd hallucinations of a fixed idea turning to madness"; he did, however, concede that such a style was, and had to be, "summoned to express all and to venture to the very extremes", and he quoted with approval Baudelaire's confessed fascination with "the phosphorescence of putrescence".

Having been haunted from its inception, therefore, by a measure of cautious intellectual treason, the Decadent Movement consisted of writers devoted to a certain sly shiftiness. They asserted that modern civilization was in irreversible decline, its essential vitality having been sapped by the luxury and comfort that had enervated its ruling classes. Unlike their predecessors and forefathers, the adherents of Romanticism, Decadent writers saw no future or virtue in rebellion against this state of affairs; they set out instead to become connoisseurs of perversity, praising the use of psychotropic drugs in the search for "artificial paradises" and complimenting the excesses of exotic lifestyles. In the meantime, they accepted, with a sigh, that the unavoidable lot of the neurotic genius—especially one whose ancestry made him victim to hereditary neurasthenia—was to struggle hopelessly under the triple oppression of *ennui, spleen* and *impuissance*.

No Decadent writer could really qualify as a Decadent genius in his own estimation, because the mere act of writing—especially if it produces an income and a living—is an avoidance of oppression. Even a character in a work of Decadent fiction is likely to have trouble going the whole hog, because the demands of dramatic tension impose a certain duty of action. A Decadent hero ought not to do very much, but he must, alas, do *something*, or his literary existence becomes unjustifiable. In any case, *ennui* will occasionally drive him from his couch in desperation, in exactly the same way that his author is driven to take up his pen. What better role is there for him to fulfill, in that case, than that of a consulting detective? A solver of occasional puzzles, of a sort that will only yield to genuine power of mind accessorized by a unique talent for lateral thinking, is surely a far more admirable Decadent hero than any mere libertine. The only leading member of the French Decadent Movement who ever wrote a detective story was Catulle Mendès; the others considered it beneath their dignity to dabble in a favorite genre of *feuilletonists*. The loss was theirs; Zaleski is at least as perfect a portrait of the Decadent genius as Joris-Karl Huysmans' Jean Des Esseintes or Jean Lorrain's Monsieur de Phocas.

Prince Zaleski is introduced as a "victim of a too importunate, too unfortunate Love, which the fulgor of the throne itself could not abash; exile perforce from his native land, and voluntary exile from the rest of men!" We are presumably intended to infer from the opening phrases that he is a homosexual, as were so many of the English exiles in France at that time, but nothing more is said on that subject. His mansion is "a vast tomb of Mausolus in which lay deep sepulchred how much genius, culture, brilliancy, power!" It is, of course, falling into ruins; "a troop, of fat and otiose rats" flees at the narrator's entrance. The only part of the house that is furnished is the tower where Zaleski keeps his apartment, in a door "tapestried with the python's skin" ("python" is derived from the Greek *pythein*, to decay).

Like Dupin's quarters, Zaleski's are maintained in semi-darkness, illuminated by "an open censerlike *lampas* of fretted gold". Even the narrator is amazed by "a certain incongruity of barbaric gorgeousness in the furnishing," but not by the fact that the atmosphere is heavy with "the fumes of the narcotic *cannabis sativa*"—of which Zaleski is a habitual user. The prince's couch is positioned next to an open sarcophagus, whose mummified inhabitant has been unbandaged to display a "naked, grinning countenance"—the ultimate *memento mori*. "The general effect," Zaleski's faithful chronicler comments, "was a *bizarrerie* of half-weird sheen and gloom"—an impression that the reader is bound to share. The final touch is supplied by a passing reference to Zaleski's taste in music. Sherlock Holmes, of course, favored the delicate distractions of the violin, but the prince is otherwise inclined: "One whole side of the room was occupied by an organ whose thunder in that circumscribed place must have set all these relics of dead epochs clashing and jingling in fantastic dances." It is, of course, only the relics—including, one presumes, the half-unclad mummy—that partake of this *totentanz*, even in the imagination; Zaleski lacks the necessary energy.

Zaleski demonstrates his existential convictions as well as his deductive skills when he solves the first two mysteries that confront him, without rising from the couch where he languishes. The first of them, although it takes the form of a vexing locked-room puzzle, yields very easily to his practiced eye because its plot hinges on a typical Decadent syndrome; it involves an aristocrat driven to extraordinary extremes by the treacherous disease that infected the art of so many Decadents while it slowly destroyed them in mind and body: syphilis. That same ailment plays a minor but crucial role in the second story, causing confusion to arise in the matter of the apparent theft of a quasi-magical jewel—whose concatenation of properties, we are told in the final judgment, may be a significant instance of scientific discoveries to come "in exact conformity [with] a general trend towards a certain inborn perverseness and whimsicality in Nature."

It is the third element in the original set of Zaleski's exploits that has attracted most attention in modern times, by virtue of the less-than-fortunate coincidence by which its title, "The S.S.", acquired a new significance in Hitler's Germany. Shiel has been suspected by some unsympathetic critics—particularly Sam Moskowitz, who included a grudging account of Shiel's pioneering work in the genre of scientific romance in his study of *Explorers of the Infinite* (1963)—of harboring fascist sympathies, and the fact that the story's Society of Sparta arouses Zaleski's attention by dabbling in negative eugenics has sometimes been advanced in support of this case. Given Shiel's pragmatic affiliation to the Liberal party, however—not to mention Mrs Gladstone's interventions on the specific behalf of the stories making up the book—the interpretation of "The S.S." as a proto-fascist fiction must be regarded as extremely dubious. In fact, Shiel's politics were considerably more radical than Lord Rosebery's; by the time he wrote *The Lord of the Sea* (1901) he was promoting a kind of socialism based in the works of the American theorist Henry George, in philosophical alliance with ideas derived from the works of Friedrich Nietzsche by such British Nietzscheans as John Davidson, who was another of Shiel's literary acquaintances, and perhaps the closest of all in spirit as well as in style.

Shiel's Society of Sparta is a company of visionaries who have discovered the Nietzschean idea of the *übermensch* (overman) but have—according to Zaleski—a mistaken notion of the methods required to bring about his advent. Zaleski—who is not to be reckoned an overman himself, although his successor in Shiel's work, Cummings King Monk, might be—reveals his limitations in coping with the threat posed by the S.S., not because he is unable to counter the menace successfully, but because he has to rise from his couch to do so; it is in this necessity that we find the crucial disability of the Decadent Detective and the effective terminus of his career. (Although Zaleski, like the murdered Sherlock Holmes, was eventually to return to literary life, he was likewise "never the same man afterwards".) The underlying purpose of Zaleski's expedition to the outside world is not really to warn the S.S. of the dangers of excessive zeal, but rather to examine his own relationship to them.

Zaleski locates the S.S. by means of one of the most astonishing (some might say preposterous) feats of deduction ever perpetrated in a detective story, by reducing the Latin motto *mens sana in corpore sano* to a coded reference to the river Thames and the name Aesop. Aesop is, of course, most famous as a composer of fables, but Zaleski analyses his character in a different way: "He was a slave who was freed for his wise and witful sallies: he is therefore typical of the liberty of the wise—their moral manumission from temporary and narrow law; he was also a close friend of Croesus: he is typical, then, of the union of wisdom with wealth; lastly, and above all, he was thrown by the Delphians from a rock on account of his wit: he is typical, therefore, of death—the shedding of blood—as a result of wisdom, this thought being an elaboration of Solomon's great maxim, 'in much wisdom is much sorrow'." [The quote is actually from *Ecclesiastes 1:18*.] It is easy enough to believe that Shiel had at least one other man besides Aesop in mind when he wrote this;

his own mother was of mixed race, the descendant of slaves; he had become a social intimate of key members of the wealthy Liberal elite; and he identified strongly with the misfortunes and sorrows of Job. Although he lived long, and occasionally prospered, many of those in his circle did not; Wilde and Dowson were dead within five years of *Prince Zaleski*'s appearance, and John Davidson killed himself—by throwing himself from a rock—in 1909.

After rowing all the way down the Thames from Wargrave to a desolate stretch "a long way past Greenwich" (Hornchurch marshes?), and having passed a fruitless and uncomfortable night in an east London lodging-house, the prince finally discovers a board bearing the fateful words DESCENDUS AESOPI. Following the advice of the first term he goes down into a kind of underworld, where he is twice challenged by a guardian with the words: "You are a Spartan?" He answers in the affirmative, the second time "emphatically". Having been admitted to a meeting of the society he takes the first opportunity to deliver his judgment on their methods—and, in response, he is drugged, with "a powerful and little-known anaesthetic" (it appears to be chloroform). The experience that he next undergoes seems quite superfluous, but cannot really be, at least in the author's mind, else it would be omitted from the story:

> The incubus of the universe blackened down upon my brain. How I tugged at the mandrake of speech! was a locked pugilist with language! In the depth of my extremity the half-thought, I remember, floated, like a mist, through my faded consciousness, that now perhaps—now—there was silence around me; that *now*, could my palsied lips find dialect, I should be heard, and understood. My whole soul rose focussed to the effort—my body jerked itself upwards. At that moment I knew my spirit truly great, genuinely sublime. For I *did* utter something—my dead and shuddering tongue did babble forth some coherency. Then I fell back, and all was once more the ancient Dark.

What, we are bound to wonder, was Zaleski enabled by this supreme effort to say? We know that when he was first seized he was attempting to tell the Spartans that he was not the only one who "shared in their secret", but he had already concluded that they would not kill him, so the utterance of that threat hardly seems worthy of the extreme urgency of this final effort, let alone of the sensations of true greatness and genuine sublimity that accompanied it. Surely it must have been some deeper truth that he voiced, some far more penetrating expression of sympathy. In searching for the Society of Sparta, beneath the mask of Aesop, Zaleski is surely attempting to confront himself, to see himself and to speak to himself—and yet, in the end, he will not tell his chronicler, or his readers, what it was he saw and said. Surely Shiel, in writing "The S.S.", was endeavoring to do something similar, but with a frustratingly identical result.

So the "ancient Dark" reclaims Zaleski, and the rest was silence...at least until Shiel was persuaded, much against his judgment, to dust off his discarded creation and permit him to deduce, in a flagrantly lackluster fashion, yet another secret address. The reader is bound to feel a certain annoyance in being teased in this way, but ought not to regret or resent it. After all, what is a sphinx without a secret? What is a Decadent without a source of *spleen* deep-rooted in his own heart? Aesop the fabulist did not always state his morals clearly, and would not have been a better writer if he had; indeed, he might be even more interesting had he refrained more often.

There is a certain irony in the fact that, so far as his posthumous reputation was concerned, Shiel did not make the wisest provision. Had he not been so concerned to avoid all mention of his black ancestors he might now be a hero of "post-colonial literature", the first great West Indian novelist. Had he not been so concerned to avoid all mention of the ambiguity of his sexual impulses, he might even be enjoying a renaissance under the academic banner of "queer studies". Given his moment and his milieu, however, it is hardly surprising that he chose to represent himself, in his life as in his work, as a thoroughly heterosexual white man. Nor is it surprising, on the other hand, that he chose to make himself exceptional in a manner that was currently acceptable—or that having so chosen, he labored wholeheartedly to take his exceptional quality to an unprecedented extreme.

Shiel succeeded in this ambition, several times over and in several different ways. *Prince Zaleski* was not his best book—he would have been utterly horrified to think it might be, given that it was apprentice-work—but it is by no means his worst, and the fact that it is as absurd as it is extraordinary should certainly not be held against it. It certainly has more Poe than Job in it, but Job is there, laying groundwork for later, more truly epic, manifestations. The book is, in its fashion, an entirely suitable monument to the glorious perversity and divine insanity that constituted the Decadent style and *weltanschauung*—which is, of course, far more relevant and pertinent today than it was in 1895.

THE BLACK-AND-WHITE MYSTERY OF *THE PURPLE CLOUD*

The first version of *The Purple Cloud* was serialized in *The Royal Magazine* in the first months of the twentieth century, running from January to June 1901. The story also marked something of a new departure for Shiel the novelist, whose previous long works had been hectic historical romances and near-futuristic war stories. Although two of the future war stories—*The Yellow Danger* and *The Lord of the Sea*—had attained climaxes of a considerable magnitude, as was not unusual in that kind of popular fiction, the bulk of their text had been devoted to conflicts of a relatively mundane stripe. *The Purple Cloud* not only features a far more apocalyptic interruption to the course of human affairs, but situates that interruption near the beginning of the story instead of the end, shifting the main body of its narrative into a very different and rather more esoteric genre of imaginative fiction.

In his previous novels, Shiel had made some attempt to tone down the conspicuously Decadent style in which the shorter stories collected in *Prince Zaleski* and *Shapes in the Fire* had luxuriated, but he gave himself much freer rein in *The Purple Cloud*—a liberation that was even more evident in the expanded version published by Chatto and Windus in September 1901. Shiel seems to have repented of his early extravagance later in his career, perhaps feeling that he had alienated too many potential readers, but he only consented to impose a slight moderation on the third, somewhat abridged, version of *The Purple Cloud* he prepared for the Victor Gollancz edition of 1929, which was reprinted in the USA by Vanguard and remained the standard text thereafter. Among all his novels, this was the one he regarded most highly; he rightly considered that the Decadent elements of its style are perfectly fitted to its philosophical import and its descriptions of the post-apocalyptic world. Although the final version is by no means unsatisfactory, the first book edition retains an extra measure of glamour that fully justifies its preservation.

* * * * * * *

As the reader of the present edition will observe, Shiel's introduction to the first book edition carried a footnote omitted from the abridged version in the 1929 edition, which identified *The Purple Cloud* as the third element of a trilogy begun with the then-unpublished *The Last Miracle* and continued with *The Lord of the Sea*, whose publication had preceded it in May 1901. All three texts are represented as transcriptions by one Dr. Arthur Lister Browne of reports made by a medium, Mary Wilson, detailing texts read by her during trances in which her consciousness was displaced into the future.

According to Browne, he has been acquainted with Mary Wilson over a period of about fifteen years, culminating in her death shortly before the date of his own letter to Shiel (May 1900). Although Browne's reinterpretation of Mary's perceived "distances within" as time spans is only tentatively calibrated, he offers the suggestion that the text of *The Last Miracle* (observed "forty-five miles within") must have been written down between fifteen and thirty years after its supposed anticipation—which must have been some time between 1884 and 1899, although the tone of the reportage suggests that it was probably nearer to the earlier date than the latter.

This means that the events described in the narrative (which must, of course, have preceded their recording) are imagined to have reached their climax some time between 1899 and the 1920s, most probably in the early 1900s. Given that we are told that Mary "never got beyond sixty-three [miles within]", the implication is that the events recorded in *The Purple Cloud* are imagined to be taking place between twenty-one and forty-two years after the supposed date of its anticipation—*i.e.*, between 1905 and the 1930s, most probably in the 1910s. This is significant in terms of the Millenarian elements that all three texts possess, and also in terms of their relationship to one another (a relationship partly spoiled by the belated publication—in 1906—of *The Last Miracle*, and greatly confused by their reissue at a later date than the imagined events described therein).

It is not improbable that the near-future scenarios mapped out in the three novels are meant to be seen as alternatives rather than elements in a sequence; they certainly do not overlap in any significant respect, as might be expected of fragments of a future history. It is, however, unlikely that Shiel had it in mind to emphasize the fact that the as-yet-unmade future always contains many alternative possibilities; it seems more probable that he intended the three works as more-or-less independent visions of three phases in an unfolding process—a process whose links were philosophical rather than chronological.

Although all three texts belong to recognizable genres of then-fashionable popular fiction—*The Last Miracle* is formulated as a thriller, *The Lord of the Sea* as a future war story and *The Purple Cloud* as a disaster story—their generic forms are at least partly calculated as sugar coats concealing potent pills. The fundamental artistic impulse that moved Shiel to produce them was obviously orientated more to the provision of nutritious food for thought than mere confections—or, more accurately, to the provision of effective *medicine* for thought-processes that had been too long fed on junk and had become sickly in consequence. All three books are, in essence, religious fantasies, whose concerns move backwards through the scriptures from the New Testament to the Old, whimsically inverting their own prophetic quality in the second element by focusing there on the messianic prophecies that allegedly forge the two parts of the Bible into a whole.

The Last Miracle describes the subversion and eventual supersession of Christ's teaching, attempting in its climax to replace his message much as he had replaced the obsolete Ten Commandments with the injunctions of the Sermon on the Mount. (Shiel realized, of course—although many Christians seem to think otherwise—that what had been involved had been an attempted replacement rather than the issue of a supplement, and that any attempt to reconcile Jesus's conspicuously tolerant teachings with the hawkishly forbidding Ten Commandments was a hopeless exercise in idiotic illogic.)

The Lord of the Sea revisits the notion of a messianic advent, and proposes that its own hero, Richard Hogarth, is in fact the messiah for whom the Jews had waited so long—which Christ clearly was not—and expressing the expectation that the true messiah would surely do a far better job (purely on the Jews' behalf) than any of those who had been mistaken for him in the past. Both books are fervently optimistic, in that the former imagines a constructive replacement of Christianity by a morally-responsible creed fully in tune with the revelations of modern science, while the latter imagines that the belatedly-redelivered Promised Land might be abundantly productive of new knowledge and higher wisdom as well as milk and honey.

At first glance, it might seem that the events described in *The Purple Cloud* serve only to dash the optimistic hopes of its predecessors into smithereens, obliterating a society that has not, after all, become wise enough. The matter is not so simple, though. The backward movement of Shiel's train of thought through the pages of the Bible is a return to fundamental issues; the impetus of the text takes it all the way back to *Genesis*, but the route, crucially, goes via *Job* and *Ecclesiastes*. Although there is a sense in which the allegory of *Job* involves dashing all human hopes and grinding the fragments to dust, the purpose of that breakage is no mere annihilation. Rather, it is the construction of an ultimate road of trials for a hero who must be tested to the absolute limit in order to be found spiritually worthy. In *Job*, and in *The Purple Cloud*, annihilation is not an end but a means, not a final Judgment but a re-Creation. Just as *The Last Miracle* and *The Lord of the Sea* had been admirably bold in their philosophical ambitions, however, so *The Purple Cloud* is not content merely to reiterate the story of Job, moral and all. Shiel's Job is also Adam, and a rebellious Adam at that—one who is not inclined to give in to arbitrary tyranny, but is ambitious to have a voice in his own destiny.

* * * * * * *

The Purple Cloud is not without literary ancestors, one of the more obvious being Mary Shelley's *The Last Man* (1826), but it owes little to any of them and it is entirely plausible that Shiel had never read any nineteenth-century post-apocalyptic fantasy save for George Griffith's *Olga Romanoff*, to which Arthur Pearson must have directed his attention as the opposition that his own future war stories were supposed to match and surpass. If Mary Shelley can be counted as an influence at all, the work from which Shiel might have taken some slight inspiration is *Frankenstein*, whose use of Robert Walton's polar explorations as a metaphor for the hazards of prideful ambition is echoed in the expedition that Adam Jeffson (*i.e.*, Jehovah's son) undertakes in the opening chapters of *The Purple Cloud*. Whereas Walton became trapped in the ice, however, reduced to playing audience for Shelley's allegory of botched creation, Jeffson actually reaches the pole and is enabled thereby to escape the doom of the world. He thus becomes the agent and substance of a potential re-creation: a Monster of sorts, to be sure, but a more ambitious Modern Prometheus than the craven Victor Frankenstein was capable of becoming.

One of the mysteries of the text is what, exactly, Jeffson finds at the North Pole. We are told that there is a pillar of ice in the centre of a lake whose fluid is alive, and that there are indecipherable words inscribed at its base, together with "a long date". Jeffson has already been warned, by "John the Baptist Redivivus," that the pole is very like the Tree of Knowledge in Eden, on account of being forbidden—and perhaps, also, on the grounds of possessing the power of limitless enlightenment—but it does not seem, at first, that he carries much enlightenment away with him on the long southward trek to the poisoned continents.

Like the passage in *Prince Zaleski* in which the eponymous hero, interrogated under the influence of drugs by the Society of Sparta, gropes his way towards some enormously important utterance that the reader is not allowed to read, the revelation to Adam Jeffson of an unreadable message seems a deliberate tantalization, a blatant tease. We must bear in mind, however, that the original Adam obtained very little *immediate* intelligence from eating the fruit offered to him by Eve. All that *Genesis* condescends to specify is that he found out that he was naked—and there is certainly a parallel to be found with that in Adam Jeffson's discovery that he is alone. (The alert reader—of which Shiel was certainly one—would have noted that the first Adam must also have spent a period of time alone, given that *Genesis* 3:23-24 is very explicit about the fact that the Lord God "sent *him* forth from the garden of Eden" and "drove out *the man*"—thus implying that Eve must have caught up with him at some later date, within the long interval covered by the text-break between chapters three and four.)

The sensible reader is bound to infer that the first Adam must have obtained far more knowledge from the forbidden fruit—even if he did not obtain it immediately—than is specified in chapter three of *Genesis*, which is mostly content to describe the curses heaped upon him by the Lord. He must have obtained a great many technical skills, given that chapter four begins with his two sons working competently as "a keeper of sheep" and "a tiller of the ground." Perhaps—one is entitled to speculate, if not actually forced to conclude—the fruit of the Tree of Knowledge from which Adam ate (even if it was only the tree of knowledge of good and evil rather than the tree of life mentioned alongside it in *Genesis* 2:9) took time to digest and integrate its substance with his. If so, then Adam Jeffson's precipitate flight from the phallic pole and its seminal lake may also be interpreted as a mere shameful prelude to a much longer process of education—a process constituted by the story told in the novel, whose entire narrative runs parallel to a small fraction of the tale left untold by *Genesis*' third text-break.

Seen in this light, the parallels between Adam Jeffson's story and Job's—and the differences between them—are somewhat altered in their significance, and in their ultimate import.

Job is a proverbial "man who has everything"—or, to be painstakingly accurate, a wife, ten children (only three of them daughters!), seven thousand sheep, three thousand camels, five hundred pairs of oxen, five hundred female asses and lots of servants—and then has it taken away, bit by bit, as a result of a wager between the Lord and a satan. The satan in question is, of course, not *the* Satan—the Jewish religion has no anti-god—but merely a hypothetical adversary, more logical antithesis than rebellious individual. The substance of the wager is the Lord's anxiety that Job's worshipful attitude towards Him is contingent on his good fortune, and that if his prayers went unanswered he would lose his faith. So it almost proves, despite the specious reassurances offered by his three "comforters", until the Lord speaks directly to Job from a whirlwind, reminding him at great length what a powerful entity He is—with the result that Job realizes that he is a worthless piece of shit, repents of his resentments, and has all his wealth returned to him by way of reward.

We are offered no suggestion as to how the satanic viewpoint might regard the morality of this story—but we are, once again, free to speculate, if not forced to conclude, that it would not be overly impressed. The satanic voice of skepticism might also have taken a dim view of the fact that three books further along (or back, in Shiel's reverse reading) the Bible-reader is assured by *Ecclesiastes* the Preacher that, even though our prayers will never be answered, and life will always be hard, and all our spiritual vanities will be vexed, and "in much wisdom is much grief, and he that increaseth knowledge increaseth sorrow," still we should "Fear God and keep his commandments, for this is the whole duty of man."

Adam Jeffson, unlike Job, is a man who has considerably less than everything—a small Harley Street practice and authorship of a successful book on *Applications of Science to the Arts*—and little enough ambition to attain more until he is urgently prompted by his not-yet-wife Clodagh, whose role model is Lucrezia Borgia. She, of course, is more Eve than satan, but Jeffson has been subject all his life to two contending inner voices, which he calls the Black and the

White out of respect to a fellow medical student of his, who always used to insist that "the black mystery of the universe" is really "the black-and-white mystery." What is taken away from Jeffson is not his relatively meager possessions but their context—the society and companionship of his fellow human beings. Of possessions, indeed, he now has an infinite supply—and he sets out to make the most of them—but he finds in the end that wealth is of far less consequence than he had hoped. Only when that lesson is well-and-truly learned is he offered a potential comforter and a potential Eve; that is when the battle between the Black and the White reaches its critical phase. The *power* of the black-and-white mystery, which might as well be called God as anything else, requires no emphasis here by any whirlwind-borne voice, but the question Adam Jeffson must answer—if he can—is whether power alone is sufficient to command respect.

Shiel the preacher had already made it clear, in the concluding chapters of *The Last Miracle* and *The Lord of the Sea*, that he was only content to echo *Ecclesiastes* in part. He agreed, by necessity, that our prayers will never be answered, that life will always be hard, and that all our spiritual vanities will very likely be vexed—but he was not at all sure that "in much wisdom is much grief, and he that increaseth knowledge increaseth sorrow." Indeed, he tended rather to the opposite opinion—that wisdom tended to ameliorate grief, and knowledge sorrow. As to whether we should "Fear God and keep his commandments, for this is the whole duty of man"—well, that depended on exactly what His commandments actually were. Given that Shiel, like Jesus before him, felt perfectly competent to update and revise those commandments, he was inclined to accept the judgment *on the right terms*. In order to determine what those terms might be, *The Purple Cloud* continues the process of renegotiation begun in *The Last Miracle*, and makes further progress—but it could not and did not conclude a matter that had to be subject to further modification by increases in wisdom and knowledge yet to come. Shiel's last preachy novel, *The Young Men are Coming!* (1937), took up the challenge again, as valiantly as ever.

Adam Jeffson's ultimate reward is, of course, far less than Job's, although it is surely he who strikes the harder bargain with the Lord. Some readers might conclude that his fate is merely the original Adam's catalogue of curses, revisited upon him by a wrathful and power-mad God, but it is not. It is a new way of seeing, which calculates the true measure of those supposed curses, and the real nutritive value of the fully-digested knowledge of forbidden fruit.

* * * * * * *

Although it is primarily a religious fantasy—and, as such, a member of a subcategory of metaphysical fantasy—those historians who have hailed *The Purple Cloud* as a classic of science fiction are not wrong. Given that metaphysics is, by definition, that which lies outside the scope of science, it may seem that metaphysical fantasy—including religious fantasy—is a genre rigorously exclusive of sf, but metaphysical systems are constructed in order to contain what is known about the world, in the hope of discovering more coherence therein than the logical extrapolation of actual observations can provide. As knowledge evolves, therefore, the spectrum of metaphysical plausibility changes in parallel, and the advancement of science inevitably gives rise to new metaphysical extensions. Such scientific disciplines as cosmology and evolutionary theory—a favorite of Shiel's—are host to as much metaphysics as physics and biology; their conscientious extrapolation demands consideration of metaphysical as well as physical implications.

For this reason, those subgenres of metaphysical fantasy that may seem quite incompatible with science-fictional speculation—religious fantasy being the most conspicuous—are actually very hospitable to it. Although "religious science fiction" is an inherently chimerical notion, the relationships between religious fantasy and science fiction have always been intimate and confused, and many texts exist that draw narrative energy and aesthetic flexibility from the calculated collision and collusion of their ideologies.

While religiously-inclined readers might think it appropriate that Adam Jeffson is tested more severely than Job, on the grounds that he was by no means as good and pious a man as Job was before the testing process commenced, readers who approach the text as science fiction will realize that the propriety lies elsewhere. For the greater part of the book Jeffson considers himself to be the instrument of the Black, recruited to that cause by virtue of the murders committed in order to sustain his ambition, but the Black is not synonymous with Evil any more than the satan of *Job* was synonymous with the Christian Satan. The satan of *Job* is not an enemy of God but a collaborator—an anxious skeptical voice from within, which doubts not only the moral worth of humankind but the moral worth of Creation—and so is Jeffson's Black.

The science fiction reader, recognizing that "God" is merely a metaphor for the evolutionary process and the fundamental dynamism of the cosmos, will see that the tests to which Adam Jeffson is subjected are harder because the universe has been discovered to be a far more hostile place than it was supposed to be in the times chronicled by the Old Testament. It would, in fast, be far too easy for Jeffson to conclude that he is a worthless piece of shit clinging to an irrelevant speck of dust somewhere in the labyrinthine depths of an infinite black mystery; the trick is not to reach that conclusion but to avoid it, without resorting to a personalized God-father—and that is the sterner test by far.

Shiel's fascination with the mythology of the Old Testament is, of course, that of a satan—not an atheist, by any means, but a challenging believer. (He declared atheism to be an impossible intellectual position to adopt, but, in order to do that, he required an exceedingly flexible notion of what the notion of deity might imply.) Much of his literary work is dedicated to the cause of disturbing and distressing conventional ideas of morality so that they might be replaced with something better. He had taken the view, in *The Last Miracle*, that "love thy neighbour" was too narrow a creed to support a world whose social horizons had been extended to a global scale; in *The Purple Cloud* he took the view that it was too simple a creed to accommodate the possibility that a man might find himself, or consider himself, devoid of neighbors.

For Shiel, deity was no mere tribal godfather prying protectively into the affairs of a chosen people; deity was the essential impetus of motion and evolution, which pertained to whole worlds and the universe entire, irrespective of tribal loyalties and mundane affections. Shiel wanted the pattern of moral obligation to extend across the generations, into a potentially-infinite future, and he asked that human goodness should base its calculations on the long-term good of the entire race, or of life itself, rather than the immediate benefit of a few individuals. That is, in essence, the mythology of progress to which modern science fiction is also committed—and which far too much modern religious fantasy unfortunately denies.

Shiel's decision to re-enact the story of Job on the widest available stage, and in the most intensely introspective manner, was both religious *and* science-fictional, as well as wholly original and entirely natural. His vivid and reckless prose style—which sometimes seemed an unnecessary affectation when he dealt with more mundane matters—was, in this instance, wonderfully appropriate, not merely in its ornate Decadence but also in its chimerical flamboyance.

There is no other book remotely like it, but it is for its accomplishments rather than its eccentricity that *The Purple Cloud* warrants serious consideration as a masterpiece of religious fantasy and of science fiction. It was not the first novel, and certainly was not the last, to construe a world-catastrophe as a punctuation mark in human history, but it still stands aloof from the vast majority of its peers in identifying that punctuation mark not as a full stop, or as the symbol used on a musical score to indicate *da capo*, or even as an exclamation mark, but rather as a conjunctive dash, more akin to an arrow than a bridge.

The fact that its hero is named Adam, Son of Jehovah, does not imply that its culmination is any mere return to square one; unlike many similar works written before and after it, *The Purple Cloud* is not a dispirited acceptance of eternal recurrence—nor any other preprogrammed change of tempo. It does not seek to imply that the best we can expect from the whole story of humankind is a sine-wave succession of rises and falls, or a re-acceptance into Eden, or mere extinction; it seeks to inform us that, no matter what, life *will* go on, and that the fact that it will never be the same again is the best news we could ever hope to obtain.

Jaunting on the Scoriac Tempests, by Brian Stableford

THE DURANCE OF DECADENCE:
THE PALE APE AND OTHER PULSES

Fifteen years separated the publication of M. P. Shiel's first collection of miscellaneous short stories, *Shapes in the Fire* (1896) from *The Pale Ape and Other Pulses*, which was published by T. Werner Laurie in 1911. A great deal had changed in the interim, not only in Shiel's life and career but in the literary marketplace that provided its context. Some of those changes are mapped in the contents of this second collection, which draws its material from the entire span of the interim period.

Like its immediate predecessor, which had chronicled the extraordinary adventures of *Prince Zaleski* (1895), *Shapes in the Fire* had been planned as a book publication to be issued by John Lane, the most important promoter of the English Decadent Movement. None of the stories in it had been published in periodicals, all of them having been designed as ornately-stylized works of a much more highbrow stripe than the common fare of middlebrow magazines. It would not have occurred to Shiel to republish therein such early magazine stories as "Guy Harkaway's Substitute" (1893) and "The Eagle's Crag" (1894). When the market for that kind of book disappeared, however—which happened almost immediately after the publication of *Shapes in the Fire*—Shiel had no alternative but to consider the possibility of adapting his future short fiction into formats in which it might obtain magazine publication, while retaining the possibility of eventual collection in book form.

The earliest of the stories included in *The Pale Ape and Other Stories* to see publication, "Huguenin's Wife," appeared in April 1895 issue of *The Pall Mall Magazine. Shapes in the Fire* had not yet appeared, although the collection had presumably been submitted to its publisher beforehand. "Huguenin's Wife" was published before the fate of the short-lived English Decadent Movement was sealed by the backlash generated by the conviction and imprisonment of Oscar Wilde; in another and kinder world Shiel might have been able to place more stories as exotic as this one in the magazines, at least for a while, but that possibility vanished along with the possibility of publishing more books like *Shapes in the Fire*.

"The Case of Euphemiah Raphash," which appeared in the 1895 Christmas supplement of *Chapman's Magazine*, might well have been written, and perhaps accepted for publication, before Wilde's downfall, but "The Spectre-Ship," which was published in *Cassell's Magazine* in September 1896, was almost certainly written afterwards. It is possible that one or two of the stories published for the first time in *The Pale Ape and Other Pulses* has also been written before the end of 1895, but had failed to find publication then—"The Great King" is the most likely candidate—but whether that is true or not, all the later materials in the collection reflect, in one way or another, the fact that English Decadent prose suffered a drastic decline in fashionability in 1896, from which it never recovered. Publishers in all sectors of the marketplace became less sympathetic to it, if not actively antipathetic; in seeking to distance themselves—publicly, at least—from Wilde's supposed moral decadence, they began to distance themselves from everything he had stood for, including the exuberant flamboyance and exoticism of his literary style and ironic wit.

Oscar Wilde's fall was not the only cause that his enemy, the Marquess of Queensberry, had reason to celebrate in 1895. As well a pursuing Wilde for the supposed ruination of his younger son, Lord Alfred Douglas, Queensberry had also been waging a campaign of hatred against the man he considered responsible for the ruination and suicide of his elder son, Lord Drumlanrig: Lord Rosebery. Queensberry was never likely to bring Rosebery down in the way that he brought Wilde down, because Rosebery was more highly placed in the peerage and had the additional advantage of being the prime minister, but circumstances beyond either man's control contrived to bring down Rosebery's government in 1895 and put an effective end to his political career.

The cloak of secrecy and subtle deceit with which Shiel cloaked his private life makes it difficult to be certain, but it seems likely that his acquaintance with Oscar Wilde was relatively slight. He probably knew Rosebery much better, having moved in the social circle of the higher echelons of the Liberal party for some years, but how intimate their acquaintance was remains a matter for speculation. The principal crack in Shiel's discretion regarding this association was the heavily disguised dialogue on aesthetic and philosophical matters contained in *Shapes in the Fire*, "Premier and Maker," in which a writer whose fictitious name borrows aspects of both Shiel's and Wilde's conducts an animated discussion with an unnamed prime minister very obviously modelled on Rosebery.

The extent to which Shiel distanced himself from all that Wilde and Rosebery stood for can be gauged by a dialogue contained in the present collection, which plays a similar role to the one contained in *Shapes in the Fire*: the middle section of "Cummings King Monk," subtitled "He defines 'Greatness of Mind'." Both Wilde and Rosebery are included among the names of those to whom Monk—here engaged in a dialogue whose first person narrator is addressed as "Shiel"—denies true greatness of mind, finding evidence of a fatal mediocrity in both. Rosebery's supposed flaws are not discussed in detail, but seem to be primarily political—Shiel, as a committed socialist, had moved considerably to the left of orthodox Liberal politics—while Wilde is condemned for his superficiality, for being a poseur in life and literature alike. Shiel's commitment to the Decadent style, and to its appropriate literary deployment, was always more earnest and intense than Wilde's.

The discussion between Shiel and his imaginary *alter ego*—a kind of über-Shiel—regarding greatness of mind is bound to seem slightly odd to a modern reader because its main specimen of examination is Cardinal John Henry Newman, a man still famous at the time—although he had died in 1890—but now completely forgotten. Newman was the most famous Victorian convert from the Anglican Church to Catholicism, who subsequently argued theological matters with the zeal that is typical of converts anxious to justify what might otherwise seem a kind of treason.

Shiel's interest in Newman might conceivably have sprung from a brief dalliance with the idea of making a similar conversion himself; his own father had been an Anglican minister, and he spent a great deal of time in Paris, where he must have become acutely aware of the fact that the author of the paradigm example of Decadent prose fiction, Joris-Karl Huysmans, had made a very public reinvestment in the Catholic faith. Huysmans had recommended such an investment in the final page of his "Decadent Bible," *À rebours* on the archetypally perverse grounds that its creed and ceremonies were such a spectacular tissue of lies and impostures. The fact that Huysmans had entered a monastic order might well have something to do with the fact that Shiel's first fantastic projection of his own personality, Prince Zaleski—whose lifestyle is even more flamboyant than that of Jean Des Esseintes, the hero of *À rebours*—had been replaced by a "King Monk."

JAUNTING ON THE SCORIAC TEMPESTS, BY BRIAN STABLEFORD

Cummings King Monk is so merciless in his analysis of Cardinal Newman's intellect that he not only denies him the greatness of mind widely credited to him in the Victorian era but diminishes him to the level of a "savage." That is not quite the unalloyed insult that it seems, since Monk also establishes that Socrates and Plato—the inventor and popularizer of the very dialogue form he is employing—are also "savages," as was Jesus himself; Newman is, however, held to have far less excuse than they, for they knew nothing of the modern science whose intellectual mastery is the key to greatness of mind, while Newman had willfully ignored it.

Monk inevitably has difficulty in finding anyone, even among his contemporaries, who meets all of his criteria of greatness of mind, but his rankings are interesting, particularly his judgment of two of Shiel's fellow socialist writers, George Bernard Shaw and H. G. Wells. Shaw is held to fall shorter of the ideal by a more considerable margin than Wells, the great pioneer of scientific romance. Shiel wrote several novels allied to the latter genre, although the best and most famous of his futuristic fantasies, *The Purple Cloud*, had been as much a religious fantasy as a scientific romance. Whenever Shiel discussed the future of religion and the philosophy of faith in his fiction—as he often did, from *The Purple Cloud* (1901) and *The Last Miracle* (1906) to *The Young Men Are Coming!* (1937), he did so in terms that attempted to replace the moral teachings of the Old and New Testament with a faith accommodated to the discoveries of modern science, which was therefore compatible with Monk's definition of "greatness of mind."

Any comparison of Cummings King Monk with Prince Zaleski is bound to find the substitute a less colorful figure, Both characters are, in essence, derivatives of Edgar Allan Poe's fantastic self-projection C. Auguste Dupin (and thus may be ranked as kissing cousins of Arthur Conan Doyle's Sherlock Holmes) and both retain the key features of their original model, but they develop those features in somewhat different directions. Zaleski is Dupin taken to Decadent extremes of which even Jean Des Esseintes only dreamed, drowning in the bizarrerie of his surroundings and languishing in a drug-assisted phantasmagoria. By contrast, Monk, although he is even richer than Zaleski, chooses to live far more modestly, exercising his exotic tastes with much greater restraint. Monk is also more active than Zaleski. Although Zaleski had been prepared to go out into the world to admonish the members of the Society of Sparta for employing murderous means to their idealistic ends, Monk is not only prepared to mount the large-scale social experiment outlined inn "He Meddles with Women" but also to take the good fight much more aggressively to the self-described "exact scientist" featured in "He Wakes an Echo."

Monk has disciplined himself to an extent that Zaleski never would have done, although he is still the ultimate *amateur*, who regards crime-fighting merely as a means of alleviating his *ennui*. He is not much interested in crimes as puzzles; his fascination with social deviance cuts deeper than that, and he sees that it is problematic in more ways than one. In that respect, he is very much in the mainstream of Shiel's evolving literary work, of which *The Pale Ape and Other Pulses* provides a fascinating cross-section.

Although "Huguenin's Wife" would have slotted very well into *Shapes in the Fire*, being as conspicuously Decadent an *hommage* to Poe as "Xélucha" and "Tulsah," the other stories in the present collection make manifest efforts to move away from the aesthetic philosophy of the earlier collection, in much the same direction that Cummings King Monk followed in subjecting Prince Zaleski to a thorough rehabilitation. "The Case of Euphemia Rakash" is a crime story cast more obviously in the Holmesian mode than any of Zaleski's adventures, although it is far more interested in crime as a product of abnormal psychology than as a threat to social order. Indeed, the notion on which its plot hinges—that of multiple personality—was to become something of an *idée fixe* of Shiel's in the years following its publication. The first short story he published in 1896, "Wayward Love," may have been omitted from this collection because its theme also hinges on dramatic personality transformation, but that did not prevent Shiel from including "A Bundle of Letters," which is a wry inversion of the same theme in the context of a popular love story. Nor did it prevent him from including "The Pale Ape" and "The Bride," both of which similarly revolve around issues of confused identity, one objective and one subjective.

There is nothing very surprising about Shiel's use of fantastic projections of himself in literary dialogues extrapolating his own internal disputes, nor his in continual dabbling with the melodramatics of multiple personality and secret identity—these are methods and preoccupations to which many writers have been exceedingly prone—but it is worth noting that Shiel's interest was considerably more focused that the average. When he had imagined himself, allegorically, as an alloy of Adam and Job in *The Purple Cloud*, he objectified the contrary impulses at war within himself as "the black" and "the white," although they do not reflect any simple contrast between good and evil. The same complexity—or, at least, obliquity—is evident in the various stories in this collection in which characters provide the focal points for internal motivational warfare. By comparison with orthodox fantasies of multiple personality modelled on Robert Louis Stevenson's *Dr. Jekyll and Mr. Hyde*, Shiel's are far more peculiar, in moral as well as psychosexual and psychosomatic terms.

The other elements of Shiel's work that continue their trajectories in this collection include his use and development of the *conte cruel*, which is the typical form of Decadent short fiction. Shiel had always cleaved closer to Poesque models of the *conte cruel* than many of the French writers who took over its evolution—including the Comte de Villiers de l'Isle Adam, who gave the subgenre its name. Such archetypal Shielian examples as "Huguenin's Wife" and "The Spectre-Ship" are tales of relentlessly-unfolding doom of which Poe would surely have approved wholeheartedly, although the latter is marked by a distinct move towards literary naturalism in spite of its exotic setting. Whereas "Huguenin's Wife" draws upon the mythical past, "The Spectre-Ship" is set in a clearly-defined historical context that forbids the kind of casual supernatural intrusion employed in the earlier story; here, the hand of fate works its will just as inexorably, but also more ironically, working through the power of the imagination rather than literal manifestation.

In the context of this shift, "The Bride," which first appeared in *The English Illustrated Magazine* in 1902, and "Many a Tear," which first appeared in the US version of *Pearson's Magazine* in 1908, offer interesting examples of the mutation of the format. "The Bride" is far the more Poesque of the two in every respect but its setting, which transposes a formula designed for use in exotic contexts into the formulaic setting of contemporary "shop girl romances"—a transposition that few writers would have found comfortable, although Shiel was never afraid of calculated oddity. The result is an evident anomaly, but the mundanity of the setting adds an extra ironic edge to the conclusion, which some readers will find uniquely delicious. "Many a Tear," by contrast, is not at all Poesque, being solidly cast in the kind of determinedly naturalistic frame that eventually gave rise to "dirty realism" and *noir* fiction, providing a harrowing account of everyday human cruelty whose moral indignation in deftly muted.

The development of these two stories mirrors a drastic shift in the pattern of demand to which the middlebrow magazines of the early twentieth century were responding. The 1890s had been an era of experimentation, when editors would try anything, but after

1900—by which time Decadent excess had already taken one mortal body-blow—the results of those experiments were generally held to have been firmly established by experience. It became a matter of editorial dogma that what the public wanted to read were crime stories and domestic dramas, which held closely to the fundamental story-arcs now typical of those genres: in the former instance, crimes committed were solved and expiated; in the latter, relationships hazarded on the basic of natural affection ultimately triumphed over social barriers inhibiting their consummation.

Neither of these formulas held any significant attraction for Shiel—whose foremost literary interest was always in their subversion by *conte cruel* assumptions and their perversion by the divers operations of abnormal psychology—but he had perforce to operate in a context of demand in which they had become familiar and in which they set the standards of thematic and stylistic normality. There is a sense in which the whole contents of *The Pale Ape and Other Pulses* show Shiel wrestling with that fact of literary life, as heroically as he could. He never gave in to the extent of producing pastiches of conventional popular fiction in large quantity, but he did find a certain fascination in various patterns of compromise. "A Bundle of Letters" is as close as he came to attempting a conventional "happy ending," and the conspicuous half-heartedness of the attempt might have prevented the story from selling to the popular magazines that must have been its envisaged market.

Of the other stories in the collection that had not been previously published in 1911, "The Great King" is the most conspicuous example of a story that was unrepentantly ill-fitted to the new publishing regime. Although its setting is only a little more exotic than that of "The Spectre-Ship," it is as firmly committed to the conventions of the mythical, rather than the historical, past as "Huguenin's Wife." Its plot is, in effect, much the same as that of "The Bride," and fits much more comfortably into its quasi-Biblical milieu than the latter does into the subrealm of the shop girl romance, but it is the sort of neat fit of which the popular magazines had become very suspicious. "The House of Sounds" is even more flamboyantly Poesque than "The Great King"—it is a calculated exaggeration to an imaginative ultimate of "The Fall of the House of Usher"—but is somewhat less extreme in its exaggeration than the story of which it is a new version, which had appeared in *Shapes in the Fire* as "Vaila."

"The House of Sounds" might have been written as a stylistic experiment, when Shiel had decided that he ought to tone down the

Jaunting on the Scoriac Tempests, by Brian Stableford

Decadent features of his prose and personality alike—which he must have done sincerely rather than as an exercise in cosmetic diplomacy—but it was more probably a straightforward abridgement written in response to some editorial offer that never came to fruition. At any rate, Shiel evidently came to prefer the second version, for that was the one he reprinted several times over. Some of the changes are purely cosmetic; for instance, the alienist in the story—who is evidently modelled on Jean-Martin Charcot, professor of neurology at the Sorbonne—is named Carot rather than Corot, presumably to avoid confusion with the painter, and the island of Vaila becomes Rayba. Others are more substantial; a considerable section is lopped out of the alienist's commentary on a hypersensitive patient, which carefully likens his malady to the extraordinary apprehension of the Supreme Being, and two sections from Harfager's discourse relating to life's endurance beyond the cessation of breathing are omitted.

Some readers (I am one) do not consider these material cuts to be the story's advantage, but there is undoubtedly a logical rationale in their making. They tighten up the story-line, and make the story more reader-friendly by reducing the exoticism of the prose, cutting out many terms borrowed from other languages and exotic spellings—the long passage represented as a quote from "Hugh Gascoigne's *Chronicle of Norse Families* uses more conventional spelling in this version than the earlier one, and many other (though by no means all) esoteric terms employed in the original story are removed or modified. The continuity of the climax is improved by the excision of a brief passage in which the narrator is seized by the intoxication of the storm, although the cost of greater consistency is the loss of the story's most high-flown speech, in which the narrator judges the tempest to be "jaunting on the scoriac tempests and reeling bullions of hell!"

"The House of Sounds" makes an interesting pair with the third section of "Cummings King Monk," which also describes a labyrinthine house in the grip of terminal decay. The references in the former story suggesting that Shiel was familiar with the work of Charcot imply that he might also have heard rumor of the ideas of Sigmund Freud relating to the symbolism of dreams, but even if he had not, his reading of "The Fall of the House of Usher" would have familiarized him with the notion of a house mirroring and incarnating the psychology of its owner. There is no shortage of such symbolic edifices in Gothic fiction, and significant new examples had been produced by Shiel's contemporaries—William Hope Hodgson's *The*

House on the Borderland had appeared three years before *The Pale Ape and Other Pulses*, and Shiel must have liked it a great deal if he had happened across it—but Shiel's dark, twisted and decaying houses trembling on the brink of annihilation are more extreme mirrors of elaborate hysteria than any others of their kind.

The not-so-stately homes featured in "The Pale Ape" and "The Strange Case of Euphemia Rakash" are markedly less exotic than those featured in "He Wakes an Echo" and "The House of Sounds," but their membership of the same symbolic subspecies is unmistakable. The edifices similarly displayed in "Huguenin's Wife" and "The Great King" are not houses in quite the same sense, but they too are elaborations of the human psyche, which pay due heed to its innate complexity and perversity. Whether they are fallen already, doomed to fall in the future, or capable of some semblance of survival, all these houses are balefully lit and direly uncomfortable to inhabit. They are all subject to unnatural vibrations, born of the storms which—by virtue of the conventional literary inversion of the pathetic fallacy—inevitably reflect the emotional turbulence of their inhabitants.

For all his hectic and inveterate extravagance, Shiel was not a man to use words carelessly, and he must have been sensible of the implications of calling the items in *The Pale Ape and Other Pulses* something other than "stories" or tales." He probably had in mind the obsolete significance of the term that is defined in Webster as "a stroke; an impact; also an attack" as well as the figurative meaning that refers to an "underlying sentiment, opinion, drift, or the like" discoverable by skill in perception. The whole point of *contes cruels* is that they are strokes or impacts—attacks, even—that aspire to perceive something underlying, unacknowledged if not properly hidden. In this sense, "pulses" is as good a word for them as any, and it is in this sense rather than in terms of regular rhythm that *The Pale Ape and Other Pulses* is a striking, as well as a heartfelt, book.

Jaunting on the Scoriac Tempests, by Brian Stableford

EDWARD LYTTON BULWER AND THE GOTHIC LIFESTYLE

That life imitates art far more assiduously than art imitates life was obvious long before Oscar Wilde offered an explicit statement of the dictum in his classic essay on "The Decay of Lying". It had first become obvious a century earlier, during the heyday of the so-called Gothic novel. The attachment of that label to the horror novels of the late eighteenth century had as much to do with the lifestyle fantasies in which Horace Walpole indulged at Strawberry Hill and William Beckford at Fonthill Abbey as with the content of their pioneering literary exercises, but the close and intricately tangled relationship between Gothic literary fantasy into Gothic lifestyle fantasy soon came to be crucially associated with the image of Lord Byron.

Even in today's world of instantaneous communication, cheap superstardom and hectic fads it would be impossible to discover such a tight feedback loop as that which existed between Byronic literary fantasies and Byronic lifestyle fantasies—a loop that became a knot when both Lady Caroline Lamb and John Polidori elected to express their spite against their former friend in the form of ludicrously exaggerated Gothic fantasies.

In exactly the same way that all fiction is fantasy, so there is a sense in which all lifestyle is fantasy, but in exactly the same way that most fiction is stubbornly mundane and slavishly mimetic, so the great majority of lifestyles are stubbornly and slavishly bound to convention and custom. It is no coincidence that the lifestyle fantasy that made the true relationship between life and art obvious was an oppositional lifestyle fantasy, calculatedly cast in defiance of commonplace social norms.

Because lifestyle fantasy is essentially a pick-and-mix business, constrained by financial means and varied by idiosyncratic taste there was at the beginning of the nineteenth century, as there is now, a broad spectrum of overlapping oppositional lifestyles whose elements are negotiable. The main definitive feature of the Gothic lifestyle fantasy is, however, easy enough to identify as an extreme adherence to a Romantic aesthetic creed, with a particular emphasis on what that creed's opponents would be likely to see as perversities.

In brief, the Gothic pose prefers the sublime to the beautiful, the wild to the ordered, emotional excess to reasonable moderation, night to day and black to color. It is intimately interested in the arcane, the occult, the supernatural and altered states of consciousness, even though it often takes a skeptical or rigorously Sadducistic view of all problematic phenomena. It applauds or attempts to carry forward the cause of literary Satanism: the philosophical position summarized by William Blake's remark that Milton was of the devil's party without knowing it, which was subsequently expanded into a manifesto of sorts in Shelley's *Defence of Poetry*.

Although the original models of Gothic lifestyle fantasy were all aristocratic, the fantasy was soon democratized. A definitive cut-price version was eventually supplied by Edgar Allan Poe's description of the lifestyle of C. Auguste Dupin in "The Murders of the Rue Morgue"—a passage still cited as "crucial" by Mick Mercer in his definitive commentaries on today's Gothic lifestyle fantasies. In the most recent of those commentaries, *The Hex Files: the Bible of Goth*, Mercer recalls a conversation he had with a motor-cycle courier who biked round some late information from the publisher.

"Is it a book about Popular Culture?" the courier asked.

"No," Mick replied. "Unpopular Culture."

That terse summation is the essence of all oppositional lifestyle fantasies, including all those describable in retrospect as Gothic.

* * * * * * *

By the time the boy who was then known as Edward Lytton Bulwer began reading, the Gothic novel was in the final phase of its fashionability, and by the time he began writing it was a dead duck. Its associated lifestyle fantasies did not long outlast it. Byron's death in 1824 robbed Gothic lifestyle fantasists of their primary role model. His good friend George Brummell—whose insulting enquiry "Who's your fat friend?", indirectly aimed at the Prince Regent, became the star item of counter-conventional dialogue—followed him into exile in 1816 but fell thereafter into far greater obscurity, at least until 1843, when his influence was spectacularly but posthumously renewed in France by Jules-Amadée Barbey d'Aurevilly's epoch-making essay on "dandyism".

JAUNTING ON THE SCORIAC TEMPESTS, BY BRIAN STABLEFORD

The path into exile pioneered by Byron and Brummell was, of course, to be followed by many other British lifestyle fantasists of an oppositional stripe, including Swinburne (temporarily) and Wilde (too late)—a necessity that speaks volumes about the awesome power and rigor of British convention. We usually refer to the fierce backlash against early nineteenth-century oppositional lifestyle fantasies as Victorianism, but it began more than a decade before Victoria acceded to the throne, and anyone who hoped to conserve a measure of respectability while remaining in England after 1825 had to knuckle under.

For Bulwer, there was never any serious question of deserting his homeland, and he spent the greater part of his life in the ruthless suppression of his own tendencies to opposition. He refused to reprint his own thin contribution to Gothic prose fiction, *Falkland*, even though he was prepared to dispute his mother's judgment that it was a horridly immoral book. He made his way across the political spectrum from freethinking reformist to steadfast Tory. When he inherited Knebworth he adopted a lifestyle quite beyond reproach, and rebuilt it in a style that was not in the least fanciful. In the meantime, however, his writing kept on picking at the scabs of his youthful indiscretions, to the extent that the existential wounds never completely healed. Ironically, his continual revisitations of certain elements of the Gothic world-view—because rather than in spite of their confused and cryptic nature—became one of the major factors in the late nineteenth-century revision and revival of the Gothic lifestyle.

If one takes Bulwer's public pronouncements too seriously, this was not merely an unintended consequence of his endeavors but one of which he thoroughly disapproved. In the collection of *Life, Letters and Literary Remains* assembled by his son, a whole page is devoted to the boast that it was Bulwer, in *Pelham*, who assassinated Byronism, there considered as a species of "foppery".

"It is a wonder," writes the son, "that Byronic sham should have been so long sustained by impostors whom nobody believed, and who could not possibly have believed in themselves.... Youths in the fresh exuberance of life supposed it beautiful and heroic to put on a woe-begone expression of countenance, and pretend that their existence was blighted in its bud. They affected to be sated and worn out by premature vice, and darkly hinted that their conscience was tortured by the stings of unutterable crimes.... The foppery of Pelham was the reverse of all this. It was frank, cheerful, and refined.... The author of *Pelham* congratulated himself on this result of his work.

Writing of it in 1840, he remarks: 'Whether it answered all the objects it attempted I cannot say, but one at least I imagine that it did answer. I think that, above most works, it contributed to put an end to the Satanic Mania—to turn the thoughts and ambitions of young gentlemen without neck-cloths, and young clerks who were sallow, from playing the Corsair, and boasting that they were villains. If, mistaking the irony of Pelham, they went to the extreme of emulating the foibles that that hero attributes to himself, those, at least, were foibles more harmless, and even more manly and noble, than the conceit of a general detestation of mankind, or the vanity of storming our pity by lamentations over imaginary sorrows, and sombre hints at the fatal burden of inexpiable crimes.'"

It is, of course, only natural that Bulwer should have taken this diplomatic line in 1840, and even more natural that his son should avoid drawing attention to the observation that anyone who used Pelham as a role-model had "mistaken the irony" of the character. But the argument should not be taken at face value. The first volume of the *Life, Letters and Literary Remains* offers abundant evidence of Bulwer's early flirtations with certain aspects of the so-called Satanic Mania, and both its narrative voices would presumably have been deeply insulted had anyone dismissed Bulwer's unhappiness over his disastrous first love affair and its subsequent literary embodiments as "the vanity of storming our pity by lamentations over imaginary sorrows".

The fact remains that *Pelham* is a deeply ambivalent work, whose ambivalence becomes even more obvious when it is considered in combination with the novella to which it was originally conceived as a companion-piece, *Falkland*, to the work that Bulwer was later to couple with it as a novel of fashionable life, *Godolphin*, and most particularly to an even later novel, which likewise grew, after several false starts, out of an early fragment that Bulwer never could put conclusively away: *Zanoni*.

There was certainly a world of difference between Byron and Bulwer, perhaps most neatly summed up in the fact that whereas Byron annoyed the hell out of Lady Caroline Lamb by tossing her aside like a worn-out sock, it was Lady Caroline Lamb who annoyed the hell out of Bulwer by subjecting him to a similar indignity, presumably because he was neither mad enough, bad enough nor dangerous enough to be worth knowing. The would-be lifestyle fantasists who were to look upon *Zanoni* as deliriously thirsty men might greet a watery mirage were, however, far more interested in what the two men seemed to have in common.

Jaunting on the Scoriac Tempests, by Brian Stableford

* * * * * * *

The circumstances of Bulwer's childhood were ideal for the making of a half-hearted outsider. Separated by his overbearing mother from his brothers, taught to despise his father thoroughly, his education begun by his bibliophilic grandfather and all-too-briefly continued by the books the old man left behind when he died, Bulwer was isolated, flattered, indulged and greatly encouraged in both independence of spirit and intellectual vanity, to the extent that his biographer, Michael Sadleir, was driven to ask: "Is it strange that this child should have grown up ill at ease with more normally-backgrounded and normally-educated men? Is it surprising that his ancestry and training should have cast him in a sort of contradictory mould, so that throughout his life he lay athwart the pattern of his age and circle, at once self-distrustful and self-confident, rightly sure of his own pre-eminence but never sure how to impose it on the world?" To which rhetorical questions the answers are, of course, negative.

Bulwer's early experiments in the role of a morbidly melancholy pseudo-Gothic poseur culminated in his pilgrimage to Ulleswater to cast himself upon the grave of the girl with whom he had had a brief secret love affair and his seduction by Lady Caroline Lamb in the aftermath of Byron's funeral. His eight-month sojourn in Paris and Versailles in 1825-26 seems—in spite of later attempts to talk it up—to have been unremittingly dull, but he made up for that in the course of his courtship of Lady Caroline Lamb's protégée Rosina Wheeler, marriage to whom made him an outcast from his home, encouraged his flirtation with radical politics and forced him to write for money as well as glory. The last was a necessary spur, not merely to his productivity but also to the ingenuity with which he sublimated his lifestyle fantasies into his work, ready for further re-cycling by readers who stubbornly persisted in "mistaking his irony".

* * * * * * *

Falkland, was first published in 1827, seven years after the last of the great Gothic novels, Charles Maturin's *Melmoth the Wanderer* and two years before William Mudford's burlesque, *The Five Nights of St. Albans*. Not until the late 1840s would there be any significant revival of the form, when its stereotypes were extensively rehashed for newly-literate readers in a profusion of penny dreadful serials.

Like many of Bulwer's early prose fictions, *Falkland* is something of a patchwork, in which several disparate and presumably pre-existent fragments are stitched together by various kinds of connective tissue. The novella begins with a series of letters in which Erasmus Falkland responds to the Honorable Frederick Monkton's unreproduced description of "the gaiety of 'the season'" with an elaborate description and explanation of his own lifestyle. He inhabits "a ruin rather than a house" amid "savage and wild scenery", having long indulged a "thoughtful and visionary nature" by wasting his hours in "dim and luxurious dreams", to the point at which his character has been irremediably stamped by a "fitfulness of temper" and an "affectation for extremes". In sum, Falkland reports, "I have rendered my mind unable to enjoy the ordinary aliments of nature; and I have wasted, by a premature indulgence, my resources and my powers, till I have left my heart, without a remedy or a hope, to whatever disorders its own intemperance has engendered."

In these early pages Falkland speaks entirely for himself, and there is no obvious reason why the reader should not sympathize with his viewpoint. Nor is there any clear indication that the reader is not expected to continue that sympathy when letters by other hands are cited and an objective narrative voice intervenes to introduce Lady Emily Mandeville, with whom Falkland quickly falls in love. Emily loves him in return, in spite of the disapproval of her family, even though her affection is threatened by Falkland's impassioned argumentative assault on the notion of the immortality of the soul. She agrees to elope with him, although the decision seems ill-starred when she suffers a stroke after reading some cautionary verses.

As the hour for the lovers' crucial defiance of morality and convention approaches, the tone of the narrative becomes increasingly hysterical. Falkland sees an apparition of Emily, who had earlier pledged to renew his faith in immortality by appearing before him as a spirit if she should die before him. She has, of course, suffered a second and conclusive stroke—dying, as any decent heroine of her era would be expected to do, before her anticipated dishonor. Falkland is unhinged by grief, and commits himself suicidally to a war of liberation waged by Spaniards against the French. As he meets this thoroughly Byronic fate he gives voice to his anguish and despair in a last unrepentant soliloquy. It was this soliloquy that Bulwer's mother held up as final proof of the book's immorality—and one cannot help suspecting that the defense to that charge set out in Bulwer's letters, to the effect that Falkland is a bad man who gets his just desserts, is a trifle disingenuous. Even so, the *Life, Letters and Literary Remains* establishes that one of several preliminary drafts of *Pelham* was begun in tandem with *Falkland*, with the clear end in view of exploring a character of a very different type.

The notion that Falkland was always intended to seem unsympathetic is somewhat enhanced by the fact that he is named after the villain of William Godwin's *Caleb Williams*, who is an evil hypocrite. His first name, though, would have been associated with contemporary readers with Erasmus Darwin, who was reckoned a great man in spite of his tendency to materialism. Henry Pelham, on the other hand, bore exactly the same name as one of the great pioneers of the Gothic revival, who had hired William Kent to rebuild Esher Place in a fashion that was subsequently held by historians to have inaugurated the new fashion in architecture and landscape gardening. The original Henry Pelham's nephew, Lord Lincoln, was one of the obsessive objects of desire cultivated by Horace Walpole, whose experiments at Strawberry Hill took some inspiration from his visits to Esher Place. Nor is it obvious, in the early chapters of Bulwer's *Pelham* (1828), that the eponymous narrator is to stand alone as its central character, given the trouble taken there to introduce the Falklandesque Reginald Glanville: "the one who, of all my early companions, differed the most from myself; yet the one whom I loved the most, and the one whose future destiny was the most intertwined with my own."

The novel as eventually developed is even more of a patchwork that *Falkland*, and the *Life, Letters and Literary Remains* goes to some pains to dismiss the Glanville patches as the least satisfactory, but it seems probable that, when the first version was begun, Glanville's tragic history was to be the heart of it. This tale of a twice-frustrated revenge, which the comprehensively-alienated Glanville attempts to take upon the man who ruined and caused the death of his first love, provides the final version of the novel with a better melodramatic counterpart to Pelham's supercilious and mildly satirical tourist-guide to contemporary high society than the absurd excursion into the criminal underworld that replaces it in the later phases. It is worth noting, too, that Pelham's guide to fashionable society takes the trouble to include a lengthy jeremiad by the exiled Lord Russelton—an obvious pastiche of Beau Brummell—whose parodic elements are overlaid on a definite sympathy. Although Bulwer and his public eventually decided to stand four-square with

Pelham, several lengthy descriptions of alternative lifestyles and world-views testify to the fact that the decision was neither so easy, nor so clear-cut, as it seemed.

Glanville, we are told—with obvious approval—"was a man of even vast powers—of deep thought—of luxuriant, though dark imagination, and of great miscellaneous, though perhaps ill-arranged erudition. He was fond of paradoxes in reasoning, and supported them with a subtlety and strength of mind which Vincent, who admired him greatly, told me he had never seen surpassed. He was subject, at times, to a gloom and despondency, which seemed almost like an aberration of intellect.... It was only then, when the play of his countenance was vanished, and his features were still and set, that you saw to their full extent, the dark and deep traces of premature decay." After considerable expansion on this theme, Pelham takes care to assure his readers that Glanville is neither artificial nor affected, and is therefore cut from finer cloth than the average Byronist, but his only complaint against Byronism at this point seems to be the inauthenticity of its contemporary adherents.

In the *Life, Letters and Literary Remains* Bulwer's son records that among the other manuscripts he found that dated from 1826, along with *Falkland* and some "sketches of life and character" that were combined with other materials in *Pelham*, was "a short fiction founded in the alleged secrets of the Rosicrucian Brotherhood" which was "quite complete, and appears to contain the germ of those ideas which...suggested *Zicci* and finally created *Zanoni*." The hastily-aborted serial *Zicci* was published in 1838, four years before its existing chapters were rewritten in the novel *Zanoni*, but Bulwer toyed half-heartedly with occult themes several times between 1826 and 1838, most notably in "The Tale of Kosem Kesamim", which was first issued as part of the satirical serial *Asmodeus at Large* in 1832, and in the novels *Godolphin* (1833) and *The Last Days of Pompeii* (1834).

The preface added by Bulwer to *Godolphin* when he included it in his collected works compares and contrasts its eponymous hero with those of *Pelham* and the Godwin-influenced crime novel *Eugene Aram* (1832), insisting that Godolphin is a deeply flawed character very much inferior in character and morals to Pelham. The text itself follows a pattern that can now be seen as consistent through all Bulwer's occult-tinged novels, losing sympathy with its hero by slow but sure degrees, until little or none is left at the death.

Godolphin, having frustrated in his love for Constance Vernon, exiles himself to Italy, where he meets a Danish astrologer and occult scholar named Volktman. He becomes briefly fascinated by Volktman's esoteric studies but cannot take them seriously. Volktman's daughter Lucilla, however, falls deeply in love with him, encouraged by a horoscope that anticipates an ominous conjunction between her natal star and his. When Volktman dies, Lucilla happily lives with Godolphin as his mistress, but is devastated when she learns that he has made contact with his former lover, now widowed and in a much more accommodating frame of mind. Lucilla renounces Godolphin, committing herself instead to the continuation of her father's researches. She eventually becomes a fashionable society occultist operating pseudonymously in London. Godolphin's marriage to Constance is blighted by the guilt occasioned by his betrayal of Lucilla, but the power of true love enables them to work through their troubles—until Lucilla reveals herself and the prophecy of the horoscope comes to its fatal fruition.

In spite of several apparent demonstrations of its power within the story, Godolphin never concedes that there is any truth in astrology, in much the same fashion that Falkland was not convinced by the promised apparition of Emily that he too was possessed of an immortal soul. Nor is the story's seeming endorsement of Lucilla's powers as wholehearted as it may seem, always keeping open the possibility that her visions are purely psychological phenomena whose accuracy is based in subconscious understanding. Bulwer was certainly fascinated by the occult "sciences", and took the trouble to assemble a considerable library to aid his researches, but he never could make up his mind how seriously to take their claims or how to explain their hold over the imagination. "The Tale of Kosem Kesamim" is a visionary allegory about a Faustian magician, and Bulwer subsequently attempted to excuse his more determined excursions into fantasy by appending allegorical interpretations that ring conspicuously hollow, but this only served to emphasize the depth of his confusion.

The Last Days of Pompeii was an obvious attempt by Bulwer to cash in on the popularity of historical novels, and to upstage Walter Scott. The story is careful to flatter conventional piety by presenting early Christianity in a favorable light and securing the eventual conversion to that faith of the novel's cultured hero, Glaucus, but by far the most interesting character in the book is its neo-Gothic villain Arbaces, a magician-priest of Isis. "The character of Arbaces," the text observes, "was one of those intricate and varied webs, in which even the mind which sat within it was sometimes confused and perplexed. In him, the son of a fallen dynasty, the outcast of a sunken people, was that spirit of discontented pride, which ever rankles in one of a sterner mould who feels himself inexorably shut from the sphere in which his fathers shone, and to which nature as well as birth no less entitled himself. This sentiment hath no benevolence; it wars with society, it sees enemies in mankind."

By the time Bulwer wrote those words he had begun to mend the breach with his mother occasioned by his marriage to Rosina Wheeler, but the marriage itself was on the rocks and he probably felt more isolated than he had before. He and Rosina returned from the continental tour during which the first three-quarters of *The Last Days of Pompeii* was written in a state of conspicuous disarray, which helps to explain why the final quarter of the novel is so weak and dispirited that even the eruption of Vesuvius cannot revivify the exhausted narrative.

The attractions of Arbaces' misanthropic world-view are more firmly rejected within the text than those of Falkland, by means of the stern insistence that he is a bad man who gets his due comeuppance. His supposed magical powers are also treated dismissively, as charlatanry supported by a measure of secret scientific knowledge and philosophical acumen. The fact remains, though, that, even in the absence of any Falklandesque rants, his is the most eloquently-expressed viewpoint in the story. It is hardly surprising that Bulwer set out four years later to write a novel about a magician-priest with *real* powers, and although he abandoned it for a further four years just as his protagonist was about to be initiated into the ancient mysteries, he did eventually bring the project to a conclusion.

* * * * * * *

Like *The Last Days of Pompeii*, *Zanoni* is a historical novel. It is set in the years leading up to the French Revolution. The Terror stands in for the eruption of Vesuvius, and Bulwer took care to incorporate into the narrative La Harpe's famous account of Jacques Cazotte's prophecies of the fates of the several of the Revolution's key figures—a prophecy that shares with all famous prophecies the unremarkable attribute of having been recorded after the event. Cazotte's meager powers pale into insignificance, however, by comparison with those of Zanoni, who is, in his turn, merely a protégé of the immortal Mejnour.

The plot of the novel involves an English dilettante named Glyndon, who has much in common with Godolphin. He is attracted to the singer Viola Pisani, but cannot consider her a suitable candidate for marriage, although it seems that marriage alone might save her from the violent attentions of a Neapolitan prince. Glyndon and the prince are both descended from scholars of the occult who lacked the moral fiber to become true adepts, and this encourages Mejnour to take an interest in them. When Zanoni steps in to save Viola from the royal rapist, Glyndon refuses to marry her, preferring to become Mejnour's pupil in a remote Gothic pile. Zanoni then feels duty-bound to sacrifice his own immortality and revert to mere humanity by binding his fate to hers. Glyndon proves, however, to be a far weaker vessel than Zanoni, failing the tests that are set for him by his tutor so comprehensively that, when he finally runs away with a gipsy mistress, he becomes haunted by the accusing and threatening stare of the monstrous Dweller of the Threshold.

A note appended to later editions of *Zanoni* includes an anonymous allegorical interpretation of the story in which the Dweller of the Threshold is said to represent "FEAR (or HORROR) from whose ghastliness men are protected by the opacity of the region of Prescription and Custom", but a different interpreter might have likened it to the censorious and ever-watchful gaze of society, eager to pounce upon all transgression, especially as it might be embodied in the gaze of a disapproving mother. At any rate, Glyndon never does cross the threshold that separates the everyday world from the attractive but costly realm of supernatural promise. Nor, despite numerous posthumous attempts to assert the opposite, did Bulwer—but the world has never been short of Byronic fools avid to rush in where honest Victorians fear to tread. Numbered among *Zanoni*'s readers were a few—perhaps more sensitive to its ironies than the majority—who took such inspiration from Glyndon's frustrated aspirations that they yearned to outdo him. The least inhibited of them was, inevitably, a Frenchman.

Alphonse-Louis Constant was, like almost every other extreme Gothic lifestyle fantasist, a failed *littérateur*. After dabbling unsuccessfully in poetry and politics he found his métier in middle age when he adopted the pseudonym Éliphas Lévi. He quickly became the great pioneer of modern occult scholarly fantasy, publishing a series of works whose star items were *Dogme et rituel de la haute magie* (1854-6; tr. as *The Doctrine and Ritual of Transcendental Magic*) and *Histoire de la magie* (1859; tr. as *The History of Magic*) with provided the earlier book with appropriately elaborate, if largely imaginary, historical foundations. The former became the principal source-book of all subsequent practical handbooks of "high magic", including those used by the "Rosicrucian lodges" that sprang up in some profusion in *fin-de-siècle* Paris, most famously the one headed by Joséphin Péladan, and those written in English by A. E. Waite (who was Lévi's translator) and Aleister Crowley. The success of Lévi's largely-imaginary history prompted the poverty-stricken historian Jules Michelet to dash off the highly imaginative potboiler that was to become the most influential scholarly fantasy of its era, *La Sorcière* (1861).

Lévi first visited London in 1854, and returned in 1861. He was later to offer carefully sensationalized and appropriately teasing accounts of his relationship with Bulwer, the only man in England of whom he approved, although he may not actually have met his local hero until he visited Knebworth during his second visit. Bulwer had very little to say on this topic, but a footnote in his second occult romance, *A Strange Story* (1862)—which certainly borrows details from Lévi's scholarly fantasies—observes that *Dogme et rituel* is "less remarkable for its learning than for the earnest belief of a scholar of our own day". We cannot know, of course, how earnest Lévi's impostures were, although the history of charlatanry does testify to propensity that even the most cynical scholarly fantasists have for falling victim to their own lines of patter. What we need not doubt, however, is that the feedback loop that connected Bulwer's literary fantasies with Lévi's lifestyle and scholarly fantasies initiated a series of echoes whose elaborate feedback extends to the present day.

All modern lifestyle fantasies of an occult stripe are part of a tradition whose real point of origin was Alphonse-Louis Constant's decision to remake himself as Éliphas Lévi, and, to the extent that Bulwer influenced that conversion, his contribution to neo-Gothic lifestyle fantasies was significant. Even if his influence had little or no causal force, his anticipation of the pattern into which modern occult lifestyle fantasies would settle is remarkable, and the key to that anticipation was the scrupulous ambivalence that ultimately prevented him from becoming any kind of neo-Byronic lifestyle fantasist himself. The great majority of modern lifestyle fantasists retain a thoroughly Victorian insistence on the fundamental virtue of their poses. Vulnerable parties defend themselves against the charge of "Satanic Mania" by insisting that Satanism is a charge unjustly leveled at them by adversaries who do not understand them, and that good magicians may thrive while the bad inevitably get their comeuppance.

Michael Sadleir's summary judgment of Bulwer, italicized for emphasis, was that "*Bulwer throughout his life was an intellect be-

trayed by character". A more sympathetic commentator might have put it the other way around, proposing that it was, in fact, Bulwer's intellect that kept getting in the way of his character. It was his intellect that always prevented him from taking the Gothic lifestyle entirely seriously, in spite of its fascinations, and rendered him immune to the folly into which enthusiastic lifestyle fantasists fall when they begin to believe in their own inventions. If Alphonse-Louis Constant and the legions that followed after him had been willing to do likewise, we would be living in a far saner but somewhat less gaudy world. There is, of course, not the slightest reason why we, who are proud to count ourselves among the sane, should regret or defame the performance art that lifestyle fantasists provide for our edification, or the inspiration that the literary fantasies of men like Bulwer provide for them.

HUMPHRY DAVY'S DREAM

The evolution of what we can now identify, in retrospect, as "proto-science fiction" was as uncertain a process as might be expected from a genre whose name is so nearly an oxymoron. "Science" is, by definition, truth acquired within a framework of understanding in which the credentials of truthfulness are established by hypothesis, logical analysis, empirical observation and experimental testing. "Fiction" is, by definition, a lie, even when set out within a naturalistic framework which demands that the liar make as much effort as possible to reproduce the texture of actual experience.

This divide is not as deep as it may seem, because the hypothetical phase of the scientific adventure is speculative and imaginative, dealing with as-yet-untested possibilities, and science can only discover new truths by means of hypotheses that are bold as well as original. The consequence of this necessity, however, is that when science ventures into the realms of fiction it has little use for those kinds of fiction that attempt to minimize their lies by clinging stubbornly to naturalistic representation of the world as known (or, at any rate, believed in). However odd it may seem, the even-more-oxymoronic term "science fantasy" might be reckoned a more honest account of the most useful literary extrapolations of science than the more familiar term. It is, at any rate, far from obvious that the "natural" or "ideal" forms of "science fiction" are the novel and the short story, whose evolution has been strongly influenced, if not actually determined, by the naturalistic doctrine.

We, of course, have grown used to the awkward fusion of scientific fantasy and novelistic narrative, but the pioneers who laid the first foundations of modern science fiction can hardly be blamed for couching their first experiments in other, more nakedly fantastic, formats. The rich tradition of proto-science-fictional traveler's tales was launched by the first and foremost champion of the scientific method, Francis Bacon, who followed the precedent set by other Utopians in embedding his incomplete account of the technologically-sophisticated society of *New Atlantis* (1627) in a fanciful traveler's tale. Another pioneer of the scientific revolution, John Kepler, was the first to couch an earnest scientific argument—a representation of the Copernican theory of the solar system—within a literary dream. His *Somnium* (1634) also includes an ingenious attempt to imagine how life on the moon might have adapted to the long cycle of day and night, anticipating evolutionary theory and ecological science. The greatest French champion of Enlightenment, Voltaire, overturned the format of the traveler's tale in *Micromégas* (1750), which adopts the hypothetical viewpoint of a gargantuan native of the planet Saturn in order to assault the delusions of grandeur maintained by contemporary churchmen, thus launching the proto-science-fictional tradition of fabular *contes philosophiques*.

The adaptation of these frameworks to the work of serious scientific speculation was by no means unproblematic. The traveler's tale, even in its Utopian mode, had inherited a chronic frivolity, and it was hard to see how it could be rehabilitated in an age that was in the process of completing the exploration of the Earth's surface. A literary dream, even if it is gravely allegorical, is by definition a mere phantom of the imagination, always threatened by ruination at the point of awakening. The moral fable's transformation into the *conte philosophique* overcame the problem of its dyed-in-the-wool conservatism but not, at first, the calculated artificiality of its carefully-distanced milieux and conventional constructs (of which anthropomorphic animals are only the most obvious). Even so, these were the resources on which early nineteenth century scientists were most likely to draw if they decided to venture into the further realms of speculation, and the examples cited above were among those most likely to influence the framing of early nineteenth century ventures. It is this context that we need to bear in mind in assessing the contribution to proto-science fiction made by Sir Humphry Davy in his last book, *Consolations in Travel; or, The Last Days of a Philosopher*, which was issued posthumously in 1830, a year after the death that is so gracefully anticipated in its pages.

* * * * * * *

Humphry Davy was one of the foremost scientists of his day. He was born in Penzance in 1778 into relatively poor circumstances, although his mother, having been orphaned in infancy, had been adopted by a surgeon named John Tonkin. Tonkin took a keen interest in his grandson-by-adoption, and when Humphry's own father died he took it upon himself to secure the boy an apprenticeship with a fellow physician in 1795. Tonkin also allowed Humphry to set up a laboratory in his garret, although he subsequently cut Davy out of his will when the young man turned his back on the medical profession. Davy had found another patron by then, who employed him as a laboratory assistant in a Pneumatic Institute he had established in Bristol.

In Bristol, Davy made the acquaintance of Samuel Taylor Coleridge and Robert Southey, and began writing poetry under their influence, which Southey included in the anthology he was then editing. His scientific publications were, however, far more prolific, his early endeavors being collected in *Researches, Chemical and Philosophical* (1800). In 1801 he was appointed Director of the Chemical Laboratory at the recently-founded Royal Institution, also serving as editor of the Institution's publications. His career went from strength to strength thereafter, winning him a series of promotions and prizes and culminating in the knighthood conferred upon him in 1812, the year in which he published *Elements of Chemical Philosophy*. This was followed, a year later, by *Elements of Agricultural Chemistry*. In 1815 he devised the miners' safety-lamp for which he is today best-remembered. In 1818 he became a baronet, and in 1820 he was elected President of the Royal Society. He continued his pioneering researches in electro-chemistry, with particular reference to the problem of preserving the copper sheathing used to protect the hulls of ships, but his health had already begun to fail and it broke down completely in 1826. He spent his last three years roaming continental Europe, partly in search of a more benign climate and partly in search of the solace afforded him by the contemplation of natural scenery and the ruins of past civilizations. His penultimate book was *Salmonia, or Days of Fly-Fishing* (1827), a celebration of his favorite hobby.

Such was the parlous state of medical knowledge in the 1820s that Davy's health problems mostly went undiagnosed as well as untreated. With the aid of hindsight and his own record of his many endeavors, however, we can form a much clearer picture than he could of the nature and causes of the physical deterioration that killed him at the age of fifty. That deterioration must have begun in his early days as an experimenter, when he undertook extensive empirical investigation of the physiological effects of nitrous oxide ("laughing gas"), which he suspected of being the "principle of contagion" responsible for the communication of disease. Although his most successful investigations were in the fields of mineral analysis and "galvanism" Davy never gave up hope of solving the problem of contagion, and his constitution suffered a more serious degradation while he was at the height of his powers, in 1812, when he contracted a dangerous fever whose cause he was trying to detect. The damage done by the fever was further exacerbated by his attempts to determine whether such contagions could be countered by inhaling curative gases. Unfortunately, the gas whose potentially-curative properties were most widely touted at the time was chlorine, whose properties were extensively investigated by Davy (although he never figured out that it was an element) long before it saw military use in the Great War as an aggressive poison.

In brief, although he may not have known it himself, Sir Humphry Davy was a casualty of his own war against ignorance. He was murdered by the strength of his devotion to the scientific method. *Consolations in Travel* is the last intellectual testament of a dying man, published as it was first written down because the author had no opportunity to make any revisions. It takes the form of a series of six philosophical dialogues, although the dialogues are frequently interrupted by long expository sequences in which the hypothetical narrator—who is eventually given the name Philalethes (*i.e.*, "love of truth")—describes various European settings and meditates on his responses thereto, and offers accounts of dreams that he has experienced at various times in his life.

The other main participants in the first two dialogues are called by the pseudonyms Ambrosio and Onuphrio, and their main function is to represent different religious standpoints; the former is a conservative Roman Catholic, the latter a moderately radical Protestant. In the later dialogues two other characters make extensive contributions to the discussion. One, described as "The Unknown" or "The Stranger", eventually speaks most explicitly and most elaborately in the voice of Davy the scientist, although that is not his first function. (His assumption of this burden certainly does not mean that Philalethes should not be taken as a projection of Davy himself; it is perfectly permissible for several or all the participants in a philosophical dialogue to be hypothetically-separated aspects of its author.) The other, Eubathes—presumably implying "good depth", although Eubathos would have been more explicit—is a keen flyfisherman who becomes the predominant voice in the final pages, when he delivers a long and eloquent soliloquy on the inevitability of mortality and decay. As philosophical dialogues go, Davy's are notably lacking in conflict and contention; his five characters spend most of their time enthusiastically agreeing with one another.

Philalethes reveals that he was a skeptic in his youth, but that he was eventually converted to belief in God. A generous proportion of the discussion within the text is given over to the reconfirmation of this decision, although a reader so inclined might judge that Philalethes emphasizes the firmness of his faith just a little too much to be wholly convincing. It is interesting that his account of his conversion identifies the root cause as a dream he had while he was delirious after contracting a dangerous fever while investigating the theory of contagion: a dream that he insists on construing as a vision of an angel. It is also interesting that he offers this dream as a reason for his belief that another and much more elaborate dream—an account of which occupies most of the first dialogue, "The Vision"—can be counted as an essentially truthful Revelation. Although it may be a slight oversimplification, the entire book can be seen as an extended attempt to discover the implications of this supposed Revelation.

* * * * * * *

The narrator (who remains unnamed throughout the first dialogue) explains to his two listeners how he sat alone in the ruins of the Colosseum in Rome by the light of the full moon, and how his situation led him to ruminate on the transitory nature of human endeavor:

> The beauty and the permanency of the heavens and the principle of conservation belonging to the system of the universe, the works of the Eternal and Divine Architect, were finely opposed to the perishing and degraded works of man in his most active and powerful state. And at this moment so humble appeared to be the condition of the most exalted beings belonging to the earth, so feeble their combinations, so minute the point in space, and so minute the period of time in which they act, that I could hardly avoid comparing the generations of man, and the effects of his genius and power, to the swarms of luceoli or fire-flies which were dancing around me and that appeared flitting and sparkling amidst the gloom and darkness of the ruins, but which were no longer visible when they rose above the horizon, their feeble

light being lost and utterly obscured in the brightness of the moonbeams in the heavens.

This reverie leads to the conscious construction of analogies between human individuals and civilizations, which give way to the vision itself:

> The ruins surrounding me appeared to vanish from my sight, the light of the moon became more intense, and the orb itself seemed to expand in a flood of splendour. At the same time that my visual organs appeared so singularly affected, the most melodious sounds filled my ear, softer yet at the same time deeper and fuller than I had ever heard in the most harmonious and perfect concert. It appeared to me that I had entered a new state of existence, and I was so perfectly lost in the new kind of sensation which I experienced that I had no recollections and no perceptions of identity.

This altered state of consciousness allows the narrator to hear the voice of a "superior intelligence", which he chooses to call the Genius, who plays the role of commentator as the narrator is carried away on a voyage through time and space.

Playing the time-traveler, the narrator sees the remote ancestors of mankind living in a wild state, without clothes or shelter, using primitive tools of flint and bone. Then, after "the birth of Time", he sees man "in his newly created state": fully clad, far better fed—having invented agriculture and animal husbandry—and properly sheltered. He sees civilization advance by degrees, witnesses the advent of metallurgy and philosophy, war and writing, conquest and colonization. The Genius explains to him how the fall of Rome to barbarian hordes was a necessary clearance and prelude to reinvigoration by hybridization, and waxes lyrical on the crucial role played in human history by natural philosophers and technological innovators: the progenitors and agents of progress.

Post-Darwinian readers can see how close the Genius comes, while advancing his theory of human progress, to the notion that social evolution is guided by natural selection, but he stops short. (Much of the subsequent discussion of the vision is dedicated to the work of reconciling the idea of progress with the accounts of the Creation and the Fall set out in *Genesis*; later in the text, the idea that fossil species might have evolved by slow degrees into the creatures that currently populate the earth is summarily rejected by the Unknown.) The Genius continues his own mission by demonstrating to the narrator what little his feeble mind can comprehend of the spiritual universe and the vast spaces outside the earth:

> Spiritual natures are eternal and indivisible, but their modes of being are as infinitely varied as the forms of matter. They have no relation to space, and, in their transitions, no dependence upon time, so that they a pass from one part of the universe to another by laws entirely independent of their motion. The quantity, or the number of spiritual essences, like the quantity or number of the atoms of the material world, are always the same; but their arrangements, like those of the materials which they are destined to guide or govern, are infinitely diversified; they are, in fact, parts more or less inferior of the infinite mind, and in the planetary systems, to one of which this globe you inhabit belongs, are in a state of probation, continually aiming at, and generally rising to a higher state of existence.

The Genius assures the narrator that he could show him the present incarnations of the spiritual essences that were Socrates and Newton, "now in a higher and better state of planetary existence drinking intellectual light from a purer source" but decides instead to conduct him to the planet Saturn, so that he might look down into its atmosphere and see its alien inhabitants:

> I saw moving on the surface below me immense masses, the forms of which I find it impossible to describe; they had systems for locomotion similar to those of the morse or sea-horse, but I saw with great surprise that they moved from place to place by six extremely thin membranes, which they used as wings. Their colors were varied and beautiful, but principally azure and rose-color. I saw numerous convolutions of tubes, more analogous to the trunk of the elephant than anything else I can imagine, occupying what I supposed to be the upper parts of the body.

The Genius explains that each of these trunk-like tubes "is an organ of peculiar motion or sensation" and that their superior sensory apparatus and intelligence have allowed the Saturnians to discover far more about the universe and its laws than mankind ever could, and to become far more virtuous. He explains to the narrator that the other planets in the solar system are inhabited by beings at various levels of intellectual and spiritual development, and that the "higher natures" that exist elsewhere in the universe make use of "finer and more ethereal kinds of matter" in their organization. After death, therefore, men—among whom scientists are those most ready for rapid advancement—will make heavenly progress by slow and measured degrees, through a series of extraterrestrial incarnations:

> The universe is everywhere full of life, but the modes of this life are infinitely diversified, and yet every form of it must be enjoyed and known by every spiritual nature before the consummation of all things.

The narrator is permitted to glimpse one other mode of existence, when he observes moving around him "globes which appeared composed of different kinds of flame and of different colors", containing figures that remind him of human faces. The Genius explains to him that he is now in "a cometary system":

> Those globes of light surrounding you are material forms, such as one of your systems of religious faith have been attributed to seraphs; they live in that element which to you would be destruction; they communicate by powers which would convert your organised frame to ashes; they are now in the height of their enjoyment, being about to enter into the blaze of the solar atmosphere.

Although they were once incarnate as men, these cometary beings can no more remember their humanity than men can remember life in the womb. The only "sentiment or passion" that the spiritual essence or "monad" carries forward through all its successive metamorphoses is the love of knowledge, whose ultimate extrapolation is the love of God. If this love is misapplied to worldly ambition the pursuit of oppressive power, the Genius explains, a spirit "sinks in the scale of existence...till its errors are corrected by painful discipline" but the narrator is not insulted by any vision of such subhuman modes of existence. The Genius concentrates on celebration of the progressive aspects of the post-human situation, insisting that the cause of progress is not merely the highest good but the source of the greatest joy of which any imaginable being is capable.

The Saturnians and the comet-dwellers, the dreamer is assured, are capable of far greater happiness than mere humans. The Genius, who is happier still, cannot take the narrator into his own world—the sun—because its brightness would prove fatal to one of his feeble constitution, and so the vision ends with the voice of Enlightenment replaced by that of a servant searching for his lost employer.

* * * * * * *

Davy's vision was not the first flight of the human imagination into the cosmos theoretically constructed by science, and the subsequent dialogues refer *en passant* to two visionaries who had undertaken more extensive odysseys: Athanasius Kircher and Emmanuel Swedenborg. The work by Kircher to which Davy refers is, however, the proto-geological study *Mundus Subterraneus* (2 vols., 1665; 1678) rather than the much less well known *Itinerarium exstaticum* (1656), and although the documents nowadays known as the *Arcana of Heaven* had been extracted from Swedenborg's notebooks for publication and translation, it is unlikely that Davy had read them. It is even more unlikely that he had read the work that had pioneered the idea of serial reincarnation in extraterrestrial settings, Restif de la Bretonne's epistolary fantasy *Les Posthumes* (written 1787-89; published 1802). Even if he had taken some inspiration from such prior endeavors, though, Davy's vision of the cosmos includes some notable original features.

What is most significant about Davy's dream, from the point of view of the literary historian, is that it bridges the borderline between religious fantasy and scientific fantasy, attempting the futile but heroic task of reconciling the two. There are, of course, enthusiastic acknowledgements of scientific discovery in the earlier fantasies cited above, but those in later religious cosmic fantasies such as W. S. Lach-Szyrma's *Aleriel* (1886) and W. S. Harris's *Life in a Thousand Worlds* (1905) became increasingly tokenistic as awareness deepened of the essential irreconcilability of the ideas that Davy was attempting to combine. Davy's dream and its supportive dialogues constitute an unusually determined attempt to place the scientific enterprise at the very heart of human endeavor and human destiny, as conceived by Christianity, thus placing human life in a cosmic perspective simultaneously accommodating everything that observation and experiment have so far proved and everything that the scriptures have supposedly revealed. It is, in this sense, not merely a work of proto-science fiction but a work of proto-hard science fiction, as well as a Christian fantasy.

It is significant that Davy's bridge between science and religion is markedly different from the bridges constructed by later writers who attempted to incorporate contemporary scientific knowledge into cosmic visions that still appointed conscious Creators as their First Causes. Edgar Allan Poe's magisterial *Eureka* (1848), begins by decrying the limitations of the scientific method and pleading the cause of individual "intuition" as a source of truth far more reliable than the supposed revelations of scripture. Although Davy's faith in the revelatory authority of the scriptures and his own dreams is certainly a kind of intuition—which, as it happens, served him more meanly than Poe's genius served him—Davy's insistence that the scientific method is the first and best instrument of the love of truth and his commitment to an Anglo-Catholic version of Protestantism require him also to insist that science cannot and may not produce any knowledge that will flatly contradict the account of Creation given in the Old Testament.

We may assume that Davy's dream had an even more powerful influence than Poe's prose-poem on the writer who made the most assertive attempt to carry their fledgling tradition forward, Camille Flammarion. Flammarion loved Poe, but he took the trouble to translate *Consolations in Travel* into French; it is the vision in Davy's first dialogue that is the true forefather of Flammarion's brilliantly imaginative *Lumen* (1887), which extrapolates all of Davy's ideative innovations (and is likewise organized into five dialogues). Flammarion was, however, writing after the publication of Darwin's *Origin of Species*, and he knew full well that the revelations of science could no longer be reconciled with those of *Genesis*; he had no alternative, therefore, but to become an outright heretic, abandoning the Catholicism of his forebears for the newly-reconfigured faith of Spiritualism.

It is not obvious that any other subsequent producers of cosmic visions took abundant inspiration from Davy, but it is possible that the vision included in William Hope Hodgson's *The House on the Borderland* is partly indebted to him for its "celestial globes", whose description and evaluation echo the "cometary intelligences" of the earlier work. Of more interest to the modern reader, however, are the manner in which Davy's attempt to make good use of his dream tackles key issues in the conflict between science and religion that have recently been re-opened—more fiercely contested than ever before—in the American bible belt, and the tentative argument it sets out for the psychological utility of science fantasy in general and hard science fiction in particular.

* * * * * * *

The principal question addressed by Ambrosio and Onuphrio in the second dialogue, when Philalethes has recounted his vision (adding, as a supplement, an account of his earlier encounter with a presumed angel) is that of whether his vision of the gradual rise of man from savagery to civilization can possibly be true, given the very different account of prehistory rendered in *Genesis*. This leads to a further discussion about the merits of different religious systems.

The arguments set out in this cause seem odd to the modern skeptical eye, in that they approach only to veer away from what seem to us like common sense anthropological explanations in much the same way that the vision approached but veered away from a quasi-Darwinian notion of human evolution. In seeking to establish that arguments from authority are (provided that it is the right authority) quite consistent with empirical arguments, leading to exactly the same conclusions, Philalethes is obviously trying to have his cake and eat it too. He is an early "Creation Scientist", although his sometimes-unilateral interpretations of the Old Testament would be bound to seem weak-kneed to a contemporary bible-belt Fundamentalist.

Having decided that he cannot doubt the fact of Creation, Philalethes is then confronted, in the third dialogue, by its eponymous hero: "The Unknown", whose first function does indeed seem to be to represent the unknown—and, indeed, the unknowable. The Unknown begins his new acquaintance by lecturing his new friends on the geology of Italy, summarizing recent discoveries, but he is soon forced by Onuphrio to justify his assertions and reconcile them with *Genesis*. Not until he has decisively rejected evolutionary theory as a retreat "into the desert and defenseless wilderness of skepticism [and] false and feeble philosophy" is he allowed to pass his own judgment on Philalethes' vision. At this point he recounts an adventure of his own, in which he met an accursed wanderer condemned to immortality—not the Wandering Jew of legend but a

Jaunting on the Scoriac Tempests, by Brian Stableford

Wandering Christian, cursed by God for attempting to rebuild the Temple in Jerusalem at the behest of the Roman emperor Julian (the Apostate), who desired to put the prophecies of the Old Testament to experimental proof. Although a devotee of the Church of England, the Unknown wears a rosary purchased in Jerusalem at the Church of the Holy Sepulcher and blessed by the pope; he reports that it has been an invaluable passport and safety-warrant during his scientific investigations in rural Italy.

In the third dialogue the Unknown seems to symbolize the limitations of scientific knowledge, setting out boundaries of mystery that ought not to be crossed; the parable of the Wandering Christian seems to be indicating that there are some matters that should not be subjected to experimental testing. When he returns to centre stage in the fourth dialogue, however—having witnessed an incident in which Philalethes and Eubathes escape death by a hair's-breadth after a fishing accident—the Unknown becomes a guide not unlike the Genius, save that his observations are restricted to matters of biology and philosophical ruminations on the nature of life. Challenged by Eubathes, he presents a robust rebuttal of materialism and a stirring defense of vitalism (to which the immortality of the spiritual essence is, in his view, a mere corollary).

It is in the fifth dialogue that the Unknown takes on Davy's voice most obviously, mounting a strident defense of chemistry as a uniquely useful field of human endeavor, summarizing its crucial contributions to human progress and waxing lyrical on the issue of its as-yet-unrealized potential. This argument is further extended in the final dialogue, where the Unknown becomes passionate in his insistence that men must work much harder to preserve their works from the everpresent effects of erosion and corrosion. Eubathes takes up this theme, arguing with equal passion that because decay is inevitable and all earthly things transient men must look beyond civilization and technology for the final justification of their efforts and endeavors. It is, however, Philalethes who must draw the final conclusion, offering a judgment based in his personal Revelation:

> Time is almost a human word and change entirely a human word; in the system of Nature we should rather say progress than change. The sun appears to sink in the ocean in darkness, but it rises in another hemisphere; the ruins of a city fall, but they are often used to form more magnificent structures as at Rome; but, even when they are destroyed, so as to

produce only dust, Nature asserts her empire over them, and the vegetable world rises in constant youth, and—in a period of annual successions, by the labours of man providing food—vitality, and beauty upon the wrecks of monuments, which were once raised for purposes of glory, but which are now applied to objects of utility.

These, it will be remembered, were the last words written for publication by a man who knew that he was dying, and might have had some inkling of the extent to which he had martyred himself for his philosophy. No one should begrudge him, even if it were utterly false, the consolation he obtained from the thought that he—a "ruin among ruins", as he acknowledged himself—might rise again in constant youth under the benign empire of progressive Nature. The real point of his vision, however, was not that it conserved his hope of an afterlife, but that it presented an idea of what that afterlife might and ought to be if, within the system of Nature, we may and should "rather say progress than change."

A modern Fundamentalist might be able to recognize Sir Humphry Davy as an intellectual ancestor, but would not have an atom of sympathy for his conscientious reinterpretation of the exact nature of the revelation to be found in the scriptures. Although Davy was perfectly willing to reject the evidence of fossils as proof of the evolution of biological species he was quite unwilling to deny the permanence and importance of change as a factor in human, earthly and universal affairs. As a natural philosopher, he saw evidence of the inescapability of change in every landscape; for him, the ruins of lost human empires sat side by side with evidence of more profound geological changes. Denial being out of the question, it is only natural that he became obsessed with the question of whether there was any consolation to be found in this heightened awareness of the inevitability of corruption, erosion and corrosion—and, if so, what sort.

Most of Davy's contemporaries, and many of his intellectual descendants, including modern Biblical Fundamentalists, understandably took the view that corruption, erosion and corrosion were natural corollaries of the Fall, and that hope could and ought to be conserved by faith in Salvation: in the faith that the "spiritual essence" of the deserving is bound for a Heaven immune to all kinds of decay. Davy considered this intellectual move to be a kind of *hubris*. The only acute disagreement in *Consolations in Travel* occurs in the fourth dialogue, when Eubathes challenges the Unknown with the assertion that the resurrection of the physical body is both guaranteed in Holy Writ and logically necessary for the administration of divine judgment. "Nothing is more absurd," the Unknown replies, and goes on to argue that the opposite is the case: that if we can only overcome the vile arrogance which makes us think that we can anticipate the judgments of God, then we would realize that the far-reaching ends of divine judgment could only be served by a much more flexible and much more generous universe.

Philalethes is, of course, enthusiastic to agree with this assessment; his vision, though vague, has revealed to him that although there are Hells of a markedly non-Dantean kind, designed for education rather than for punishment, it is the gloriously long and uphill climb to Heaven that is paved with our best intentions. In the scheme revealed to Philalethes we shall not be so unfortunate as to make the transition from life to Eternal Light with a single bound, but will instead be permitted to engineer our own transition by slow but sure steps, buoyed up all the while by the particular joy of learning—a process of self-education for which the scientific method is our God-granted instrument.

It is the moment at which the reader sees the sense of this crucial argument that enables him to see the full meaning of Davy's title. It is certainly concerned with the immediate consolations to be obtained by intellectually-enhanced tourism, but its real concern is the necessity of seeing human existence as one small step on an immensely long journey of literal as well as metaphorical Enlightenment. This was a message that fell, for the most part, on deaf ears, although it had sufficient fervor to strike the young Camille Flammarion with the force of revelation. In order to conserve its central tenets in a post-Darwinian era, however, Flammarion found no alternative but to abandon Davy's respectful attitude to Holy Writ and embrace Spiritualism, while modern Fundamentalists—including "Creation Scientists"—went to the opposite extreme of abandoning Darwin and clinging even harder to the security-blanket of Holy Writ. Now that Spiritualism has gone the way of all briefly-fashionable heresies there are very few people around to argue Flammarion's case, but, if it were still feasible to publish philosophical dialogues, it might be worth while using such a medium to interrogate the question of whether it was actually necessary for Flammarion to make that move in carrying Davy's argument forward. It is, at any rate, worth wondering how Davy might have modified his own position had he refrained from poisoning himself in pursuit of a principle that turned out to be false, and had lived instead to the ripe old age of eighty.

The one thing we need not doubt, of course, is that Davy would have admitted the force of Darwin's arguments. He was a scientist, and he knew a compelling argument when he saw one. By 1859, the mass of evidence was so great that he would have felt obliged to concede the truth of the evolution of species as soon as a plausible mechanism for its operation was suggested, and there is evidence enough in *Consolations in Travel* to assure us that he would immediately have realized the explanatory power of the principle of natural selection (just as he would immediately have realized the explanatory power of Pasteur's version of the germ theory of disease had he lived to be a hundred). We can also be certain that if the dead were able to return to us in the manner permitted by Flammarion's *Lumen* (even if such returns were merely metaphorical) then Sir Humphry would have been back long ago to give us the benefit of his posthumously-acquired wisdom. The fact that he has never played the Genius in anyone else's dreams enables us to conclude that he was absolutely right in the one point of insistence that Flammarion refused to carry forward: that whatever "spiritual essence" is carried forward from the individual life by the process of universal progress cannot and does not include any kind of "self-consciousness".

Given all this, I think we can say with some confidence that the correct extrapolation of the philosophy expounded by Sir Humphry Davy during his last days—correct, that is, in the sense that it is the one of which Davy would have approved—would run along the following lines:

The interpretation of scripture that modern Fundamentalists would reject as insufficiently literal is, in fact, worse than insufficiently metaphorical. As a map of the Divine plan, *Genesis* is not merely useless but worthless. Original sin does not consist of attempting to dine on the Tree of Knowledge and the Tree of the Knowledge of Good and Evil, but in refusing to do so. A balanced diet would assure us, not only that there is a great deal more to be learned about the world and universe in which we find ourselves than our ancestors could imagine, but also that anyone who imagines that the account-books of good and evil are restricted to listing the petty sins and good deeds of individuals, so that shades of those individuals can be committed to Eternal Reward or Eternal Punishment, is a moral imbecile.

Jaunting on the Scoriac Tempests, by Brian Stableford

Neither the good nor the evil that men do is interred with their bones to await the resurrection of the body; it lives after them, to take effect in the course of human history, and, if they have been virtuous, that effect will be progressive. Furthermore, even if humankind should turn out in the fullness of time to be a blind alley, doomed to extinction, we should try to live as if it were not—as if our remotest descendants might yet be able to take a hand in the progressive fashioning of universal history. We should be prepared to accept, in the light of modern scientific knowledge, that nothing will survive of us but the effects that extend through future time of those of our actions that are significant enough to serve as causes; whatever honest consolation is to be found in our earthly travels and travails is to be found there or nowhere.

There *is* honest consolation, though, to be found in both travel and travail. As Davy insists in the pages of *Consolations in Travel*, education towards enlightenment is an inherently joyful process, and the greatest real triumphs of all human beings lie in the depth of their vision: in their ability to see beyond the superficialities of landscapes and objects to the history and natural processes that underlie their temporary aspects; and in their ability to dream while fully awake of the possibilities that those temporary aspects contain.

Today, a man who killed himself by breathing chlorine in order to test the hypothesis that it might counter the principle of contagion would be a fool. He would be a fool because Sir Humphry Davy, who was as far from being a fool as any man his age produced, helped pave the way for a proper understanding of the properties of chlorine and a proper understanding of the nature of disease. It might be a pity if Davy were remembered today only for his invention of a now-obsolete safety lamp and the work he committed to his pioneering attempted analysis of *The Elements of Chemical Philosophy*. Although it too has to be read with some sensitivity to the context of relative ignorance in which it was produced, *Consolations in Travel* is, in its fashion, an important and inspiring work. The "Vision" with which it begins stands in need of correction, but, once corrected, has more to offer the modern reader than the great majority of the idols that have been set up in its stead.

RESISTING PANTHEA'S SIREN SONG: ROBERT HUNT AND THE POETRY OF SCIENCE

As I described and discussed in an essay in *Foundation* 10 (June 1976), the term "science-fiction" was first coined by William Wilson, and the implications of that coinage were first explored in two chapters of his 1851 publication *A Little Earnest Book Upon a Great Old Subject*. The "great old subject" in question was poetry, and the two chapters outlining Wilson's prospectus for science-fiction were headed "The Poetry of Science": a title that he had borrowed from a book published in 1848 by Robert Hunt.

The one example of science-fiction cited by Wilson is *The Poor Artist* (1850) by Richard Henry Horne, a romantic fantasy in which the impoverished hero wins the hand of a fair lady by making a series of sketches of a coin as it would be differently viewed by the eyes of seven animal observers. This seems a rather odd paradigm example of "science-fiction" by any standards, but the most peculiar thing of all about its choice is that there was a much more obvious candidate for inclusion in its stead: the novel with which Robert Hunt followed up *The Poetry of Science*: *Panthea, the Spirit of Nature* (1849). Wilson presumably had not read it, and probably did not know of its existence—which is a pity, because it might have given him a broader and rather different notion of the inspirational quality of "the poetry of science" and the potential of "science-fiction".

Wilson is not the only one to have overlooked *Panthea*. Like *The Poor Artist* it is omitted from both E. F. Bleiler's *Checklist of Science-Fiction & Supernatural Fiction* (2nd ed., 1979) and Darko Suvin's *Victorian Science Fiction in the UK* (1983), although it is annotated—and recommended for further study—in George Locke's *A Spectrum of Fantasy* (1980). Hunt's scientific work has also slipped into obscurity, although he was reckoned sufficiently important to warrant an entry in the *Dictionary of National Biography*, a project to which he also contributed. Although one could not recommend *Panthea* as a work of great literary merit, Locke is entirely right to judge that it is of some importance as a historical document in the history of science fiction, recording as it does a crucial phase of conflict in the evolution of natural philosophy, religion and Romanticism. Set against the background of the author's life and work it reveals some fascinating tensions.

* * * * * * *

The most useful sources of biographical information about Robert Hunt are R. E. Anderson's article in the *Dictionary of National Biography*, the introduction to Hunt's *Popular Romances of the West of England* (1865; expanded 1881) and a brief article in Frederic Boase's *Modern English Biography* (1892). Unfortunately, their accounts of the chronology of Hunt's early life are rather vague; none has more than the barest details of his family. Although some of the missing data can be filled in with the aid of genealogical data available at rootsweb.com a few significant lacunae still remain.

Robert Hunt was born in September 1807 in what was then known as Plymouth Dock but soon became Devonport. He was named after his father, a naval officer whose ship, *H.M.S. Mocheron*, had gone down with all hands in the Mediterranean in April of that year. His mother's maiden name was Honor Thomas; I have been unable to ascertain whether she remarried. The naval officer must have had a brother because the younger Robert had a cousin named Richard William Hunt, who eventually settled in Leeds (where Robert was visiting him at the time of the 1851 census).

After attending school in Plymouth and Penzance, Hunt was "placed with a surgeon practicing in Paddington, London" (*DNB*); this appears to have occurred when he was only twelve years old (*PRWE*). There followed a nine year period of "close labour" (*PRWE*). He studied anatomy under Joshua Brookes (*DNB*) and worked as a physician and medical dispenser before "failing health" (*PRWE*) and the inheritance of a small property in Fowey (*DNB*) caused him to return to Cornwall, apparently in 1828.

While he was in London, Robert Hunt made the acquaintance of "Radical Hunt", who "helped to direct his studies" (*DNB*). The namesake in question was not—as modern readers might be inclined to assume—the famous Radical journalist Leigh Hunt, but Henry

Hunt (1773-1835), a friend of William Cobbett's whose main claim to fame was that he had just stepped up to address the crowd gathered in St Peter's Fields on 16 August 1819 when the so-called Peterloo Massacre began. Henry Hunt was imprisoned in the wake of that incident, but was elected to parliament as M.P. for Preston in the early 1830s. (Leigh Hunt, who became annoyed when confused with his rival, preferred to term him "Bristol Hunt").

It is not clear exactly how Henry Hunt "directed" Robert Hunt's studies, but the coincidence of names and the fact that the younger man forged an intimate acquaintance with the works of the Romantic poets tempts one to recall that Leigh Hunt had once taken a young medical student under his wing—John Keats—and helped him become a Romantic poet. *The Poetry of Science* and *Panthea* are shot through with references to the English Romantics and the latter contains some original poems in the same vein; *Panthea*'s title is borrowed, with due acknowledgement, from Shelley's "Prometheus Unbound"—in which Panthea is the "Oceanide" whose last rhapsodic monologue celebrates the enlightenment of modern science—and the quote supporting its subtitle is drawn from an essay by Coleridge.

When Hunt first returned to Cornwall he produced a volume of poems entitled *The Mount's Bay* (1829) and "studied the folklore of the district" (*DNB*). The latter study included a ten-month walking tour, in which he visited "each relic of Old Cornwall" and "gather[ed] up every existing tale of its ancient people" (*PRWE*). Although this odyssey was undertaken partly for the reinvigoration of his health and the results remained unpublished until 1865, Hunt was as much a pioneer as a folklorist as he was to be in more than one field of experimental science (he takes care to note in *PRWE* that his work preceded that of Mrs Bray, who collected the *Traditions, Legends and Superstitions of Devonshire* in 1835 and published them in 1838). Having recovered his strength, though, he opened a pharmacy in Penzance in 1833 (*MEB*).

In March 1834 Hunt married Harriet Swanson (born 1809), whose younger sister Jane (born 1811) married his cousin Richard. Both Swansons, like both Hunts, had been born in Devonport; the four of them may well have been acquainted since childhood. The Swanson family owned a boot-making business which was eventually inherited by Harriet's younger brother William. Harriet Hunt bore five children: Robert (born 1835), William (born 1836), Charlotte (born 1842), Harriette (born 1843), and Emma (born 1845).

Jaunting on the Scoriac Tempests, by Brian Stableford

Soon after his marriage Hunt returned to London, obtaining employment with a firm of chemical manufacturers. Thanks to an accident of timing, he was given work to do that made him one of the earliest investigators of the chemistry of photography. In 1840, however, he moved back to Cornwall again when he was appointed secretary of the Royal Cornwall Polytechnic Society "by the operation of causes beyond my control" (*PRWE*). He settled with his family in Falmouth. Hunt's interest in the education of the working class had always been strong—he had helped to found a Mechanics' Institute in Penzance—and he became increasingly enthusiastic in that cause, particularly on behalf of Cornish miners. Save for two atypical publications (of which *Panthea* was the first and *Popular Romances of the West of England* the second) the remainder of his life was devoted to the causes of education and science.

Hunt's *Popular Treatise on the Art of Photography* (1841) was the first to be issued in the British Isles; it was to go through six editions and was revised and expanded in 1851 as a volume of the *Encyclopedia Metropolitana*—a project explicitly based on a plan devised by Coleridge. The first edition of his *Researches on Light in its Chemical Relations* (1844) was almost exclusively devoted to photography, but his experiments soon ranged further afield. He took a particularly keen interest in the subtly-different chemical effects of colored light rays separated by prismatic refraction; when a second edition of the *Researches on Light* issued in 1854 it was much broader in its scope, embodying the abundant experimental results he had obtained in the intervening decade.

In 1845 Hunt received the government appointment of Keeper of the Mining Records, a post he was to hold for the next thirty-seven years. Although the duties attached to the position were by no means trivial he found time to publish *The Poetry of Science* and *Panthea* before becoming a lecturer in Mechanical Sciences in the Royal School of Mines at Redruth in 1851. He published a textbook of *Elementary Physics* in the same year. After two years in this post he succeeded to the chair of Experimental Physics. He continued to spend a good deal of time in London, actively involving himself in the organization of the Exhibitions of 1851 and 1862, for which he produced handbooks explaining the scientific and technological background of the items in the catalogues. He contributed to the scientific column of the *Athenaeum* as well as maintaining a steady stream of statistical and educational publications.

Some time before the 1881 census Hunt moved back to London, establishing himself in St Leonard's Terrace, Chelsea, where he died in 1887; Harriet survived him, inheriting his modest estate (£1,605 6s 8d). His friends in London and Cornwall established a Robert Hunt Memorial Museum in Clinton Road, Redruth and the Redruth Mining School dedicated a wing to his memory. These establishments housed his collection of mineral specimens until the school closed in 1953; it was then transferred to the Geological Museum at the Camborne School of Mines, where it can still be seen. Although the *Encyclopedia Britannica* dropped its entry on Hunt half a century ago, his inclusion in the recently-updated *DNB* and the Camborne exhibition continue to ensure that Robert Hunt the scientist is not entirely forgotten.

* * * * * * *

Hunt's most enduring work has proved to be *Popular Romances of the West of England.* This was initially issued in two volumes in 1865 with decorations by George Cruikshank; a single-volume edition followed from Chatto & Windus in 1871, which was enlarged and revised in 1881. Chatto & Windus issued further editions in 1896, 1916 and 1930, and the text was reprinted yet again by another publisher as recently as 1990. It is conceivable that *Panthea* was begun in the latter phase of the same sojourn in Cornwall that produced the notes for this study. Although the final chapter of the novel was almost certainly written shortly before its publication, the early chapters give every indication of having been written in a very different mood under the influence of very different convictions; the publication of *The Mount's Bay* proves that Hunt was involved in other literary endeavors in the late 1820s.

There is a strong resemblance between the plot of *Panthea* and that of Edward Bulwer's anonymously-issued *Godolphin* (1833), under whose immediate influence it might well have been written. Bulwer was an active radical during the late 1820s and early 1830s—although he became a Tory after changing his signature to Bulwer-Lytton—and his tenure as a radical MP coincided with Henry Hunt's. It is possible that Henry Hunt introduced his protégé to Bulwer's works, if not to the man himself, although there is no record in the Bulwer-Lytton archives of any correspondence between Bulwer and either Hunt. Before publishing *Panthea* Hunt would also have had the opportunity to read Bulwer's Rosicrucian romance *Zanoni* (1842), which may also have had an influence on its subject-matter, but the resemblances to Bulwer's earlier novel are far stronger. Interestingly, *Godolphin* exhibits a seemingly-decisive change of mind on the part of its author, which the writing of the novel may have helped to bring about, and *Panthea* does the same. Both novels begin by enthusiastically embracing an occult worldview that their heroes—together with the impersonal narrators commenting on the heroes' careers—eventually renounce.

Bulwer never could entirely overcome the allure of the occult, and he went on to produce other seemingly-credulous works in the same vein as *Zanoni*. If *Panthea* reflects an authentic conversion experience—and it certainly invites consideration as an autobiographical allegory—then Hunt's long career as an experimental scientist proves that the conversion in question was more wholehearted and durable than Bulwer's. It is, therefore, all the more remarkable that the flamboyant exuberance of *Panthea*'s early visionary sequences is bolder than anything Bulwer ever contrived. Given that *Panthea* was published after *The Poetry of Science*, however, it is probably best to delay detailed consideration of its contents until the work that inspired William Wilson to imagine a new genre of "science-fiction" has been subjected to further analysis.

* * * * * * *

In 1848, when Hunt produced the first edition of *The Poetry of Science*, there was no such publishing category as "popular science". It was not until Camille Flammarion published the first edition of his *Astronomie populaire* in 1880 that the idea of "the popularization of science" really took off. Hunt was, therefore, a significant pioneer of this kind of enterprise. Although the success of *The Poetry of Science* was moderate, it was reprinted in the USA (in an edition published in Boston by Gould, Kendall and Lincoln in 1850) and went through two further editions in England, the last being revised and enlarged for release by a new publisher, H. G. Bohn. The main text of *The Poetry of Science* is conscientiously addressed to ordinary readers, although the footnotes and scholarly references aggregated at the end include an impressively wide range of early scientific journals—including several published in French—as well as all the major reference-books in the various fields of the book's concern.

If Hunt was a pioneer in one sense, however, he was slightly old-fashioned in another. There was nothing particularly unusual in the fact that a man of his time should be interested in both poetry and science, or in the poetry of science; several leading Romantic poets had been fascinated by new scientific discoveries, and many leading scientists of a slightly earlier era, including Erasmus Darwin and Humphry Davy, had dabbled in poetry and visionary fantasy. By 1848, however, specialization and the evolution of modern scientific discourse were beginning to make a much clearer distinction between science and the arts. The literary style of *The Poetry of Science* is as awkwardly poised on the brink of the new era of separatism as its hybrid subject-matter. *Elementary Physics*, which he published only three years later, with a similar audience in mind, is much more closely akin to modern introductory texts.

Various references in Hunt's works to the life and works of Humphry Davy lend evidential support to the natural supposition that Hunt must have read Davy's last, posthumously-published, book *Consolations in Travel* (1830), which is elaborately described in the preceding essay. The morals that Hunt draws from the contemplation of the geological discoveries of James Hutton, Charles Lyell and others echo Davy's so closely that Hunt must have thought of himself and Davy as kindred spirits. Hunt, like Davy, appears to have set aside early flirtations with radical free thought in order to become a devout and steadfast Christian. Like Davy, therefore, he is very reluctant in *The Poetry of Science* to read the evidence that the surface of the earth had undergone enormous changes in past eras as a challenge to the religious view of humanity as a special and direct creation of a Divine Architect.

Another work to which *The Poetry of Science* clearly invites comparison is Edgar Allan Poe's *Eureka—An Essay on the Material and Spiritual Universe*, which was published in the same year. The two books are particularly interesting in juxtaposition because they are so strikingly complementary. Poe's long essay—which he requested his readers to judge as a poem—is a rhapsodic account of the revelations of the only physical science that receives tokenistic attention in *The Poetry of Science*: astronomy. Hunt's reluctance to speculate much on astronomical matters—although he quotes extensively from the writings of John Herschel, Poe's primary inspiration—is based in a firm determination to respect the bounds of experimental verification. The speculative "method" employed in *Panthea* is, however, much closer in spirit to the intuitive method championed by Poe in *Eureka*. It is extremely unlikely that Hunt had read *Eureka* before finishing *Panthea*, let alone before starting it, but that only serves to emphasize the sturdiness of the Romantic roots that separately nourished the two works.

* * * * * * *

Jaunting on the Scoriac Tempests, by Brian Stableford

Hunt's purpose in writing *The Poetry of Science* is robustly stated in the first paragraph of its preface: "An attempt has been made in this volume to link together those scientific facts which bear directly and visibly on Natural Phenomena and to show that they have a value superior to their mere economic applications, in their power of exalting the mind to the contemplation of the Universe." (Hunt 1848, p. v) He admits that "For the purpose of exhibiting the great facts of Science in their most attractive aspects, the imagination has been occasionally taxed," but insists that "it has never been allowed to interfere with the stern reality of Truth." (Hunt 1848, p. vi) This is, of course, the fundamental tenet of what is nowadays called "hard science fiction".

As promised in this prospectus, each of Hunt's sixteen chapters sets out to acquaint the reader as to what facts have been discovered in each of the fields of physical and chemical science and what theories have been induced therefrom, together with a careful and reverent account of what the sum of these conclusions suggests as to the nature of the universe and humankind's place therein. Hunt continually contrasts the revelations of modern science with the speculations of classical philosophers and the inventions of folklore, consistently appealing to what later writers have called "the sense of wonder" in order to prove the superiority of the scientific revelation.

The central assertion of Hunt's argument is that, contrary to popular opinion, science has an inherently "poetic" character, his notion of the "poetic" being derived partly from the Romantic theorists Coleridge and Shelley and partly from his activities as a folklorist. The two are, of course, related; the German Romantic theorists from whom Coleridge drew much of his inspiration placed a high value on folklore as a key to the *volksgeist*, and Hunt's Introduction to *Popular Romances of the West of England* waxes lyrical on the subject of the as-yet-indelible stamp that ancient Pantheistic religion has made on "the Celtic Mind". (Hunt 1881, p. 24)

Hunt reiterates this fundamental assertion continually throughout *The Poetry of Science*, but seems to think himself on particularly safe ground when he considers the manner in which our knowledge of chemistry and electricity informs our view of a drop of water:

> It has been argued by many that the realities of science will not admit of anything like a poetic view without degrading its high office; that poetry, being the imaginative side of nature, has nothing in com-

87

mon with the facts of experimental research, or with the philosophy which generalizes the discoveries of severe induction. If our science was perfect, and laid bare to our senses all the secrets of the inner world; if our philosophy was infallible and always connected one fact with another through a long series up to the undoubted cause of all: then poetry, in the sense we now use the term, would have little business with the truth; it would, indeed, be lost or embodied, like the stars of heaven, in the brightness of a meridian sun. But to take our present fact as an example, how important a foundation does it offer on which to build a series of thoughts, capable of lifting the human mind above the materialities by which it is surrounded; of exalting each common nature by the refinement of its fresh ideas to a point higher in the scale of intelligence, of quickening every impulse of the soul, and giving to mankind most holy longings.

What does science tell us of the drop of water? Two gases, the one exciting life and quickening combustion, the other a highly inflammable air, are, by the influence of a combination of powers, brought into a liquid globe. We can from this crystal sphere evoke heat, light, electricity and actinism in enormous quantities; and beyond these we can see powers and forces, for which in the poverty of our ideas and our words we have not names; and we learn that every one of those principles is engaged in maintaining the conditions of each drop of water which refreshes organic nature, and gives gladness to man's dwelling-place.

Has poetry a nobler theme than this? Agencies are seen like winged spirits of infinite power, each working in its own peculiar way, and all to a common end—to produce under the guidance of omnipotent rule the waters of the rivers and the sea. As the great ocean mirrors the bright heaven which overspreads it, and reflects back the sunlight and the sheen of the midnight stars in grandeur and loveliness; so every drop of water, viewed with the knowledge which science has given to us, sends back to the mind reflections of yet distant truths which, rightly followed, will lead us upwards and onwards in the tract of higher intelligences—

"'To the abode where the eternals are.'" (Hunt 1848, p. 173-175; the quote within the quote, uncredited by Hunt, is a slightly-misrendered version of the closing words of Shelley's "Adonais", in which "Eternal", though clearly plural, has no terminal "S".)

This was the argument that snared William Wilson's imagination; the exemplary quote that he reproduces as the essence of scientific wonder comes from the same lyrical passage.

The notion that there are hidden elementary forces holding matter together and determining its transactions is promoted ever more enthusiastically by Hunt as a quasi-deistic substitute for the more haphazard fancies of poetic myth:

> The spiritual beings, which the poet of untutored nature gave to the forest, to the valley and to the mountain, to the lake, to the river, and to the ocean, working within their secret offices, and moulding for man the beautiful or the sublime, are but the weak creations of a finite mind, although they have for us a charm which all men unconsciously obey, even when they refuse to confess it.... The poetical creations are pleasing, but they never affect the mind in the way in which the poetic realities of nature do. The sylph moistening a lily is a sweet dream; but the thoughts which rise when first we learn that its broad and beautiful dark-green leaves, and its pure and delicate flower, are the results of the alchemy which changes gross particles of matter into symmetric forms....
>
> The flower has grown under the impulse of principles which have traversed to it on the beam of solar light, and mingled with its substance. A stone is merely a stone to most men. But within the interstices of the stone, and involving it like an atmosphere, are great and mighty influences, powers which are fearful in their grander operations, and wonderful in their gentler developments. The stone and the flower hold, locked up in their recesses, the three great known forces—light, heat and electricity; and in all probability others of a more exalted nature still, to which

> these powers are but subordinate agents. Such are the facts of science, which, indeed, draw 'sermons from stones' and find 'tongues in trees'. How weak are the creations of romance, when viewed beside the discoveries of science! One affords matter for mediation and gives rise to thoughts of a most ennobling character; the other excites for a moment, and leaves the mind vacant or diseased. The former, like the atmosphere, furnishes a constant supply of the most healthful matter; the latter gives an unnatural stimulus, which compels a renewal of the same kind of excitement, to maintain the condition of its pleasurable sensations. (Hunt 1848, p. 262-264)

This particular repetition of Hunt's argument is significantly infected by a new note. Hitherto, such pleasantries as "the sylph moistening the lily" have been considered charming but outdated; now, the suspicion is raised that indulgence in fancies of that nature can leave a mind "vacant or diseased" and can also be perilously addictive. The poetry of science, it seems, is not merely superior to the poetry that went before but medicinal against its ill-effects. It is not entirely clear how these remarks relate to Hunt's "studies in superstition", but they may offer a clue as to the reason why those studies were set aside in favor of a renewed commitment to scientific endeavor.

The Poetry of Science moves on to consider the physical make-up of living organisms, from a viewpoint that has no knowledge of organic chemistry on which to draw (and which is not yet convinced that oxygen or nitrogen is an element) and not even the most rudimentary ecological concepts to invoke:

> We have seen that animals and vegetables are composed of four gaseous principles, oxygen, hydrogen, nitrogen and carbon. We have examined the remarkable manner in which they pass from one condition—from one kingdom of nature—into another. The animal perishing and dwindling by decomposition into his elementary state, mingling with the atmosphere as mere gas, gradually becomes part of the growing plant, and by like changes vegetable organism progresses onward to form a portion of the animal structure.

> A plant exposed to the action of natural or artificial decomposition passes into air, leaving but a few grains of solid matter behind it. An animal, in like manner, is gradually resolved into 'thin air'.... Our dependency on the atmosphere is therefore evident. We derive our substance from it—we are, after death, resolved again into it. We are really but fleeting shadows.... The sublime creations of the most gifted bard cannot rival the beauty of this, the highest and truest poetry of science. (Hunt 1848, p. 287)

The idea that humans are "really but fleeting shadows" forged by the atmosphere sees Hunt approaching a purely materialistic philosophy, and it is not the last time he flirts with that possibility. When he contemplates the revelations of geology, it is not the evidence of drastic change that first presents itself to Hunt's mind's eye, but rather the evidence of the constancy by which the fundamental forces governing matter have supervised and organized the progression of the epochs:

> Thus have we preserved for us, in a natural manner, evidences which, if we read them aright, must convince us that the laws by which creation has ever been regulated are as constant and unvarying as the Eternal mind by which they were decreed. Our earth, we find, by the records preserved in the foundation stones of her mountains, has existed through countless ages, and through them all exhibited the same active energies as prevail, at the present moment. By precisely similar influences to those now in operation, have rocks been formed, which, under like agencies, have been covered with vegetation, and sported over by, to us, strange varieties of animal life. Every plant that has grown upon the earliest rocks which presented their faces to the life-giving sun, has had its influence on the subsequent changes of our planet. Each trilobite, each saurian, and every one of the mammalia which exist in the fossil state, have been small laboratories in which the great work of eternal change has been carried forward, and under the compulsion of the strong laws of creation, they have been made ministers to the great end of forming

a world which might be fitting for the presence of a creature endued with a spark taken from the celestial flame of intellectual life....

Geology teaches us to regard our position upon the earth as one far in advance of all former creations. It bids us to look back through the enormous vistas of time, and see, shining still in the remotest distance, the light which exposes to our vision many of nature's holy wonders. The elements which now make up this strangely beautiful fabric of muscle, nerves, and bone, have passed through many ordeals, ere yet it became fashioned to hold the human soul. No grain of matter has been added to the planet, since it was weighed in a balance, and poised with other worlds. No grain of matter can be removed from it.

Under the forces we have been considering, acting as so many contending armies, matter passes from one condition to another, and what is now a living and a breathing creature, or a delicate and sweetly scented flower, has been a portion of the amorphous mass which once lay in the darkness of the deep ocean, and it will again, in the progress of time, pass into that condition where no evidences of organization can be found, again, perhaps, to arise clothed with more exalted powers than even man enjoys. (Hunt 1848, p. 324-325 & 329-330)

This is, however, as close as Hunt dared come towards the philosophy of evolutionism in 1848. He does admit that similar observations to these have combined "to deceive poor man into the belief that he is a material being, and the inhabitant of a material world" but he will not go so far himself. The imagery of these passages, like much other imagery in *The Poetry of Science*, recalls certain passages in Shelley's "Queen Mab" (1821)—*e.g.*, "There's not one atom of yon earth/But once was living man;/Nor the minutest drop of rain,/That hangeth in its thinnest cloud/But flowed in human veins." That poem testifies self-consciously to Shelley's flirtation with atheism, but, if Hunt was similarly tempted by his first encounter with it, the temptation was one he overcame, at least temporarily. Hunt's denial of materialism in *The Poetry of Science* is based on an experimental scientist's defensive insistence that "every argument [supporting it] is based on an assumption without a proof; every assumption being merely a type of philosophy itself, a baseless fabric, a transcendental vision." (Hunt 1848, p. 396).

The early phases of *Panthea* are perfectly content to deal in transcendental visions, albeit of a slightly different stripe—another reason for suspecting that its visionary chapters might have been written before Hunt wrote *The Poetry of Science*—but its final chapter is much more closely in tune with the argument presented in *The Poetry of Science*. Indeed, it takes the argument a step further, lending credence to the notion that it must have been written later.

The Poetry of Science itself ends with a ringing restatement of its central thesis:

> Every motion which the accurate search of the experimentalist has traced, every principle of power which the physicist has discovered, every combination which the chemist has detected, every form which the naturalist has recorded, involves reflections of an exalting character, which constitute the elements of the highest poetry. The philosophy of physical science is a grand epic, the record of natural science a great didactic poem.
>
> To study science for its useful applications merely, is to limit its advantages to purely sensual ends. To pursue science for the sake of the truths it may reveal, is an endeavour to advance the elements of human happiness through the intelligence of the race. To avail ourselves of facts for the improvement of art and manufactures, is the duty of every nation moving in the advance of civilization. But to draw from the great truths of science intelligible inferences and masterly deductions, and from these to advance to new and beautiful abstractions, is a mental exercise which tends to the refinement and elevation of every human feeling....
>
> Experiment and observation instruct us in the discovery of a fact;—that fact connects itself with natural phenomena,—the ultimate cause of which we learn from Divine revelation, and receive in full belief,—but the proximate causes are reserved as trials of man's intelligence; and every experimental truth, discovered by induction, is an exemplification of the

fresh-springing and all-enduring POETRY OF SCIENCE. (Hunt 1848, p. 397-398)

* * * * * * *

Before proceeding with an analysis of *Panthea* it may be useful to summarize the plot of the book that its own plot closely resembles, *Godolphin*. The preface added to that novel when Bulwer included it in his collected works insists that Godolphin is a deeply flawed character, but the story follows a pattern that is consistent in all Bulwer's occult-tinged novels, in which an initial sympathy with its hero is gradually forsaken, until little or none is left at the death.

Godolphin, having been frustrated in his love for Constance Vernon and estranged from his family, exiles himself to Italy, where he meets a Danish astrologer and occult scholar named Volktman. He becomes fascinated by Volktman's esoteric studies. Volktman's daughter Lucilla falls deeply in love with him, in spite of an ominous quality in the horoscope that reveals a crucial conjunction between her natal star and his. When Volktman dies, Lucilla lives happily with Godolphin as his mistress, but she is devastated when he re-establishes contact with Constance, who is now widowed.

Lucilla renounces Godolphin and commits herself obsessively to the continuation of her father's researches, eventually becoming a fashionable society occultist operating pseudonymously in London. Meanwhile, Godolphin's marriage to Constance is blighted by the guilt occasioned by his betrayal of Lucilla. The power of love enables them to work painstakingly through their domestic troubles, but matters cannot be conclusively settled until Lucilla reveals herself and the prophecy of the horoscope comes to its fatal fruition.

In spite of several apparent demonstrations of its power within the story, Godolphin ultimately refuses to concede that there is any truth in astrology, or in Volktman's other arcane studies. The narrative's endorsement of Lucilla's prophetic powers is also a trifle querulous, always leaving open—albeit unconvincingly—the possibility that her visions might be purely psychological phenomena whose accuracy is based in subconscious understanding.

These uncertainties reflect Bulwer's own. He was fascinated by the occult "sciences" but never could make up his mind how seriously to take their claims, or how to explain their hold over the imagination. He settled in the end for the service of more commonplace ambitions. Robert Hunt's life is far less extensively-chronicled than Bulwer's, but if *Panthea* can be taken seriously, there must have been some intriguing similarities in their intellectual histories.

****

The protagonist of *Panthea* is Lord Julian Altamont, the only son of the Earl of Devonport. Several siblings having died in infancy, Julian has one surviving younger sister, ominously named Euthanasia. Julian's tutor, Mr. Cheverton, was once an experimental scientist, although he is now a clergyman; in spite of his own religious orthodoxy and the strong objections of Lord Devonport, Cheverton has encouraged Julian to seek further enlightenment from an unorthodox scholar named Laon Ælphage, or Laon the Mystic. Laon is said to be "a follower of Jacob Behmen [who had declared] his firm conviction of the truth of many of the views entertained by the Rossicrucians [*sic*]" (Hunt, 1849, p. 4). ("Jacob Behmen" is the German mystical philosopher Jacob Boehme, who began writing at about the same time as the first appearance of the notorious "Rosicrucian manifestos" in the 1610s; he attempted to refresh the sternness of Lutheran religious philosophy with an injection of alchemical symbolism.)

The first chapter of the novel—which follows an apologetic preface and a Prelude in verse that uses a verse-form similar to that of "Adonais"—finds Laon and Julian deep in philosophical discussion, the former criticizing the latter for his worldliness and finding in him a symbol of the times:

> Julian, you are a type of the age. The giant element of thought, which grows strong with toil, is enervated by indulgence. The eagle eye of the soul, which should gaze steadily on the fixed centre of truth, is weakened by looking on the ground, and the flickering of puny stars now dazzles it, Unable to comprehend, to reach the reality, man contents himself with the semblance. Without the will to raise itself from the surface, and nobly wing its flight through the purer air, the mind hurriedly flutters over the low earth, and is satisfied with the superficial search of an irregular flight.... As man, knowing good and evil, stood bewildered at the gate of Eden, surveying the second chaos which his rashness had produced, he now stands on the frontier of the land he

would conquer, proud but nearly powerless (Hunt 1849, p. 6-7).

Conventional scientific endeavors appear to be diminished by this argument as a matter of paying too much attention to the trees and not enough to the wood. At this point in the story the reader is given no reason to doubt the authority of Laon's judgment on this or any other matter. Although Julian admits that "I cannot follow you" (Hunt 1849, p.12) he is quick to beg for further instruction, in order that he might.

Laon takes Julian home, to a cottage where they discover Laon's daughter Æltgiva "bending with an expression of intense delight over a water-lily, glistening with dew or spray" (Hunt 1849, p. 16-17)—a sight that immediately prompts Julian to compose a poem addressing her as "Maiden Sylph". In *The Poetry of Science* it was exactly this image that led Hunt into his reflections on addictive imagery and diseased mentality, but here the meeting seems a wholly fortunate one.

Although he is supposed to be in love with the eighteen-year-old Eudora Spencer, the daughter of one his father's neighbor landowners, the slightly older but exceedingly lovely Æltgiva makes a deep impression on Julian. She seems to him to be haloed in "mystic sanctity", and when she offers to initiate him into the mysteries of "the mighty PANTHEA"—the spirit of nature—he is extremely eager, and writes to his father to say that he is going on a journey of discovery with Laon.

Having received this letter, Lord Devonport looks for and finds evidence of what he considers to be Cheverton's treachery, in annotations carelessly made by Julian in the margin of a book entitled *Fama Fraternitatis* signed "Andrea". (Johann Valentin Andreae was the undoubted author of a pamphlet translated as *The Chemical Wedding of Christian Rosenkreutz*, 1616, and the probable author of the two Rosicrucian "manifestos" published in 1614 and 1615; *Fama Fraternitatis* is the abbreviation of a much longer title by which the first of those manifestos is generally known.) Lord Devonport reacts angrily to this discovery, while his wife is driven by sadness to seek consolation in her Bible. Euthanasia, on the other hand, is happy because she has chanced to meet Æltgiva and has been reassured that Julian will soon return.

* * * * * * *

Julian's far-ranging journey of discovery changes him considerably:

> It appeared to Julian that he had entered upon a new state of existence. His thoughts were of a higher order, and his feelings of a more sensitive character. His powers of perception were more accurate, and his reflective faculties capable of closer and more enduring exercise. He could now direct his powers of observation to the most microscopic phenomena, and without difficulty connect them with the extended operations of creation. A veil had been removed from his eyes; all things appeared more clear; a greater transparency was, as he thought, exhibited in nature.
>
> Beauty was in and around all things; as a flood of light it diffused itself over the whole world.... His eye was brighter than before, and liquid as with light or tears. His cheek, now almost as white as marble, was, with every thought, tinted by a blush; the current of mind was seen to flow in mystic brightness before that transparent skin. His voice was very altered in its tone,—it had acquired more of that soft and spiritual melody which was so remarkable in Æltgiva, and it had lost those commanding tones which formerly distinguished it.
>
> The man, young and impetuous, had become staid and patiently enduring. The proud, the bold, the obstinate, was transformed into the humble, the meek, the yielding. A man's strength had given way to an almost womanly delicacy; and with it assumed all the divine beauty of feminine spirituality. (Hunt 1849, p. 47-48)

This geography of this journey—like that of Bulwer's *Asmodeus at Large* (1833), with which it has certain affinities—seems to be metaphorical rather than literal. It reaches its climax in tropical South America, where Laon and Julian pass at hectic speed through a fern-forest, across a prairie and a cactus-strewn desert into a dense and richly-populated rain-forest. Their destination is a mountain whose slopes are briefly barred to them by a monstrous ape, which chatters and laughs wildly as the attenuated air causes Julian to slip into a trance state. He passes into the interior of the mountain through a cavernous passage lit by phosphorescence, and finds himself in a damp Underworld veined with precious metals and encrusted with gems (there is a similar Underworld in *Asmodeus at Large*). It is here, while he languishes in Laon's protective arms, that Julian is urged by a kiss upon his forehead and a magical song to send his spirit forth into a supernatural light:

> The brightness increased upon him, and he was soon involved in the splendour of rays, refracted from myriads of ærial prisms, forming, by combination, circles of the utmost chromatic beauty and intense brilliancy, revolving around a centre of the purest brightness.
> Under the influence of the powers of sound and light, Julian's consciousness was slowly restored. He was now moving through the stellar space, and saw world after world rolling on its infinite path in that intercommunion of brightness which chains the material creations into one universal whole....
> He felt that he approached the central sun. With his exalted powers of vision he could now scan the immensity of space; and looking through myriads of planetary systems, which obeyed the influence, as it now appeared to Julian, of that power which was so rapidly impelling him onward, he perceived, as a small speck of light, his own Earth amid the congregated band of planets forming the little solar system, of which he knew himself a part, although he felt no earthward longing. (Hunt 1849, p. 64-65)

When he hears the voice of the "Universal Power" Julian fancies that it is Æltgiva's, but after a considerable preamble its owner introduces herself as Panthea, the Spirit of Nature, and commands him to open his eyes and behold her. When he does so he sees her as "a beautiful embodiment of angelic grace" with furled wings. He seems to be back home, in the valley where he disputed with Laon in chapter one, but Panthea has replaced Laon by his side. She informs him that, although she is indeed a Universal Power, she remains subordinate to the Eternal Presence whose servant and instrument she is.

Panthea bears Julian aloft in a car of cloud. The imagery of this sequence, like some of the more high-flown passages in *The Poetry of Science*, is strongly reminiscent of that of "Queen Mab", which involves a similar visionary odyssey by means of a magical flying "car"—although Shelley's invocation of the "Spirit of Nature" in that poem is somewhat different. Panthea's car carries Julian into space to a viewpoint from which he can observe and study the creation, formation and evolution of the Earth under the influence of the elemental forces of Gravitation, Magnetism, Heat and Electricity. Then comes Light to "animate the scene", first producing vegetable life, then animal life, while continents shift and break up, sea replacing land and land replacing sea. All this is the natural gestation of a "Sacred Paradise", but Panthea—unlike Queen Mab—is careful to stress that its further augmentation requires the direct intervention of the Eternal Presence.

When Julian first beholds "the mighty Adam" amid the trees of paradise Adam is splendid, but a mere animal: "he saw but with his sensual eyes—he heard but with his mechanical ears. Without a thought...the parent of the human race passed before the eyes of Julian as a melancholy example of a soulless man." (Hunt 1849, p. 88) Once ensouled, however, Adam looks about him in a very different way, "all-absorbing" and admiring, but frustrated in the expression of his feelings for want of a mate. Left to his own devices, Panthea tells Julian, Man would become a demon—another Lucifer—but with the bonds of Woman's affection to restrain him he might do better. On the first advent of Adam and Eve the natural food chain is temporarily suspended—the Lion plays innocently with the Lamb—while the Celestial host sings their praises. But it does not last; nor does Julian's vision.

* * * * * * *

Dawn finds Laon and Æltgiva reunited, ascending a "Druidic way" to a Bardic Temple (a circle of stones) where they make their Pantheistic religious observances. They are approached by Eudora Spencer, who has also been Laon's pupil, in search of news of Julian. It is at this point that the reader learns that Æltgiva is in love with Julian and considers Eudora a rival, although she is careful not to let Eudora know it. Laon promises that the reawakened Julian will be home very soon, and so he is—but he is "an altered man".

Mr. Cheverton, chastened by Lord Devonport's criticisms, determines to bring Julian back into the Christian fold, and denounces Laon as a false prophet. He insists that there are limits to what men might learn, and boundaries to what science can reveal. His speech

(Hunt 1849, p. 126) echoes a slightly atypical passage in *The Poetry of Science* (Hunt 1848, p. 91), but the possibility that the passage in *Panthea* is the original and the other the copy is suggested by the fact that Julian's reply—insisting that he has actually seen the Eternal Mystery—is so definite.

At this point, and throughout the dispute that follows, the author's sympathy still seems to lie with Julian the Mystic. This chapter is, however, followed by an Interlude whose head quote is taken from a poem by Elijah Fenton (1683-1730) entitled "Impotence of Human Wisdom", and it may have been at this point that Hunt first set *Panthea* aside for a while; the text never recovers the energy of the first part and its subsequent progress is a patchwork series of fits and starts.

In the Interlude, entitled "Modern Science", Lord Devonport—who is as disappointed to discover that his son is "not Worldly" as the Countess is to discover that he is "not Holy"—dispatches Julian to London to further his education. Julian is disappointed in his turn by London society, which seems to him to be obsessed by trivialities, but he is entranced by the world of science. He soaks up all the newly-solved mysteries that are mapped in *The Poetry of Science*, but longs for more: in particular, for the additional wisdom and greater context that might be provided by Laon Ælphage. He yearns for the gift of "some process of inspiration" that will allow him to "see through nature by a species of *clairvoyance*" (Hunt 1849, p. 148). When Lord Devonport and the Countess visit Julian in London they are dismayed to find him as obsessively lost in his new studies as he had been in those from which they had hoped to distract him. After favoring them with a long lecture on his current state of mind and his philosophical ambitions he determines to return to Altamont.

"Book the Second" begins with Æltgiva and Laon anticipating Julian's return, but their first visitor is Eudora Spencer. Eudora has not heard from Julian for some time and is desperate for reassurance that he has not forgotten her. Æltgiva and Eudora see an omen that leads Æltgiva to confess that it is her own love for Julian that is drawing him home, and then to beg Panthea's—and Eudora's—forgiveness for that selfish sin.

When Julian does return he finds Laon deeply engrossed in alchemical endeavors, arguing for the possibility of transmutation with a passion Julian never found in the chemists of London. Because Julian is hungry for a similar enlightenment, Laon offers him a drug that will provide it: "the essence of the Indian Flax" whose "strange powers...have been known in the East for many centuries"

(Hunt 1849, p. 204). By this hallucinogenic means Julian hastens to the revelation of his second vision. (The reference to "Indian Flax" is presumably to the plant more familiarly known as Indian Hemp, or *Cannabis sativa*; the fact that the text subsequently refers to a variety of *Cannabis* by its Latin name may indicate that the two passages in question were written at different times.)

At first, Julian finds himself in a dark and desolate landscape, surrounded by "the mighty monuments of the Past", but a nebular light soon appears in the sky, from which Panthea descends to meet him. After chiding him for faltering in his vocation she takes up the thread of his earlier vision and displays to him a synoptic history of mankind after Adam's fall: a panorama of social progress guided by the twin lights of scientific discovery and religious revelation. This sequence is neither as long nor as lyrical as the first vision, but it retains a defiant Shelleyesque quality.

Julian eventually wakes to find Laon asleep, the Mystic's alchemical experiment unfortunately having failed. Making his way home thereafter, Julian finds Æltgiva and Eudora in a stone circle once used by the Druids as a place of sacrifice, called the Kistvaen. (This term is not to be found in an extensive chapter on standing stones in *Popular Romances of the West of England* but it does have an entry in Brewer's *Dictionary of Phrase and Fable*, which quotes Walter Scott's *The Betrothed*—published in 1825—where a "Kistvaen" is apparently defined as a granite-faced burial mound). Having reconciled himself with Eudora, Julian walks her home, then resumes his own homeward journey just as a violent storm breaks.

At this point the text undergoes a marked change of character, suggestive of the fact that its resumption was delayed for some considerable time. The storm calls forth a peculiar echo in Julian's own being; seemingly struck by lightning, he falls unconscious. Laon catches him as he falls, but when Julian regains consciousness he is delirious, and charges Laon with having driven him mad. He now sees his former mentor as a demonic tempter, and seems convinced when Laon contrives to guide him home that he has made a pact with the devil.

A physician and a surgeon are summoned to attend to Julian but in a rare moment of black comedy they proceed to disagree violently as to the treatment of his malady. In order to resolve their disputes—they cannot even agree whether laudanum or acetate of morphia is a better opiate—Mr. Cheverton eventually volunteers to treat the patient with *Cannabis indica*. The drug puts Julian to sleep again, but there is no sign of Panthea in his subsequent dreams, which are vivid but terribly confused. Much later, the narrative assures us, he was to think of them as his own version of the temptations of St Anthony. Laon fears that Julian will never recover, but Æltgiva—who has concentrated on astrological researches while her father has been absorbed in alchemical experiments—assures her father that the testimony of the stars is that his strength will be rekindled, albeit at the cost of two other deaths.

The next chapter, "The Teachings of Affliction", describes how the stricken Julian is initially cheered by the devotions of his little sister, whose subsequent sudden demise can be no surprise to the reader who has taken due note of her name. Euthanasia's death is eased by the ministrations of Æltgiva, but it is Mr. Cheverton who takes over the comforting of Julian, and soon persuades him to take a new attitude to life and work. Having conceived a new respect for the prospect of honest toil, and repented of his dreamy indolence, Julian begins to reconcile himself with his father's worldliness, although he insists on maintaining his independence from Lord Devonport's staunch Toryism.

In the final chapter, which is more synoptic and far more hurried than its predecessors, Julian embarks upon a war against Poverty, which he intends to fight with the weapons best suited to the task: scientific and technological innovation, based on assiduous experimentation, and technical education. One matter still remains to be settled, however, and it is to the self-prophesied death of Æltgiva—her return to Panthea—that the final pages of the narrative are dedicated. Laon, Eudora and Julian are all at her death-bed, but their reactions are very different. Although Julian cannot help recalling his visions of Panthea with a certain nostalgia, he now dismisses Æltgiva's demise, rather rudely, as "a choice sacrifice at a false shrine" (Hunt 1849, p. 358). When Laon bids him to "dream on" Eudora counters with an injunction to "awake and work" and it is to the latter instruction that Julian immediately pledges his allegiance.

This is an end that no reader could have anticipated during the early chapters, which seems ill-fitted both thematically and stylistically even to the chapter immediately preceding, where Julian—despite his alleged moral rearmament—is still happy to follow flights of philosophical fancy with Mr. Cheverton. The apparent disjunction lends credence to the idea that the novel was written in at least two and probably more distinct phases, the final chapter being added in 1848 or 1849 to a work that might have been begun at least fifteen years earlier and further supplemented at infrequent intervals. There is no doubt that the resolutions made by Julian in the final chapters echo resolutions that Robert Hunt actually made in real life, and the probability therefore seems strong that the contrary tendency of the earliest chapters and the confused irresolution of the penultimate ones also reflect psychological phases through which he had passed.

Once he had arrived at the conclusions summarized in the final chapter of *Panthea*, Hunt had no alternative but to set aside not merely the Romantic flights of fancy that fill the early pages of the story, but story-writing itself. As a work of speculative fiction, *Panthea* is as self-effacing as Æltgiva: it resolves its central argument by fatally undermining its own initial purpose and method. To the extent that it serves as the first work of a kind of "science-fiction" inspired by *The Poetry of Science*, it is also ambitious to be the last, because its conclusion is that "science-fiction"—or perhaps "science-fantasy" would be a more appropriate term—is a waste of mental effort: effort that ought to be directed by more practical ends. It is, however, difficult for the reader to sympathize with the act of abortion that attempts to terminate all the narrative's discussions; too much has been said in the early chapters in favor of Laon and Æltgiva to allow the rude dismissals of the final chapter to seem anything but flagrantly unjust.

* * * * * * *

The Poetry of Science sets out to inform its readers that science is not merely poetic but more poetic than poetry. It seems to follow that, if science is virtuous because it is poetic, then poetry must itself be virtuous, but that is a point on which Hunt seems slightly confused. He does not hesitate to secure the impression that he was a poet before he was a philosopher—an impression supported by the record of his publications as well as by the fact that Julian Altamont describes himself in exactly those terms in *Panthea*—but there is something slightly excessive in his rededication to science. That excess reveals itself in the final pages of *Panthea* as clearly as it had revealed itself in the passage in *The Poetry of Science* that spoke of the poetic imagery of superstition "[leaving] the mind vacant or diseased" and "[giving] an unnatural stimulus, which compels a renewal of the same kind of excitement, to maintain the condition of its pleasurable sensations."

The critic in search of hypotheses to account for the existential malaise that preceded Hunt's conversion to zealotry in the cause of science is by no means short of alternatives. *Panthea* obligingly provides evidence of his familiarity with hallucinogenic drugs, to which he would have had ready access while he was a dispensing pharmacist in London in the late 1820s and in Penzance in 1833-34. The account of the hallucinatory odyssey of discovery that Julian undertakes in the company of Laon Ælphage, as quoted above, includes some distinct homosexual undertones, although his subsequent hesitation between Æltgiva and Eudora is suggestive of a very different conflict of erotic interests. Then again, the absurd altercation between the surgeon and the physician over their equally useless treatments, coupled with the tragic account of the ill-fated Euthanasia, suggests another possible reason for Hunt's disenchantment with a medical "science" that still lacked a convincing experimental basis in 1849.

It is, of course, possible that none of the characters in *Panthea* bear any resemblance to actual people who figured in Hunt's lifestory. The DNB refuses to inform us as to whether he had a stepfather or a stepsister (although we do know that he had an uncle who was living in Devonport while he was in his infancy there) but it is difficult to imagine that there could have been real-life equivalents of Laon Ælphage and Æltgiva, especially when one bears in mind that models for both of them were readily available in *Godolphin*. Nor are the names of Laon and his daughter much help in attempting to make their significance more precise, although Eudora and Altamont are almost as obvious in their implications as Euthanasia. The use of the Æ diphthong is presumably meant to emphasize Old English (but not Cornish) origins, but it seems unlikely that Ælphage is intended to recall Ælfheah, the bishop of Winchester who became St Alphege. "Elf Age" might be a more plausible reading, given the assertion in *PRWE* that a Cornish popular creed unites fairies with Druids (Hunt 1881, p. 81). Had Leigh Hunt been Robert's mentor instead of Henry, "Laon" might have been taken as a suggestive contraction, but he was not; a likelier inspiration is the eponymous wandering alchemist of William Godwin's philosophical occult fantasy *St Leon* (1799).

The Introduction to *Popular Romances of the West of England* does, however, suggest that there might have been an actual model for at least one of the younger female characters. "When a very boy," Hunt writes, "I have often been taken by a romantic young lady, who lives in my memory—

'So bright, so fair, so wild'

"to seek for the fairies on Lelant Towans. The maiden and the boy frequently sat for hours, entranced by the stories of an old woman, who lived in a cottage on the edge of the blown sandhills of the region. Thus were received my earliest lessons in fairy mythology." (Hunt 1881 p. 22; the quote within the quote is attributed to Coleridge). If, as seems likely, Eudora Spencer was partly modelled on Harriet Swanson, this unnamed female might be the distant model of Æltgiva.

Whether or not *Panthea* can be read as a *roman à clef*, however, there is no doubt that its underlying theme—of the ideative clashes within a mind part-molded by ancient superstition and reinspired by modern science—was something that Hunt really felt. "Those wild dreams which swayed with irresistible force the skin-clad Briton of the Cornish hills," he wrote in *Popular Romances of the West of England*, "have not yet entirely lost their power where even the National and the British Schools are busy with the people, and Mechanics' Institutions are diffusing the truths of science. In the infancy of the race, terror was the moving power; in the maturity of the people, the dark shadow sometimes rises, like a spectre, partially eclipsing the mild radiance of that Christian truth which shines upon the land." (Hunt 1881, p. 25). The same passage provides a memorable image of Hunt, resting after a descent into a mine on scientific business, indulging in a little intellectual trade; his zeal for the education of the miners was counterbalanced by his desire to hear tales that they had learned from their grandfathers, of which they were already "beginning to be ashamed." (Hunt 1881, p. 23)

Although *Panthea*, like *The Poetry of Science*, ultimately celebrates the supersession of an inferior world-view by a superior one, its early chapters are clearly groping for a possible synthesis of the two, striving for a mystical perspective that might fuse them in eclectic combination. Perhaps Hunt discovered that possibility in Bulwer's fiction, and was only ever entranced with it in the limited context of his soon-forsaken literary adventures, but while he *was* entranced with it he tried to bring far more *science* into it than Bulwer ever could, even in his final Utopian satire *The Coming Race* (1871).

Panthea does not much resemble modern science fiction, although it does resemble earlier visionary fantasies part-guided by science—which category must include "Queen Mab" and "Prometheus Unbound" as well as *Consolations in Travel*. There is, however, some evidence in *The Poetry of Science* that Hunt could have written something much more like modern science fiction had he so wished. There is one remarkable passage of Utopian futurology in that book, when he takes leave to wonder whether the development

105

of better communications technologies might put an end to war: "May we not hope that the electrical telegraph, making, as it must do, the whole of the civilized world enter into a communion of thought, and, through thought, of feeling, with each other, will bind us up in one common brotherhood, and that, instead of misunderstanding and misinterpreting the desires or designs of each other, we shall learn to know that such things as 'natural enemies' do not exist?" (Hunt 1848, p. 198)

This passage proves that Hunt had leanings towards technological determinism, the philosophy that tacitly underlies most hard science fiction. His brief speculation as to whether future epochs might replace mankind just as mankind has replaced trilobites and saurians might also have given rise to proto-Wellsian speculations had he not been so wary of that kind of irreligious indulgence. The fact remains, though, that he would not be tempted in that direction. If he was not already a confirmed utilitarian in 1848-9 he certainly became one afterwards, having put away idle dreaming for good. It may, however, be worth observing that his pioneering endeavors in the analysis of the chemical effects of light were already behind him; his subsequent contributions to science were rather more pedestrian, and certainly less "poetic".

Might Hunt the scientist have done better in the latter part of his life if he had indulged his poetic imagination a little more freely? We cannot know—but there is a certain tragedy as well as a definite triumph in the renunciations of *Panthea*. Julian Altamont gave up more than he knew when he renounced Laon Ælphage's methods and madness. In giving up poetry for science he seems to have given up more than he knew of the poetry *of* science. He surrendered the power of visionary extrapolation which led others to materialist and evolutionist conclusions that he dared not embrace, although they led many other men of science to profitable conclusions. Perhaps "Radical Hunt" could not teach him to be radical enough.

On the other hand, any good utilitarian would be bound to judge that Hunt's contributions to science and education were worth infinitely more than any further contribution he might have made to literature or lyricism. Nor was his philosophy ossified in 1849; indeed, there is every reason to suppose that *The Poetry of Science* does not represent his final opinion on evolutionism. In 1855 Hunt entered into correspondence with Charles Darwin, initially with reference to Hunt's theories regarding the different make-up of sunlight in different latitudes (because of selective absorption of particular wavelengths by the atmosphere) and the use of colored glass to simulate these differences. The archive of Darwin's correspondence held at the University of Cambridge Library holds no other relevant items dated before 1867, but in May of that year Darwin supplied Hunt with his biographical details in order that Hunt might write an account of him for an anthology of articles (this appears to have been a new edition of *The Men of the Time...or, Sketches of Living Notables, Authors, Architects, etc*, whose first edition had been issued in 1852—the volume to which Hunt contributed his essay on Darwin was edited by Edward Walford). Hunt would hardly have agreed to do this had he disagreed with the thesis of *The Origin of Species*. The same archive reveals that Hunt sent Darwin a copy of *Panthea* in 1880, when both men had grown old. (The preceding article proposed that Humphry Davy would surely have been a convert to evolutionism had he lived long enough to read *The Origin of Species*; the fact that Hunt—whose argument for Creationism read the geological evidence in a very similar way—appreciated the force of Darwin's arguments provides some slight support for this contention.)

Given that his ideas moved on, presumably falling more into line with those which prompted Samuel Butler, Grant Allen and H. G. Wells to become pioneers of scientific romance, it is a pity that Robert Hunt never wrote another work of speculative fiction after *Panthea*. Had he done so, we would surely reckon him among the founders of modern science fiction, whereas *Panthea* probably ought to be reckoned an occult romance rather than a work of "science-fiction" even in the Wilsonian sense. It set out to be more than that, but its failure to live up to its own ambitions is freely acknowledged by the hasty deflation of its last chapter.

Having said that, though, the fact needs to be emphasized that no other occult romance ever dared to come as close as *Panthea* to the seemingly-contradictory world-view of hard science fiction. Nor has any other ever tried so hard to find within the poetry of science a substantiation of John Keats' dictum, spelled out in *Ode on a Grecian Urn*, that "Beauty is truth, truth beauty—that is all/ Ye know on earth, and all ye need to know." Among all the myriad works of proto-science fiction, therefore, *Panthea* has a uniquely peculiar voice, as full of yearning as it is of frustration.

HAUNTED BY THE PAGAN PAST: VERNON LEE

Violet Paget, who published almost all of her literary work as Vernon Lee, was born at Château St. Leonard, near Boulogne in France in 1856. Her mother, Matilda Adams, had previously been married to one Captain Lee-Hamilton, who was reputed to have married her for her money; he had died in 1852. Violet's father, who went by the name of Henry Ferguson Paget, was the tutor who had been entrusted with the education of Eugene Lee-Hamilton, the only child of that first marriage, born in 1845.

When Violet adopted the masculine pseudonym Vernon Lee for her writings she forged an extra link with her half-brother, who became a poet of some small reputation. The assumed name also served to distance her from her father—a colorful character of mysterious ancestry who was far fonder of shooting and fishing than literature and learning, and whose tendency to transplant the family at regular intervals seems to have been symptomatic of a congenital restlessness—but this may not have been her original intention; the first version of the pseudonym, which never made it into print, was H. P. Vernon Lee, and one of her earliest publications appeared under the signature H. Vernon Lee. At any rate, she and her half-brother developed their literary talents under the near-exclusive influence of their despotic mother, a fervent rationalist whose considerable intellect was somewhat undermined by her compulsive faddishness. The fact that Eugene was always his mother's favorite was as significant to Violet's character-development as it was to his.

Violet was a precocious child whose first literary productions were in her second and third languages, French and Italian (German was her fourth). "Les Aventures d'une pièce de monnaie" (1870) appeared in a Swiss newspaper when she was thirteen, and three articles on English women novelists appeared in an Italian journal while she was in her later teens. The literary career of Vernon Lee was launched in 1877 with an article on "Tuscan Peasant Plays" in the February issue of *Fraser's Magazine*. Her first book, a well-researched and intelligently-argued collection of *Studies of the Eighteenth Century in Italy*, appeared in 1880, two years in after Eugene's first collection of *Poems and Transcripts*.

Eugene left Oxford in 1866 without taking a degree and went into the Diplomatic Service. He was unlucky enough to be attached to the British Embassy in Paris during the siege of 1870—his mother and half-sister rushed to join him there before the embassy was relocated—and his heart was never in his work thereafter. Under threat of being sent to Buenos Aires in 1873 he developed a debilitating but probably psychosomatic illness that consigned him to a sofa for the next twenty years. As with other career invalids, he now had plenty of time to write but too little energy to produce much more than the occasional poem. He did, however, serve as an anchor suppressing his family's wanderlust, causing them to settle more-or-less permanently in Florence.

Violet, who was sixteen when Eugene fell ill, became his lectrice and amanuensis for several years, although she tore herself away more frequently and for longer periods during the 1880s, when she was often in London. She usually carried his manuscripts with her, shopping around for publishers for him as well as for her own work. After defying the diagnostic talents of many doctors, including the great Jean-Martin Charcot, Eugene decided to get better in 1894 and soon asserted his newly-regained independence in the traditional family manner by setting off on his own travels. He visited England, but that was too close to home and he soon went on to Canada and the USA. He married the popular novelist Annie E. Holdsworth in 1898 and spent the last few years of his life—he died in 1907—completely estranged from the half-sister who had served him so devotedly in the years before her literary reputation far eclipsed his.

Violet was somewhat prone to neurasthenic disorders herself, but rarely had the luxury of retreating to her bed in order to be looked after. Her bouts of illness never suppressed her literary activity for long, nor the restlessness that made her a lifelong compulsive tourist, nor the argumentative verbosity that energized her conversation as well as her multitudinous essays extrapolating her responses to various works of art. Having decided never to marry she never made the slightest effort to cultivate feminine mannerisms and maintained a rather androgynous appearance—habits that inevitably gave rise to speculations and rumors about her sexuality. We can only guess what Charcot, the forerunner of Freudian psychoanalysis, actually had to say about her hysteria-stricken family, but he was probably far too diplomatic to suggest that the intensity of her passion for art might be a kind of displacement, let alone that the literary arena in which the mechanisms of that displacement were most likely to reveal themselves would be supernatural fiction. The fact remains, though, that erotic impulses, whether evident or disguised, are the nearest thing to supernatural agents that everyone encounters in the routines of daily existence.

* * * * * * *

Vernon Lee's early critical work was heavily influenced in its attitude and manner by Walter Pater's *Studies in the History of the Renaissance* (1873). Pater, the great pioneer of the English Aesthetic Movement, had yet to publish *Marius the Epicurean* (1885) at the time when Lee began to publish voluminously, but his insistence that art should be valued for its own sake had already made a deep and indelible mark on her, as it was also to do on the most famous of all Pater's disciples, Oscar Wilde. Lee first met Pater when she visited England in 1881, shortly after her first encounter with Wilde, but she was less impressed by his "plain, heavy and dull, but agreeable" presence than she had hoped to be. Her essays are extraordinarily discursive, frequently wandering off into extended flights of fancy that often dabble so extensively in dialogue, fable or exemplary anecdote that they stray into the grey area between essay and fiction.

Lee's first fiction publication in English, issued at the same time as *Studies of the Eighteenth Century in Italy* by the same publisher, was an anonymous collection of *Tuscan Fairy Tales* allegedly "taken down from the mouths of the people", although the inspiration she took from the activities of the Bothers Grimm extended to a similar tendency to rewrite and polish the traditional tales for the benefit of a modern audience. It was followed by her first venture into supernatural fiction, a story published in the January 1881 issue of *Fraser's Magazine* as "A Culture-Ghost; or, Winthrop's Adventure", whose earliest version had been written in 1874. She had already written the novella *Ottilie: An Eighteenth-Century Idyl* [sic], but that did not see print until 1883, the same year as *The Prince of the Hundred Soups: A Puppet Show in Narrative*.

Ottilie, whose preface describes it as an account of "phantoms" beckoning to the author out of the past as if in a vision, is a curious tale of the mutual dependency of two half-siblings. The narrator

Christoph, who is much younger than his eponymous half-sister, calls his account of their relationship "a confession". Having been delivered into her care at an early age, he casually ruins the opportunities of both her potential suitors, but, after failing to complete his university education because he cannot bear to be separated from her, he marries himself. The marriage is, however, a miserable failure, and he eventually is glad to return to Ottilie's chaste embrace; she has grown old but he tells her that "we should not complain of Time and his doings, since he has taught us that we were made only for each other". This is the conclusion of the story, but an introduction set in a later era has already shown the pair living contentedly and inseparably to a ripe old age. "His works," that introduction says of Christoph, "with the exception of a little volume of verse and some collections of popular legends which he had taken down from the mouth of the peasantry, were mostly tales of the fantastic, humorous and pathetic style, slightly monotonous, and to our mind childish, which had been so popular in the time of Jean Paul and Hoffmann, and which are now well-nigh forgotten."

The Prince of the Hundred Soups is a children's story in "the fantastic, humorous and pathetic style", which redeploys some of the stock characters of the *commedia dell'arte* in a fanciful account of the redemptive advent of the opera-singer Signora Olimpia Fantastici to the state of Bobbio. It was issued in the USA in 1886 in an omnibus with *Ottilie*, under the title *The Prince of 100 Soups*. It was rapidly followed by a very different work: Lee's only venture into the three-decker novel, *Miss Brown* (1884). This intoxicated and perhaps ill-judged satirical *roman à clef* is set in the contemporary literary circles of London, which Lee had just encountered for the first time.

Like most Victorian novels, *Miss Brown* ends with the heroine's marriage, but that climax is a capitulation rather than a completion, her ambition being sacrificed on the altar of imagined duty. The novel was dedicated to Henry James, whom Lee admired and had met on several occasions; he was initially gratified, although his attitude cooled considerably once he had read the book. He felt slighted by it, although he accepted that no insult was intended, and his eventual verdict was that the book was a "deplorable mistake". When Walter Pater diplomatically withheld his own judgment, Lee decided that she had indeed overstepped the mark, and that satire and the novel of manners might best be avoided in future—at least for a while.

When she published "A Culture-Ghost" in 1881 Lee had already set out a manifesto for the writing of supernatural fiction, in an article published in the *Cornhill Magazine* in the previous year, "Faustus and Helena: Notes on the Supernatural in Art". This rhapsodic essay, which was subsequently reprinted in *Belcaro, Being Essays on Sundry Aesthetical Questions* (1883), was prompted by contemplation of the very different versions of the Faust-conjured Helen of Troy formulated by Christopher Marlowe and J. W. Goethe. It proposes an original and rather fanciful account of the relationship between art and the supernatural, involving the thesis that art's various attempts to render the supernatural explicit are bound to obliterate exactly those qualities that surpass the natural, and that the supernatural can only retain its quintessential power over the imagination if it is allowed to remain obscure, ambiguous and paradoxical.

This theoretical stance, which is perfectly consonant with Lee's admiration for the surreal works of E. T. A. Hoffmann, anticipates the theoretical approaches to the role of the fantastic in art taken by other admirers of Hoffmann, including Sigmund Freud and Tzvetan Todorov. It informed most of Lee's own supernatural fiction, helping to establish its best examples as pioneering works whose darkly ambiguous yet flagrantly passionate like had rarely been seen in English fiction before.

Lee was not entirely happy with "A Culture-Ghost", so she produced "A Wicked Voice", a much more polished version of the same story, for publication in her first and best collection of supernatural fiction, *Hauntings* (1890). The collection also reprinted the novella "Oke of Okehurst", which had been issued as a book in 1886 under the title *A Phantom Lover: A Fantastic Story*, and added two more stories set, like "A Wicked Voice", in Italy: "Amour Dure" and "Dionea".

Although it has affinities with Walter Herries Pollock's novella "Lilith" (1874-75; reprinted in 1883 as *The Picture's Secret*) and some of Mrs Oliphant's better ghost stories, the psychoanalytic element of "Oke of Okehurst" is much more self-conscious than anything to be found in the work of Lee's contemporaries. It is a strikingly modern work, which has more in common with the knowing and teasing psychoanalytical ghost stories of such American writers as Henry James and Edith Wharton than with other British works of the period. Its unreliable narrator is modelled on the portrait painter

John Singer Sargent, who had been a childhood friend of Lee's in Florence.

The other three *Hauntings* all deal with the seduction of contemporary characters by animated fragments of the past, dramatically exaggerating the process described in the preface to *Ottilie*. Their apparitions are sharper in focus than the highly ambiguous ghost featured in "Oke of Okehurst", but the only one that achieves the solidity of flesh in the story's present—the eponymous "Dionea"—sacrifices her supernatural qualities, in full accordance with the thesis of "Faustus and Helena", until the time comes for her to reclaim her true nature.

Like "Dionea", "Amour Dure" is a dramatic tale of a *femme fatale* who lays waste to modern moral standards in a cavalier fashion, being possessed of a glamour that no actuality of today's world can match. The story was originally an outline sketch for a novel to be entitled *Medea da Carpi*, but when Lee had submitted the outline to William Blackwood, the publisher of *A Phantom Lover*, he had objected to the proposed hybridization of fact and fiction, so she retailored the material to its published form. "Amour Dure" is as modern in its way as "Oke of Okehurst", particularly in its forthright celebration of masochism; "Dionea" is only slightly less so, although its sly advocacy of pagan ideals was something of a *fin-de-siècle* fad.

"A Wicked Voice" is the only story in *Hauntings* to feature a male seducer rather than a female, but the fact that he is a castrato whose instrument of temptation is his unbroken voice lends some support to the notion that Lee's understanding of desire was intimately bound to the contemplation of unmasculine objects. Lee eventually reprinted the 1881 version of the story as "Winthrop's Adventure" in *For Maurice: Five Unlikely Stories* (1927), explaining that, in spite of all its narrative faults, it was truer to her youthful impressions of Italy and "the ineffable sense of the picturesqueness and wonderfulness of everything one came across: the market-place with the stage coach of the dentist, the puppet show against the Gothic palace, the white owl whom my friend John [Sargent] and I wanted to buy and take home to the hotel...a land where the Past haunted on, with its wizards, sphinxes, strange, weird, *curious*." That same introduction explained that, by 1927, Lee had become dissatisfied with "A Wicked Voice", despite its evident literary superiority to earlier versions, because it was a story "of Yellow Book days", only brought up to date as far as the day of "Tourgueneff's *Chant de l'amour triomphant* and Wilde's *Salome*".

Such references make it abundantly clear that, in 1890, Lee had considered herself to be firmly in the vanguard of the English Aesthetic Movement while it took aboard the influence of French "Decadence", although she followed the example of many others who rejected the label when the trial of Oscar Wilde brought the wrath of the public down upon it. Like other pioneers of English Decadent prose fiction—notable examples include Arthur Machen, R. Murray Gilchrist and M. P. Shiel—Lee went on to produce work of a very different stripe after the turn of the century, sacrificing a certain fervor of style as well as the more extreme aspects of her ironic moral skepticism.

* * * * * * *

By the time *Hauntings* appeared Lee had published another deeply ironic tale of exotic infatuation, "The Virgin of the Seven Daggers" (1889). This was the most consciously Decadent of all Lee's works: a calculatedly sacrilegious tale in which one of the two images playing the role of *femme fatale* is the virtuous mother of Jesus. Although the Virgin wins the vote against the ancient Islamic princess who competes with her for Don Juan's heart—thus guaranteeing the legendary rakehell an unlikely place in Heaven—it is far from obvious that he favors her for the kind of reasons of which a devout Christian would have approved. The tale remained uncollected until it was reissued in *For Maurice* in 1927, when Lee defended its outspoken profanity on the grounds that "if I have anywhere in my soul a secret shrine, it is to Our Lady.... For is she not the divine Mother of Gods as well as God, Demeter or Mary, in whom the sad and ugly things of our bodily origin and nourishment are transformed into the grace of the immortal spirit?"

"The Virgin of the Seven Daggers" recalls the lush Romantic fantasies of Théophile Gautier, and it anticipates the heartfelt syncretism of the short stories Rémy de Gourmont wrote after his features were destroyed by lupus. Like "A Wicked Voice" it was very much a story "of Yellow Book days", and as such it has much in common with the novella "Prince Alberic and the Snake Lady", which actually appeared in *The Yellow Book* in July 1896 before featuring as the weightiest item in Lee's second collection of fantasies, *Pope Jacynth and Other Fantastic Tales* (1904). Although this volume was initially issued by Grant Richards it was reprinted a few years later, along with *Hauntings*, by *Yellow Book* publisher John

Lane, who was later to be the publisher of *Louis Norbert* and *For Maurice*.

Like "The Virgin of the Seven Daggers", "Prince Alberic and the Snake Lady" is an ironic subversion of Gautieresque Romanticism. It uses the same classical source from which Gautier had borrowed the plot of "Arria Marcella" and John Keats had adapted the story of "Lamia": Philostratus' account of a supernatural seductress, half-woman and half-snake, detected and banished by Apollonius of Tyana. Like Gautier and Keats, Lee takes the side of the tempting serpent against those who would banish her, and sees her removal from the world—representative of a reluctant acceptance of brute reality—as a tragedy best delayed for as long as humanly possible. She had long been fascinated with the story's central motif, having described a chimerical "Serpent King" in an outline for a story called "Capo Serpente", which she submitted to a magazine publisher in 1870.

Although Lee's commitment to the Aesthetic Movement was firm enough during the first half of the yellow nineties, she remained a mere dabbler in Decadent fantasy. After Wilde's fall from grace she swiftly returned to the production of naturalistic fiction in the manner of Henry James. The first two novellas collected in *Vanitas: Polite Stories* (1892) both make careful reference to James's work, and his influence is also detectable, albeit more subtly, in the third, "The Legend of Madame Krasinska", which had been published in the *Fortnightly Review* in 1890.

Lee's dedication describes the central characters of all three stories in *Vanitas* as "frivolous women", and they certainly testify to the extent to which Lee had taken aboard James's sly misogyny along with the exhortations contained in his classic essay on "The Art of Fiction" (in *Partial Portraits*, 1888). Unfortunately, the book's subtitle did not prevent it from causing offence; the first novella therein, "Lady Tal", was sufficiently close in method and spirit to *Miss Brown* to have the same effect on various persons who thought that their habits and ideas were being mocked. The distress of Alice Callander, who saw herself in the female lead, Lady Atalanta Walkenshaw, was only slightly less than that of Henry James, who thought the male lead, Jervase Marion, a cruel caricature of himself. His sense of injury was so deep that he felt obliged to send "a word of warning" about Lee to his brother William when the latter visited Italy in 1893, "because she is as dangerous and uncanny as she is intelligent, which is saying a lot.... She's a tiger-cat!" When

William passed this intelligence on, Lee was deeply contrite, and never repeated the error again.

"The Legend of Madame Krasinska", the only supernatural item in *Vanitas*, pointed the direction that Lee's fantastic fiction was to follow during the next few years, building on foundations foreshadowed in "Dionea" and "The Virgin of the Seven Daggers" but more firmly laid down by one of the most imaginative of her essays on Italian Renaissance art, first published in 1891 and reprinted in *Renaissance Fancies and Studies* (1895) as "A Seeker of Pagan Perfection, Being the Life of Domenico Neroni, Pictor Sacrilegus". This essay strays far enough into narrative to have been reprinted as a story in a Grove Press collection, *The Snake Lady and Other Stories* (1954), which helped renew interest in Lee's work among modern connoisseurs of supernatural fiction, but it does so as an imaginative exercise of the kind identified in the preface to *Ottilie*. In a broader context, this kind of attempt to forge sympathetic links with the past is an exaggeration of the philosophy of history which argues that the essence of historical understanding is the ability to identify with actors in history, thus to appreciate the rationale of their actions.

"A Seeker of Pagan Perfection" offers a speculative biography of the Volterran sculptor Domenico Neroni, venturing a hypothesis as to the sequence of events that led to his being burned at the stake in July 1488 for the crime of desecrating a church and using its apparatus for the purposes of witchcraft. Lee puts herself in the shoes of a brilliant and progressive artist living in fifteenth-century Rome, whose struggle to reconcile his profound aesthetic appreciation of pagan art with his shaky Christian faith leads him by inexorable degrees to a heretical desire to see the old gods as their ancient representers saw them, no matter what the cost.

The necessity of combining an aesthetic delight in Classical pagan artifacts with an orthodox regard for Christian morality was an affliction that weighed heavily on all Victorian critics. It had been the central obsession of John Ruskin, and Walter Pater's attempts to escape the trap had eventually faded into capitulation—as noted in the "Valedictory" appended to *Renaissance Fancies and Studies*, which observes, without making its regret too obvious, that Pater "began as an aesthete and ended as a moralist". Oscar Wilde was forced to the same conclusion by two years' hard labor, and such feeble resistance as Lee could muster in 1900 was expressed in the irony of such tales as "The Legend of Madame Krasinska", which indulge in playful but fundamentally respectful satirization of the inspirational anecdotes of *The Golden Legend*—the most preposterously imaginative of all the enterprises by which pious Christians had turned the legacy of pagan folklore to their own advantage.

By far the sharpest of Lee's perverted legends, "Marsyas in Flanders"—whose title and theme echo and subvert Honoré de Balzac's "Christ in Flanders" (1831)—also made its first appearance in 1900, but Lee chose not to reprint it until it appeared in *For Maurice*. The two similar items collected in *Pope Jacynth and Other Fantastic Tales*—the title story and "St. Eudaemon and His Orange Tree"—are somewhat lighter in tone, cast in the same whimsical mould as the mock-legendary fantasies of Anatole France and Richard Garnett. *Sister Benevenuta and the Christ Child*, a more earnest story closer in spirit to "The Legend of Madame Krasinska", was published in book form in 1906.

The fifth story in *For Maurice*, dated 1900, is "The Doll". It is odd without being supernatural, and, like the three remaining stories in *Pope Jacynth and Other Fantastic Tales*—"A Wedding Chest", "The Lady and Death" and "The Featureless Wisdom"—it is a relatively slight anecdote inspired by a work of art. The more meditative tales from *Pope Jacynth* are slightly more interesting in the context of fantastic fiction, although the *conte cruel* "A Wedding Chest" is the only one likely to appeal to aficionados of horror fiction. In much the same way that the legendary fantasies had been preceded by the more substantial "Legend of Madame Krasinska", these meditative pieces had been preceded by a more extensive account of "Ravenna and Her Ghosts" (1894), more essay than story, which Lee eventually chose to add to a 1908 reprint of her non-fiction collection *Limbo and Other Essays*, whose first edition had been issued in 1897.

* * * * * * *

The vogue for supernatural fiction that encouraged many dabblers in the late 1880s and early 1990s faded out as the dawn of the new century approached. Many British writers found it politic to suppress the supernatural aspects of their fiction after 1900, and Lee was no exception. As the end of the nineteenth century approached she became deeply depressed by the failure of her work to find a wide audience, and she toyed with the notion of giving up, while simultaneously attempting to diversify her output into more commercial channels. Her best-known works were published at around this time, beginning with the light essays in travel journalism making up *Genius Loci: Notes on Places* (1899).

Peter Gunn, the author of *Vernon Lee: Violet Paget, 1856-1935* (1964), considers *Ariadne in Mantua: A Romance in Five Acts*—which was written in 1899-1900 although it was not published until 1903 and remained unproduced until 1916—to be her most self-revealing work. In support of that claim, he argues that it is the melancholy Duke of Mantua, who has turned misogynist since being disappointed in love, rather than his opposite number—a self-sacrificing girl disguised as a male singer—who serves as the primary mouthpiece for the author's own feelings.

Penelope Brandling: A Tale of the Welsh Coast in the Eighteenth Century (1903) was a further attempt to do popular commercial work, although it was not nearly as successful as its immediate predecessors. It is a non-supernatural Gothic romance in which a spirited young bride is terrorized by a family of wreckers whose menacing spearhead is a sinister clergyman. It is melodramatic enough, but its brevity—it is a novella published in the same slim format as *Ottilie*—counted against it. Lee's inability to spin the tale out to novel length is probably testimony to the discomfort she felt in keeping her intellectual impulses under a tight rein; no further experiment of this kind appeared until 1914, when the more substantial *Louis Norbert: A Two-fold Romance* was published (although Gunn suggests that it was probably written some years earlier).

If *Penelope Brandling* may be considered a direct ancestor of Daphne du Maurier's *Jamaica Inn*, then *Louis Norbert* is the most obvious literary ancestor of A. S. Byatt's *Possession*. It is an epistolary novel whose subject-matter and narrative method were far better suited to Lee's interests and temperament, taking the form of correspondence between the middle-aged Lady Venetia Hammond and a much younger male identified only as "the Archaeologist". The correspondence relates their separate discoveries in England and Italy concerning the life of one Louis Norbert de Caritan, whose tomb they have discovered together in Pisa, bearing a date (1684) two years later than that attached to a portrait of him that hangs in Lady Venetia's old home, in what is known as "the Ghost's room".

The two correspondents set out to recover, to the extent that they can, the story of the unfortunate young man's life, attempting to penetrate the secret of his true identity and to figure out the exact manner of his premature death. The difference in their methods—he is a painstaking skeptic, while she relies on visionary intuition—is mirrored in their attitudes to the relationship that develops between them. The hopes and possibilities inherent in that relationship are eventually slain as cruelly as poor Louis Norbert, who died not knowing that he was—if Lady Venetia's intuitions can be trusted—the son of the Sun King and the rightful heir to the throne of France. By far the most heartfelt passage in the novel describes the Archaeologist's inarticulate panic as he approaches a crucial meeting with the woman to whom he is now desperately attracted—a passage that suggests that he is far more closely modelled on the author than Lady Venetia.

Although Louis Norbert is only a metaphorical ghost there is a certain kinship between his story and that of "Oke of Okehurst". The claustrophobic intensity of the earlier novella is, however, replaced by a far more playful delight in recalling the political intrigues of the seventeenth century and mixing the staple ingredients of historical romance. It might have fared far better in the marketplace had the ending not been so determinedly frustrating. This insistent anti-romantic note echoes the one sounded in an even lighter work that Lee had produced a year earlier: the last and most distinctive of all her fantasies, "The Gods and Ritter Tanhuser". This was the story she chose as the lead item in *For Maurice*, presumably because she thought it closest in spirit to the work that the book's dedicatee—the writer Maurice Baring—had enjoyed so much as a child, *The Prince of the Hundred Soups*.

"The Gods and Ritter Tanhuser" is the most relaxed and comical of Lee's many tales of Christianity and Paganism in conflict. Whereas "The Virgin of the Seven Daggers" and "Prince Alberic and the Snake Lady" had looked back from the heyday of the Decadent movement at the legendary recapitulations of Romanticism, "The Gods and Ritter Tanhuser" looks back contentedly and conservatively at an erotic legend that had been recapitulated more than once by the great exemplars of Decadence, most notably in Aubrey Beardsley's *Under the Hill* (1897). Its lightness belies the reputation Lee had acquired by this time of being an irascible, argumentative and relentless pursuer of mostly-unfashionable causes, many of which had been displayed in her two collections of sociological essays, *Gospels of Anarchy and Other Contemporary Studies* (1908) and *Vital Lies: Studies of Some Varieties of Recent Obscurantism* (2 volumes, 1912).

Although Lee's crusading efforts won her some new friends—including H. G. Wells, who addressed her as "Sister in Utopia"—they also made her enemies. The fervent pacifism that cost her a few of her English friends during the Boer War was to cost her a lot more during the Great War. She was moved by the latter tragedy—whose tragic nature she anticipated long before the majority of her contemporaries were forced to recognize it—to pen a critical allegory, *The Ballet of the Nations: A Present-Day Morality* (1915), which she expanded after the war's end into *Satan the Waster: A Philosophic War Trilogy* (1920), but these works should not be reckoned as examples of supernatural fiction.

* * * * * * *

Vernon Lee never saw her supernatural stories as central elements of her literary endeavor—they were always diversions from more serious work—but they have lasted far better than her essays on art, most of which now seem relentlessly dull as well as maddeningly unfocused. Lee could never put her heart into the composition of fiction with the same wild intensity that her half-brother Eugene Lee-Hamilton brought to his magnificently lurid historical novel *The Lord of the Dark Red Star* (1903), but this did not work entirely to her disadvantage. It was her scrupulous refusal to give way entirely to the fever of creativity, and her insistence on maintaining a carefully-controlled distance from passionate involvement, that gave her best supernatural fiction its balance, force and flavor.

The fact that Vernon Lee forbade any biography, and insisted that her early letters to her family should be kept safe from public scrutiny until 1980, lent further fuel to the rumors that circulated while she was alive to the effect that she had something to hide. Peter Gunn, who offers the usual biographer's excuses for violating the prohibitions his subject had laid down, is careful to avoid overmuch prurient speculation, but he scrupulously lists all of her close female friends. He states that she formed a "passionate attachment" to a married woman named Annie Meyer in 1878 and alleges that she was subsequently very disappointed when Mary Robinson married James Darmsteter in 1887. He opines that Lee's regard for her sometime collaborator on various works on aesthetic theory, Clementina Anstruther-Thomson, who preferred to be known as Kit, was "stronger than mere affection" and that Lee "wanted something deeper" than Anstruther-Thomson was eventually willing to provide.

Anstruther-Thomson, in whose company Lee spent at least half of every year from 1889-98, nursed Lee through one of her most protracted neurasthenic episodes. She also tended to Lee's mother and half-brother—Gunn credits her with partial responsibility for Eugene's recovery—before suffering a breakdown of her own in 1897. When, after recovering, she decided that her first duty in future should be to another sick friend, Christine Head, Lee was devastated—but only for a while.

Gunn concludes, on the basis of this sort of evidence, that "Vernon Lee was unable to recognize in herself the natural human desires, or to express them in a natural, human way. If the presence of bodily wants could not be denied, still those wants could be to all intents and purposes ignored, and that was what she did. But the imagination and emotions were real, and, try to curb them as she might, they dominated her to the very end."

This might be true, although it is unlikely to seem so to anyone who holds the view that there is no way to express "natural human desires", whether they are recognized as such or not, that is more natural or human than writing. The pattern of Lee's published works suggests, however, that she was better equipped to deal with whatever "bodily wants" she had than this summary is prepared to credit, and she seems to have been well able to subject both her imagination and her emotions to the dominion of her intellect. It is at least possible that the spectrum of Lee's desires and the extent of her self-knowledge were more extensive than her biographer was prepared to concede. The combination of secret frustration and the power of her imagination may help to explain why the supernatural fiction she wrote is so distinctively intense, but the fact that she wrote so little of it, and that it changed its character so markedly as her career progressed, is surely testimony to her success in subjecting her inner life to a workable discipline.

In common with many other writers whose sexuality was troubled, ambiguous or unorthodox, Lee dressed her early literary accounts of sexual passion with a pretended objectivity that tended to represent erotic attraction as a dangerous fever and evaluated its effects with a clinical and cynical sarcasm. It is the qualified fervor of this attitude that gives the four stories making up *Hauntings* their power, and it was the gradual relaxation of that fervor that reduced the intensity of her later work, allowing its ironic element to dissolve by slow degrees into measured slapstick. *Hauntings* remains one of the landmark collections of British supernatural fiction, and its readers may well regret that Lee never produced another like it, but the best of the rest of her supernatural fiction serves to provide a flirtatious philosophical counterweight to its steadfast grimness, and to testify that she was ready and able to learn such lessons as were to be found in it.

When, late in life, Vernon Lee was invited to contribute to the series of "Today & Tomorrow" pamphlets launched by J. B. S.

Haldane's *Daedalus; or, Science and the Future* her offering was *Proteus; or, The Future of Intelligence* (1925). There, with her customary dry wit, she observed that: "Intelligence...has quietly stripped from our moral valuations that half-supernatural, half-aesthetic halo which is but the shrunken religious involucrum wherein they came into the world. The 'problem of evil' has already become the problem not of its toleration by God, but of its diminution by man." There is no better account or explanation of the evolution of her supernatural fiction from "Winthrop's Adventure" to "The Gods and Ritter Tanhuser", via "Amour Dure".

J. G. BALLARD

James Graham Ballard was born in Shanghai, China on November 15, 1930. His father, also named James, was a chemist in the textile industry who had been appointed managing director of the China Printing and Finishing Company the year before. His early upbringing was privileged, as befit the son of well-to-do British expatriates, but his situation began a slow deterioration a few days short of his seventh birthday, when invading Japanese troops captured Shanghai.

Although the invaders respected the privileges of Shanghai's International Settlement, the Ballard home in Amherst Avenue was outside its boundaries. The city became a virtual war zone and the family was ultimately forced to move into the French sector of the Settlement. After Pearl Harbor, when Japan became embroiled in World War II, the Ballards returned to Amherst Avenue for a while, but they were interned early in 1943. Ballard lived with his parents and his sister Margaret—who was then only five years old—in a single room in the Lunghua Civilian Assembly Center for the next two and a half years.

It was in Lunghua that Ballard grew to adolescence, living on a daily ration of rice, congee and sweet potatoes and attending a makeshift school. Although his parents found conditions very harsh and Margaret nearly died of dysentery, Ballard was later to recall—usually without any manifest perplexity or shame—that he rather enjoyed life in Lunghua. The Japanese guards were friendly, at least until the war began to go badly, and the cosmopolitan mix of the internees fascinated the boy who had previously been sheltered from so many aspects of adult life by the zealous servants appointed to look after him.

Following his release from the internment camp, Ballard spent several more months in Shanghai before being sent to England to attend Leys School in Cambridge. Always a voracious reader, he had found the limited and rather haphazard stocks of reading matter that had been passed around the internment camp somewhat frustrating, and he was delighted by the fact that he now had access to the entire heritage of nineteenth and twentieth century literature. "In the next four of five years," he reported in an essay he contributed to Antonia Fraser's anthology *The Pleasure of Reading* in 1992, "I stopped reading only to go to the cinema."

Ballard went on from Leys to King's College, Cambridge to study medicine, with a view to becoming a psychiatrist, but he found the training uncongenial and left after two years without a degree. The experience left a deep impression on him, which mostly derived from his training in the dissecting room. He found a particular fascination in the way in which a once-living body could be taken apart and separated into individual components, utterly transformed by exploration and reductive analysis.

Although his mother and sister had also returned to England, Ballard's father had remained in Shanghai, convinced that the threatened communist takeover would peter out. It did not, and the elder Ballard was put on trial for anti-communist activities. "Fortunately," Ballard reported, "he was able to quote enough Marx and Engels to convince the magistrates that he had seen the error of his ways. He was acquitted and a year later escaped to Hong Kong." The elder Ballard spent his remaining years in England—where he died in 1966—and the younger did not see Shanghai again until 1991, when he returned at the behest of BBC TV, to supply footage for a "Bookmark" documentary about his life and career.

Ballard's first published short story, "The Violent Noon" (1951), appeared in the Cambridge student magazine *Varsity*. After leaving the medical school he read English for a year in London but dropped out again and worked for brief periods as a copywriter and encyclopedia salesman while trying to sell short stories to literary magazines. He then volunteered for the Royal Air Force and became a trainee pilot; his lifelong fascination with flying had been abundantly fed during the war years, when he had watched American, Chinese and Japanese warplanes in operation over Shanghai. He was posted to Moose Jaw, Saskatchewan in Canada for basic training, and it was there that he first encountered the science fiction magazines that were to provide his first literary market. Unfortunately, he found life in the RAF no more congenial than any of his earlier attempts to build a career. He wrote his first science fiction story, "Passport to Eternity", while he was still in Canada awaiting his discharge, but it did not sell until 1962.

Jaunting on the Scoriac Tempests, by Brian Stableford

When Ballard returned to England in 1955 he married Helen Mary Matthews, and worked for a while as a librarian before becoming a script-writer for a scientific film company. His son James Christopher was born in 1956 and the family settled in Chiswick in west London, although Ballard did not much like the environment. Having formed an impression of the capital from his parents' nostalgic reminiscences he had been deeply disappointed to arrive in 1946 to find "a London that looked like Bucharest with a hangover". When he subjected the city to a severe new broom in his first novel he told the readers of *New Worlds* that "anyone wondering why I've chosen to destroy London quite so thoroughly should try living there for ten years". In fact, he only lived there for five, until he moved to the small Thames Valley town of Shepperton in 1960. In the meantime, his family was augmented by two daughters: Fay, born in 1958 and Beatrice, born in 1959.

Ballard's first professional sales were made in 1956, to the British science fiction magazines *New Worlds* and *Science-Fantasy*. Their editor, E. John Carnell, helped him to find work in the field of trade journals; he was briefly assistant editor of *The Baker* and eventually became the assistant editor of *Chemistry and Industry*—a post that he held for more than three years. He continued to sell stories to Carnell, whose magazines remained his only market until 1962, when he achieved the crucial breakthrough that enabled him to concentrate entirely on his writing.

****

In a profile accompanying his first publication in *New Worlds* Ballard revealed that his first novel had been written immediately after "The Violent Noon", but that it had been "a completely unreadable pastiche of *Finnegans Wake* and the *Adventures of Engelbrecht*". He was later to comment on more than one occasion that, although *Ulysses* had made a deep impression on him in his teens, James Joyce had been a totally unsuitable model for his own work, and that it was not until he discovered surrealism that he found a philosophy and method more appropriate to his interests and ambitions. Ballard was, however, always more interested in surrealist art than literature. He was deeply intrigued by the way in which surrealist painters like Giorgio de Chirico, Salvador Dali and Max Ernst seemed to fuse visual reality with the substance of dreams and nightmares, creating an alien but seamless whole.

Such imagery had a far more powerful influence on Ballard's literary work than the leading surrealist writers, who included André Breton, Alfred Jarry and Guillaume Apollinaire. He was, however, prepared to borrow occasional inspiration from surrealist prose, as he did when he employed a modern version of Jarry's "The Crucifixion of Christ Considered as an Uphill Bicycle Race" as the final section of the most avant-gardist of his books, *The Atrocity Exhibition* (1970), which is titled "The Assassination of John Fitzgerald Kennedy Considered as a Downhill Motor Race".

The 1956 *New Worlds* profile mentions a novel called *You and Me and the Continuum* as a work in progress, but it was not until 1966 that a short story of that title was published, subsequently to be incorporated into *The Atrocity Exhibition*. If the short story borrowed more than the title of the aborted novel Ballard must have begun practicing exotic experiments in prose long before anyone was ready to publish them. One experimental work from the same period which did eventually see print was the prose collage "Project for a New Novel", written in 1958 and published in 1978.

Even Ballard's commercial work seemed rather outré to the readers of Carnell's sf magazines, who were used to straightforward action-adventure stories. His first story in *New Worlds*, "Escapement", details the existential crisis suffered by a man who finds himself living the same interval of time over and over, and that it is shrinking with every repetition. His debut in *Science-Fantasy*, "Prima Belladonna", was the first of what became a series of tales featuring exotic *femme fatales*, set in the louchely decadent artists' colony of Vermilion Sands. The enigmatic anti-heroine of "Prima Belladonna" is Jane Ciracylides, whose disturbing presence has a remarkable effect on the musical flowers sold by the protagonist. These two stories were followed by "Build-Up" (1957; reprinted as "The Concentration City"), in which the world's population has increased to several trillion and the "free space" for which the young protagonist is drawn by his dreams to search can no longer be found. In "Manhole 69" (1957) the subjects of a sleep-deprivation experiment find their experience of quotidian reality becoming nightmarish as they descend into a quasi-catatonic withdrawal state.

Even in these early, works the emergence of the manner of presentation and set of concerns, which were eventually to license the invention of the adjective "Ballardian", can clearly be seen. The three key elements of "Ballardian" work are a type of protagonist, a type of setting and a narrative voice. The protagonist, who is always male, is passively detached and almost invariably haunted by dreams of a mysterious but not imaginary past. He usually falls prey to the psychological attraction of his dreams without ever being moved to urgent or constructive action. The setting may be a city or a wilderness—or, fairly frequently, a city that is in the process of returning to wilderness—but its fixed artifacts are almost invariably decaying (its swimming pools are always empty, or nearly so). Its movable artifacts, especially those which ought to offer the possibility of rapid transit, are usually broken-down and abandoned. If birds are not abundant their absence is usually conspicuous, and they will often turn up dead; like the lush vegetation that is ever apt to spring up abruptly, they offer ambiguous omens of new beginnings and terminal decay. The narrative voice is coolly clinical, even in first-person narrative, reporting without any considerable emotional involvement and no great sense of astonishment, although it is usually possessed of a quietly dignified awe and an itchy inquisitiveness.

Ballard must have been disappointed to find that the editor of the British sf magazines was the only man willing to entertain his intense existentialist nightmares and ironic decadent fantasies, and that Carnell was only interested in the more accessible examples. Such stories as "Track 12" (1958) and "Now, Zero" (1959) are casually quirky comedies slightly slanted to the marketplace, but Ballard's willingness to compromise was severely limited and he was later to recall, wearily, that he collected a lot of rejection slips. Although he knew full well that the vast majority of magazine sf stories were tales of interplanetary adventure Ballard could not bring himself to take such themes seriously. "The Waiting Grounds" (1959), the first of only two stories he wrote with an extraterrestrial setting—the other, "The Time-Tombs" (1963), is a delicate homage to Ray Bradbury—extrapolates existential *angst* to a cosmic time-scale, thus adding an extra dimension to its alienating effect.

The profile accompanying "The Waiting Grounds" summarized Ballard's attitude to science fiction at that time: "What particularly interests me about science fiction is the opportunity it gives for experimenting with scientific or psycho-literary ideas which have little or no connection with the world of fiction, such as, say, coded sleep or the time zone.... Just as psychologists are now building models of anxiety neuroses and withdrawal states in the form of verbal diagrams—translating scientific hypothesis into literary construction—so I see a good science fiction story [as] a model of some psychic image, the truth of which gives the story its merit.

"In general, stories with interplanetary backgrounds show too little originality, too much self-imitation. More important, the characters seem to lack any sense of cosmic awe—spanning the whole of space and time without a glimmer of responsibility.... It's just this sense of cosmic responsibility, the attempt to grasp the moral dimensions of the universe, that I've tried to describe in 'The Waiting Grounds'" (*New Worlds* vol. 30 no. 88, November 1959, inside front cover.)

Ballard's fascination with the mysteries of "the time zone" were more elaborately displayed in the dystopian comedy "Chronopolis" (1960), about a future city from which tyrannical clocks have been banned, and "The Voices of Time" (1960; revised as "News from the Sun", 1982). In the latter piece, which became the most striking paradigm example of his concerns and literary method, signals from a distant galaxy have been intercepted by Earthly radio-telescopes, but the only intelligence they contain is a countdown to the end of the universe. Adventures in genetic engineering offer glimpses of the possible evolution of life on Earth, but the story's protagonists are consumed as they are by their own existential crises, one of them sleeping increasingly longer hours while the other cannot sleep at all. Some of Carnell's readers complained bitterly about the story's gnomic imagery and sense of futility, but it caught the imagination of other writers who were anxious to break the pulpish mould in which sf had long been cast, most notably Brian Aldiss and Michael Moorcock.

As science fiction expanded out of the magazines into paperback books it began to offer new commercial possibilities to its writers. Ballard dashed off his first sf novel during a two-week vacation in 1961. He sold an abridged version to *New Worlds*, where it appeared as "Storm-Wind", and the full-length version, *The Wind from Nowhere* to the US paperback company Berkley for 1962 publication in the USA. Although the story uses multiple narrative viewpoints, its central figure is the immensely rich and powerful Hardoon, who responds to the advent of a world-scouring wind by constructing a gigantic pyramid in which he can maintain a luxurious haven of calm. The attempt is futile, and the mysterious wind does not begin to abate until it has toppled this final symbol of human *hubris*.

Superficially, *The Wind from Nowhere* is a disaster story of a kind that had amply demonstrated its potential in the UK by courtesy of works by John Wyndham and John Christopher, which had acquired a measure of critical respectability as well as healthy sales. "Perhaps because of their climate," Ballard observed in the profile accompanying the *New Worlds* serialization, "English writers seem to have a virtual monopoly of the [cataclysmic story] genre, one or two of the contemporary ones producing almost nothing else". He stuck to the template himself for two further novels, but, whereas Wyndham and Christopher had written grim survivalist tales in which the traditional English virtues of decency and industry eventually withstand all manner of trials, Ballard's accounts of environmental change took it for granted that resistance is useless. His stories accept as axiomatic that the sensible response to abrupt and irresistible environmental change is psychological adaptation, no matter how drastic.

Ballard was now hitting his stride as a professional writer. Carnell published six of his shorter pieces in addition to "Storm-Wind" in 1961, and his stories began to appear in the American sf magazines in the following year. His delicate quasi-fabular account of "The Garden of Time" was in *The Magazine of Fantasy & Science Fiction* and he had five stories in the magazines edited by Cele Goldsmith, whose sympathy for stylish quirkiness allowed her to play a key role in the careers of such writers as Fritz Leiber and David Bunch—although Goldsmith, like Carnell, was prone to offer him "good" advice about those aspects if his work that he ought to set aside and replace with something more robust. By far the most important breakthrough was the sale of *The Wind from Nowhere* to Berkley, whose editor thought sufficiently highly of Ballard to publish three more of his books in the same year, including two story-collections as well as his second novel.

These sales allowed Ballard to fulfill his long-held ambition to become a full-time writer, and he immediately set about the business of bending his work further towards his own agenda. The wind from nowhere had relented in the end, but there was no such easy let-off for the characters in his next novel, *The Drowned World* (1962). As the novel opens, Earth's mean surface temperature has risen dramatically and is still inexorably rising. Water released by the melting of the ice caps has inundated much of the land, and dense tropical jungle has spread rapidly through what were once the temperate zones, rendering them all but uninhabitable. The world is, in effect, undergoing a temporal retrogression that is restoring the environment of the Triassic period.

The story's protagonist is Robert Kerans, a biologist monitoring the changes from a research station in a submerged metropolis. The psychological effects of the world's transfiguration begin to manifest themselves as dreams in which Kerans sees a version of himself that is no longer human wandering in a primitive world dominated

129

by a huge, fierce sun. These dreams, he concludes, are a kind of memory retained within the cellular heritage of mankind, now called forth again by the appropriate stimulus. They threaten—or promise—to free his nervous system from the domination of the recently-evolved forebrain, whose native environment is now gone, restoring the innocent harmony of primeval proto-consciousness and archaic environment.

As the eventful but rather enervated story proceeds, Kerans watches his various eccentric neighbors trying to adapt in their own ways to the circumstances in which they find themselves, but he comes to understand that all their strategies are hopeless. Eventually, he accepts the pull of destiny and sets off southwards, submitting to a psychic devolution that strips away his humanity by degrees, until he becomes "a second Adam searching for the forgotten paradises of the reborn sun".

Some American readers and critics who protested against the "downbeat" ending of *The Drowned World* felt that Ballard's insistence that it was nothing of the sort was adding insult to injury. American editors like John W. Campbell Jr. and Donald A. Wollheim regarded science fiction as propaganda for the enabling power of science and technology, and they demanded active protagonists who would tackle problems decisively and triumph over all adversity. Subscribers to that ideology deemed Ballard's protagonists to be supinely passive in meekly adapting themselves to changing circumstances, and considered their attitudes—which never aspired to anything more heroic than detached fascination—irrational as well as unconstructive.

Given the nature of his experiences in Shanghai, especially in Lunghua, the intellectual stances adopted by Ballard's viewpoint characters are easy enough to understand, but it is also easy enough to understand why they struck more resonant chords in Britain than they did in the USA. In Britain *The Drowned World* and *The Four-Dimensional Nightmare*—a collection combining the best stories from his first three Berkley collections—were issued in hardcover by Victor Gollancz in 1963. *The Drowned World* was enthusiastically reviewed by Kingsley Amis—who had persuaded the aging Gollancz that he ought to issue *The Drowned World* in the science fiction line rather than packaging it as a literary novel—and it went into a second printing a month after publication.

When Ballard assembled a second collection for Gollancz, *The Terminal Beach* (1964) he included five stories that he had been unable to sell to the magazines, including the title story, but when Carnell heard that it would be thus employed he rushed it into print in *New Worlds*. One of the others, "The Drowned Giant"—a brilliant quasi-Borgesian description of the dismantling of a giant corpse washed up on a beach, based on Ballard's experiences in the dissecting room at Cambridge—was reprinted the following year in *Playboy*, the highest-paying short fiction market in the world.

* * * * * * *

On 18 March 1962 Ballard took part in a radio discussion on the BBC's Home Service chaired by Wilfred De'Ath, in which he debated the significance of modern science fiction with John Wyndham, Kingsley Amis, Brian Aldiss, John Brunner and Kenneth Bulmer. Ballard waxed lyrical on the need for sf writers to abandon tales of space travel and concentrate instead on the exploration of "inner space"—a case he had already made out in an as-yet-unpublished essay that eventually appeared as a "guest editorial" in the May 1962 issue of *New Worlds*. It was here that he made the oft-quoted remark that "the only truly alien planet is Earth" and provided a definitive elaboration of the prospectus for the future evolution of the genre that he had laid out in 1959:

"I'd like to see s-f becoming abstract and 'cool', inventing completely fresh situations and contexts that illustrate its theme obliquely. For example, instead of treating time like a sort of glorified scenic railway, I'd like to see it used for what it is, one of the perspectives of the personality, and the elaboration of such concepts as the time zone, deep time and archaeopsychic time. I'd like to see more psycho-literary ideas, more meta-biological and meta-chemical concepts, private time-systems, synthetic psychologies and space-times, more of the remote, somber half-worlds one glimpses in the paintings of schizophrenics, all in all a complete speculative poetry and fantasy of science." (*New Worlds* vol. 40 no 118, p.118).

This document became one of the central theses of the "new wave" of British science fiction, for which New Worlds became the main vehicle when Michael Moorcock took over its editorship in 1964. "The Voices of Time" and *The Drowned World* were appointed as two of the key examples of new wave sf.

Ballard's antipathy to space fiction became a significant bone of contention between supporters of the new wave and the traditionalists, and Ballard defended his argumentative ground with considerable vigor. The rocket scientists who had laid the groundwork for the endeavors of NASA had all taken their inspiration from science fiction, and the sf magazines had provided a hospitable refuge for such ardent propagandists for space travel as Willy Ley and Arthur C. Clarke; many contemporary sf writers, most of them American, felt that they had a moral duty to carry forward that inspirational and propagandist function. When Ballard wrote "Cage of Sand" (1962), the first of many near-future stories in which the US space program has been abandoned as a brief folly of futile ambition, he knew that it would be regarded as a kind of intellectual treason within the sf community. As early as 1974 he began to rejoice in the casual observation that "as far as manned flights are concerned...the Space Age, far from lasting for hundreds if not thousands of years, is already over" and he continued to celebrate his foresight until 1988, when he was able to assemble a whole collection of his skeptical stories under the title *Memories of the Space Age*.

Ballard continued to publish short fiction prolifically during 1963 and the early months of 1964 but the flow dried up abruptly in the middle of the latter year. Just as his career was achieving a whole series of crucial breakthroughs, his life suffered a terrible setback. The reason for the brutal interruption of his creative flow was the sudden death of Helen Ballard, who contracted pneumonia while the family was on holiday in Spain. Ballard was left with three young children to bring up single-handedly. That would in itself have affected his productivity, but the loss of his wife also had a profound effect on the nature and temper of his subsequent work. Although the account of the incident given in Ballard's quasi-autobiographical novel *The Kindness of Women* (1991) is carefully fictionalized, the following chapters of the novel presumably offer a genuine insight into the effect that the unexpected death had upon a man who was still laboring in the psychological shadow of his experiences in the Far East. The character of his work would undoubtedly have changed anyway as he repositioned himself within the literary marketplace, but the after-effects of his wife's death undoubtedly helped to determine the direction and extent of that change.

In the summer of 1964 Ballard had already completed his third novel—or, at least, the version of it that was published as yet another original paperback by Berkley in the USA as *The Burning World* in that year—and he had also begun work on *The Crystal World* (1966), at least to the extent of producing the sequence which appeared as the short story "The Illuminated Man" in the May 1964 issue of *The Magazine of Fantasy & Science Fiction*, but it is hardly surprising that the completed novel was markedly sketchier than its predecessor, or that Ballard's work showed a sharp change in direction thereafter.

An extensively rewritten version of *The Burning World* appeared in the UK in 1965 from Jonathan Cape, one of the most prestigious British publishers of literary fiction. The new version was titled *The Drought*. Here, the pattern of physical change mapped out in *The Drowned World* is casually reversed. Earth's continents become vast deserts because industrial pollutants have produced a molecular film that covers the surface of the oceans, inhibiting evaporation. The concrete city-deserts are isolated, surrounded by expanses of hot sand, while the sea retreats from the land to expose new wildernesses of crystalline salt. Civilization shrivels, uncheckable fires reducing forests and towns alike to white ash. Ransom, the novel's protagonist, is one of the stubborn few who are most reluctant to follow the seas. He watches the river on which his houseboat is moored dwindle away, leaving behind the dregs of the social and natural order.

Eventually, Ransom and most of his remaining neighbors are driven to seek refuge in the "dune limbo" of the new seashore, where they take their allotted places in a repressive and rigidly stratified social order, whose polity is dominated by the need to extract fresh water from the reluctant sea. In the final section of the story, however, he chooses to go inland again, to discover that the mad and monstrous city-dwellers who were even more stubborn than he was have contrived to keep themselves alive, following a way of life that is thoroughly nasty but nevertheless appropriate to the now-universal aridity—which is, of course, an aridity of the soul as well as of the land.

Ballard was not the only British sf writer to achieve a crossover to apparent respectability in the mid-1960s, nor was he the only one avid to make use of the opportunity to institute a new literary *avant garde* that would import aspects of the science fictional lexicon of ideas into literary fiction, but he was the one best equipped to make use of the opportunity. Having ensconced himself at Cape, Ballard also formed an association with Martin Bax, the proprietor of the literary magazine *Ambit*, becoming its "prose editor". Most of the short stories Ballard produced during the 1970s appeared in *Ambit*, although he also became a contributing editor to Emma Tennant's literary magazine *Bananas* in 1975.

The idea of "post-modernism" had yet to get off the ground in the late 1960s, but Ballard was already thinking along those lines. When Moorcock's *New Worlds*, having lurched towards extinction in a paperback-sized format, was re-launched in 1967, with the aid of an Arts Council grant, as a heavily-illustrated A-4 magazine, the propagandistic zeal of its chief contributors was unleashed. In a notable article, which passed itself off as a meditation on the surrealism of Salvador Dali, published in 1969, Ballard dismissed the idea that the attitudes and concerns of "the Modern Movement" were typical of the twentieth century:

> On the contrary, it seems to me that the Modern Movement belongs to the nineteenth century, a reaction against the monolithic Philistine character of Victorianism, against the tyranny of the paterfamilias, secure in his financial and sexual authority, and against the massive constraints of bourgeois society. In no way does the Modern Movement have any bearing on the facts of the twentieth century, the first flight of the Wright brothers, the invention of the Pill, the social and sexual philosophy of the ejector seat. Apart from its marked retrospective bias, its obsession with the subjective nature of existence, its real subject matter is the rationalisation of guilt and estrangement. Its elements are introspection, pessimism and sophistication. Yet if anything befits the twentieth century it is optimism, the iconography of mass-merchandising, and naivety. (*New Worlds* 187, February 1969, p. 27-28)

At first glance, this may seem to constitute a renunciation of the outlook of Ballard's early novels. *The Drought* certainly seemed to most of its readers to be as introspective, pessimistic and sophisticated as anything the Modern Movement had ever produced, and the same seemed to be true of such stories as "The Terminal Beach", whose protagonist strands himself in the derelict landscape of Eniwetok, an island formerly used as a base for H-bomb tests. It must be remembered, however, that Ballard had refused to concede that *The Drowned World* was as downbeat as its detractors claimed. The detached attitudes of Kerans and Ransom do qualify as a kind of calculated naivety whose open-mindedness is carefully contrasted with the "sophistication" of Hardoon's successors. This open-minded quality is more extravagantly developed and celebrated in *The Crystal World*, in which the environmental "disaster" that begins to overtake the world is much more obviously represented as a surreal and perhaps hopeful metamorphosis.

In *The Crystal World* selected areas of the Earth's surface are subjected to a strange process of crystallization as some mysterious substance is precipitated out of the ether. The first area to be affected is in Africa, where the novel's protagonist, Sanders, is the assistant director of a leper colony. Sanders is initially horrified when he finds his mistress and some of his patients joyfully accepting the process of crystallization into their own flesh, but he comes to realize soon enough that the lepers have found a better alternative to the kind of decay that is already consuming them. Eventually, he accepts that no other destiny is appropriate, even for healthy people. What seems to be happening is that time and space are becoming supersaturated with matter and enclaves from which time has "evaporated" are being transformed by precipitation. Within these regions, living things cannot continue to exist in the manner to which they have become accustomed, but once they have been transubstantiated they cannot die.

The Crystal World draws some inspiration from Graham Greene, a writer whose work Ballard admired greatly, although its scintillating account of the birth of a new light within the heart of darkness is a far cry from Greene's restless religious orthodoxy. The lush romanticism of the novel's imagery, tending towards an unrepentant gaudiness, is replicated in several near-contemporary short stories with a decadent flavor, many of them set in Vermilion Sands. Ballard had first returned to that setting in the beautifully melancholy "Studio 5, the Stars" (1961) but three new additions to the series, all possessed of a sharper sense of tragic irony, were published in 1967: "The Cloud-Sculptors of Coral-D", "Cry Hope, Cry Fury!" and "Venus Smiles". Other stories lavishly dressed with the same bitterly mournful romanticism are "Storm Bird, Storm Dreamer" (1966), "Tomorrow Is a Million Years" (1966) and "The Day of Forever" (1967). Published alongside these finely-crafted and dreamlike stories were the first elements of *The Atrocity Exhibition*, a literary collage that attempted to carry forward the prospectus outlined in his 1969 attack on Modernism with uncompromising resolution.

The pieces making up *The Atrocity Exhibition* seemed to many readers to be even less optimistic and naive than the catastrophe novels, but they certainly set out to tackle "the iconography of mass-merchandising", attempting to encapsulate and evaluate the key images and technologies of the twentieth century in a new way. They retained nothing of the dreamy and elegiac quality of the Vermilion Sands stories, parading instead a grimly uncompromising consciousness of the way in which all the world's tragedies had been packaged and transformed by the mass media and the fantasies of their avid audience.

* * * * * * *

The principal literary influence on the "condensed novels" making up *The Atrocity Exhibition* was William S. Burroughs, whose ruthlessly cynical view of the affectations of Americanized global culture Ballard extrapolated in a remarkable series of fragmented narratives. Ballard provided a schematic diagram of the method of these prose fancies in his article on Dali, which began by summing up the core of the artist's achievement in the following terms:

> Dali's paintings constitute a body of prophecy about ourselves unequalled in accuracy since Freud's "Civilisation and its Discontents." Voyeurism, self-disgust, biomorphic horror, the infantile basis of our dreams and longings—these diseases of the psyche which Dali rightly diagnosed have now culminated in the most sinister casualty of the century: the death of affect.
> This demise of feeling and emotion has paved the way for our most real and tender pleasures—in the excitement of pain and mutilation; in sex as the perfect arena, like a culture-bed of sterile pus, for all the veronicas of our own perversions; in our moral freedom to pursue our own psychopathology as a game; and in our ever-greater powers of abstraction—what our children have to fear is not the cars on the freeways of tomorrow but our own pleasure in calculating the parameters of their deaths. (p. 25-26)

The proposition that media consumers might appropriate and exploit the manufactured glamour of public figures and luxury consumer goods for erotic purposes seemed shocking to critics who protested against *The Atrocity Exhibition*, although it is arguable that their horrified attitude was based in willful blindness. The studious eroticization of images of Marilyn Monroe and Jackie Kennedy, the use of sexuality in the advertising of cars and the erotic elements of fictional depictions of gunplay were already too obvious to carry any real shock value. In Europe, where the American content of the mass media had always seemed graphically alien, the grotesquerie of *The Atrocity Exhibition* seemed natural enough, if a trifle unhealthy in its preoccupations, but the view from within the great glamour-factory of American culture was far more problematic. The novel was scheduled for US publication in 1970 by Doubleday, but Nelson Doubleday ordered the print run to be destroyed a fortnight before publication when he learned that it contained a section entitled "Why I Want to Fuck Ronald Reagan". The next publisher who took it on, E. P. Dutton, had no objection to that ambition or its phrasing, but its directors were apparently dismayed by references to controversial consumer champion Ralph Nader. The book ultimately appeared in the USA in 1972 from the Grove Press—publisher of William Burroughs, the Marquis de Sade and other assorted erotica—as *Love and Napalm: Export U.S.A.*. Burroughs provided a defensive preface for what he complimented as a "profound and disquieting book".

Ballard continued to pursue, in various ways, the implication that the image of the world collated and conveyed by the mass media qualifies as an "atrocity exhibition". He was particularly fascinated by the development of Anglo-American culture's love-affair with the motor car and by the manner in which the landscapes of modern civilization were being transformed by the advent of motorways. In an article for the car magazine *Drive*, published in 1971, he observed that "the car crash is the most dramatic event in most people's lives" and suggested—following a speculative method established by the best-selling pop psychologist Eric Berne—that rather than being unfortunate accidents, crashes might be regarded as the real subconscious objective of fast drivers. "If we really feared the crash," he noted, "most of us would be unable to look at a car, let alone drive one."

In pursuit of this perverse insight, Ballard had already mounted, in 1970, an exhibition of crashed cars at the New Arts Laboratory in London. His first substantial TV appearance was in a twenty-minute film for the BBC entitled *Crash* (1971). The final product of the temporary preoccupation was the novel *Crash* (1973), which set out to explore the orgastic possibilities of reckless driving and crash-associated masochism.

Crash was the first novel that Ballard wrote in the first person—a device that he took care to emphasize by giving the protagonist his own name. After being seriously injured in a car crash that results in a man's death, the narrator becomes intimately involved with the dead man's widow, Dr Helen Remington, and the obsessive "hoodlum scientist" Vaughan, whose death is announced in the first sentence and described in more detail in the final chapter. The narrative's careful eroticization of every aspect of the car, and its careful equation of crashes and orgasms, is clinical rather than pornographic. The narrator maintains a dispassionate pose as he adds a careful psychoanalytic gloss to his account of the development of his new perversity, but it is obvious that his passive neutrality is a mask and that his recollections are charged with submerged excitement.

Cape's blurb-writer described *Crash* as a "cautionary tale" but it is anything but alarmist in its import; it is disturbing not because it warns of dark things to come but because it insists that the psychopathology it describes is already established, although only a few pioneers have yet acknowledged and embraced it. The publication of the book in Britain and America did not give rise to any considerable furor, although a few critics took a strong dislike to the novel. It attracted a great deal more attention in France, where it achieved a remarkable *succès d'estime* and established Ballard's reputation as an important modern novelist. The fires of scandal were belatedly fanned a quarter of a century later, when David Cronenberg's relatively faithful but rather diffident 1996 movie version was initially denied a certificate by the British censors, but the protest soon petered out.

Although it carries forward the same fascination with the impact of cars and roads on modern life and modern relationships, the much more placid existentialist fable *Concrete Island* (1974) excited far less hostility than *Crash*. This novel and its immediate successor, *High-Rise* (1975), are curious "robinsonades" whose characters become castaways in the heart of urban civilization, always remaining within sight and earshot of the metropolitan hordes but isolated nevertheless. Unlike the most celebrated Crusoes of legend and literature, the hero of *Concrete Island* is so successful in making the best of his situation, stranded on a traffic island at a complex intersection, that he refuses the opportunity to leave when the flow of passing traffic finally relents. The high-rise apartment block in the latter novel succeeds so well in providing a comfortable microcosm in which its well-to-do residents can escape the stressful world of work that it swiftly becomes a private empire one course for independence—a empire that immediately begins to decay into violent anarchy and barbarism.

JAUNTING ON THE SCORIAC TEMPESTS, BY BRIAN STABLEFORD

If *Concrete Island* is seen as Ballard's first extended version of *Robinson Crusoe* then *High-Rise* was his first extended version of *The Lord of the Flies*. all the more shocking because it translocates the social decline of Golding's novel from a remote island to suburbia, while taking it for granted that intellectually sophisticated adults are just as prone to revert to savagery as children who know no better. After the intensity and clinicality of *Crash*, however, both novels seem slightly tongue-in-cheek, as if neither narrative is able to take itself entirely seriously. Their return to the kind of matter-of-fact third person narrative that Ballard had used in his earlier novels seems slightly half-hearted, perhaps because their interest as psychological "case-studies" is markedly reduced by their being set against relatively ordinary backgrounds. Even so, they continued the extended analysis of what he had called the "death of affect" that is constituted by all Ballard's works of the early 1970s.

The "death of affect", as Ballard conceives it, is a sterilization of the emotions, whose chief corollary is moral anesthesia. He proposed in his fiction and non-fiction alike that this was a condition of the modern world: a trend whose continuation into the future had to be taken for granted. *The Kindness of Women* freely admits, however—and it could hardly have been otherwise—that some of Ballard's acquaintances were convinced that it was a more personal thing, which he was merely projecting on to the world as a whole, and from which he might one day contrive a recovery. Either way, it is understandable that the greatest positive achievement available to the characters in the stories and novels Ballard produced in the early 1970s is a kind of ataraxia, a "calm of mind" rather different from the one Plato held up as an ideal. Only those who can live alongside all manner of horrors without being moved to fear or pity can operate within the world that is in the process of being born, and those who will adapt most successfully to the coming era are those who can welcome the opportunities opened up by the separation of erotic experience from emotion and moral responsibility. His later deployments of this theme, however, became more heavily ironic, and most are possessed by a certain dry humor which tacitly concedes that the announcement of the universal death of affect might have been a trifle premature.

The tongue-in-cheek element of such works as *High-Rise* was by no means unprecedented, and might almost be regarded as a reversion to type. Although he rarely wrote outright comedies, Ballard's early short fiction had always displayed a sharp if somewhat mordant wit, which began to reappear in fuller measure such satires

139

as "The Greatest TV Show on Earth" (1972) and "The Life and Death of God" (1976). In the final work of the phase of his career begun by *The Atrocity Exhibition*, "The Intensive Care Unit" (1977), Ballard sarcastically adopts a quasi-anthropological pose to examine the awful fate of a family living in a comprehensively privatized world, who decide, very unwisely, to try to rediscover the lost joys of intimacy.

Having taken this train of thought to this terminus, and being no longer able to take it seriously, Ballard had little alternative but to make another new beginning. Given that necessity, and his earlier insistence that an authentic twentieth century literature ought to be optimistic, it is not surprising that he began to consider the possibility that the future might yet be redeemed from awful aridity and the death of affect.

* * * * * * *

This process of redemption began in *The Unlimited Dream Company* (1979), a messianic posthumous fantasy in which Ballard's home town of Shepperton is exalted far above suburban mundanity. The novel's protagonist, Blake, crashes a stolen aircraft into the Thames at Shepperton. Although his dead body remains trapped in the cockpit he finds himself miraculously reincarnated on the river's bank. In the moment of his death he has glimpsed a number of people on the bank who are now appointed as his "family". These include Dr Miriam St Cloud, a young woman who has care of three handicapped children. (In *The Kindness of Women* the narrator's wife is called Miriam.)

After making several unsuccessful attempts to leave the town, a series of visions finally convinces Blake that he has a mission to fulfill, which must be undertaken there and there alone, with the aid of the healing powers with which he has been gifted. He must teach the people to fly, so that they can transcend their earthly existence and achieve a mystical union with the vegetable and mineral worlds, dissolving themselves into eternity much as the chief characters eventually did in *The Crystal World*. Although the name of the central character is significant, the novel's theme is also strongly allied with the paintings of the defiantly eccentric Stanley Spencer, who lived in the Thames-side village of Cookham and delighted using its mundane scenery as a backdrop for apocalyptic motifs and images of transcendence.

JAUNTING ON THE SCORIAC TEMPESTS, BY BRIAN STABLEFORD

The Unlimited Dream Company is the first of Ballard's novels to feature a hero who is unreasonable in the sense specified by George Bernard Shaw's "maxims for revolutionaries". Instead of adapting himself to changes in the external world, Blake must force the world—or Shepperton, at least—to adapt to the opportunities provided by his own godlike status. Although the novel is not autobiographical in any strict sense it is deeply personal; like *Crash* it is a first-person narrative. Although Blake is shot by the enigmatic funfair-proprietor Stark and his mission is rejected by the wary citizens of Shepperton, he comes through his time of trial with flying colors, in more than one sense of the phrase. In the end, Miriam precedes him into the next world, leaving him alone with his body still confined in his crashed plane, but he is not disheartened. "There I would rest," he announces, "certain now that one day Miriam would come for me."

The Unlimited Dream Company was followed by the light-heartedly satirical *Hello America* (1981), which describes the "rediscovery" in the twenty-second century of a largely abandoned America by an oddly assorted expedition from Europe. The apparatus of the twentieth-century mythologies that once ruled the world is here reduced to a series of shattered relics. The significantly-named protagonist, Wayne, dreams of resurrecting America's technological optimism and returning its glamorous consumerism to operational status, but his quest is futile in a world that has at last outgrown such follies.

Hello America was not a seriously-intended work—its production was prompted by a misguided suggestion by its publisher—but it is similar in spirit in some important respects to its immediate predecessor, and it helped to pave the way for Ballard's next new departure. His remark in the 1969 article about Dali about "our moral freedom to pursue our own psychopathology as a game" had suggested in advance that Ballard's extensive analysis of "the death of affect" might be regarded as a strategic self-indulgence; once his fictions began to find scope for the redemption of the world it was probably inevitable that they would eventually begin to home in on their real target: Ballard's own seemingly-atrophied emotions.

Although *Empire of the Sun* (1984) can certainly be categorized as an autobiographical novel, in that it follows the exploits and adventures of a boy named Jim interned by the Japanese during World War II, it makes no bones about the fact that it is no mere documentary reconstruction. The narrative is carefully distanced from the authorial voice, by virtue of being told in the third person, as if Ballard

141

regarded his younger self as a mystery still in need of unraveling. Comparison of certain key incidents that are also mentioned in Ballard's non-fictional reminiscences—especially the attempted breakout and the incident in which Japanese soldiers murder a Chinese man at a railway station—suggests that the Jim of the novel is markedly more enterprising and more actively-engaged in his experiences than the real Ballard ever contrived to be. Although the character is by no means sanitized, he is allowed to take on certain insights and responses of which Ballard himself was incapable in the 1940s. One of the differences between the story told in *Empire of the Sun* and Ballard's own reminiscences of internment is that Jim actually witnesses the atmospheric after-effects of the explosion of the atom bomb that destroyed Hiroshima, although he does not understand what it is. Here, as in several other instances, he benefits from his creator's hindsight, making a little more sense of what is happening to him than his real analogue was able to accomplish at the time.

Empire of the Sun was nominated for the Booker Prize and won both the *Guardian* Fiction Prize and the James Tait Black Award. It became a best-seller in Britain and its celebrity was further enhanced when the film rights sold to Steven Spielberg, who produced and directed the movie himself. The *enfant terrible* reputation won by *The Atrocity Exhibition* and *Crash* was set aside, at least for a while, on the grounds that Spielberg's endorsement was an ironclad guarantee of the new Ballard's suitability for children. Although the novel is markedly less sentimental than the film, which takes aboard Spielberg's constant preoccupation with the innocence and wonder of childhood, its portrayal of young Jim is far less clinically scarifying than the psychological dissections of the protagonists of Ballard's earlier novels. The narrative does recapitulate, to some extent, the tone and ambience of the early disaster novels, and it has obvious affinities with his tales of corrosive psychological confinement, but it is quite distinct from those earlier works. It does, however, cast some light on certain preoccupations of Ballard's early works which had seemed at the time to be strange and rather pointless. In *Empire of the Sun*, the psychological significance and symbolism of empty swimming pools, dead birds and abandoned military hardware is perfectly clear and straightforward; no one who has read the novel is likely to find such tales as "The Voices of Time" and "The Terminal Beach" as unrelentingly gnomic and bizarre as the unprepared English readers who first encountered them in the pages of *New Worlds*.

JAUNTING ON THE SCORIAC TEMPESTS, BY BRIAN STABLEFORD

Empire of the Sun is unique among tales of Japanese internment camps—most of which are unremittingly grim and almost all of which embody an understandable but utterly conventional sense of outrage—by virtue of the eerily objective and accepting viewpoint that had long been Ballard's hallmark. What seems to the other characters in the novel, and also to the reader, to be a horribly unexpected and unmitigated catastrophe is to the adolescent Jim merely one more change in a routinely change-afflicted existence, which he simply takes aboard. The camp *becomes* his world, and the responses of the other prisoners—who cannot help but see their imprisonment as a cruel and intolerable subversion of the ordinary course of affairs—seem as unfathomable to Jim as any other adult behavior. It may be, however, that the more important acceptance is the narrative's concession that it is neither wrong nor unnatural for Jim to feel this way, and that the extent to which he is out of step with his fellow prisoners is not evidence of his being some kind of monster. The fact that Jim is allowed to do some of the things that Ballard apparently failed to do in similar circumstances might be regarded as a kind of self-indulgence, but the likelihood is that it is more akin to belated self-approval. *Empire of the Sun* was, in a sense, the novel that Ballard had avoided writing for forty years, and which finally materialized as a redemptive reconstruction of his own memories: a calculated, if long-delayed, act of self-forgiveness.

****

Ballard followed *Empire of the Sun* with *The Day of Creation*, a return to the Africa of *The Crystal World*, which is here more explicitly revealed as the symbolic continent of Joseph Conrad's seminal psychodrama *Heart of Darkness*. The plot concerns the emergence of a new river whose seemingly-miraculous flow begins after the uprooting of a tree at the end of the airstrip near Port-la-Nouvelle, a town in the border region between Chad and Sudan. The National Geographic Society registers it as the River Mallory, naming it after a doctor working in a local World Health Organization clinic. Mallory has dreamed repeatedly of a "third Nile" whose tributaries might bring new life to the desert sands of the Sahara and he is quick to "buy" the spring from a local warlord, Captain Kagwa, while it is still a narrow and feeble steam.

As its flow increases, the river Mallory fills the dry basin of Lake Kotto and drowns Port-la-Nouvelle. Its advent has political repercussions, increasing the stakes in the festering conflict between

143

Kagwa and his chief rival, General Harare. Following the suggestion that the river's true source is two hundred miles away in the Massif du Tondou, from which its waters have been liberated by a seismic event that has elevated the water table, Mallory sets off in the ferryboat *Salammbo* to follow the waters upstream. Alas, the new life to which the river has given birth begins to die almost immediately as the flow, having reached its maximum, begins to abate again. By the time Mallory and his companions reach the tantalizing source, nothing remains of the river's hope and promise but an exhausted expanse of primeval mud.

The ending of *The Day of Creation* has something in common with Ballard's endings of the early catastrophe novels, but the political allegory of the novel is much more elaborately developed than the psychological allegory and the significance of the river's drying up is more general than personal. With the exception of *The Kindness of Women*, all Ballard's subsequent novels can be interpreted as sarcastic sociopolitical allegories—in a 1996 interview Ballard classified them as "social critiques". Instead of regarding "the death of affect" as the central trend of modern society, these late novels suggest that the people of the modern world are "anaesthetized" in a merely apathetic way, unprepared for change and challenge.

The novella *Running Wild* (1988) makes some slight pretence to be a mystery novel, although the only real mystery is why the narrator—a forensic psychiatrist—cannot persuade the Home Office that the obvious answer to the puzzle is true. In a small Thames-side enclave named Pangbourne Village—not the actual village of Pangbourne but an exclusive, fenced-off luxury estate designed to provide its wealthy middle-class professional inhabitants with peace of mind—every adult has been killed and all their children have disappeared. Even when one of the missing children turns up in a traumatized state, unable to explain what happened, no one but the psychiatrist and a lowly sergeant in the Thames Valley Police will accept that the only people who could have committed the crime are the children.

The reason for this refusal is that the children, never having been abused, have no motive; the narrator is the only one who can understand that they were not rebelling against hate and cruelty but its opposite: "a despotism of kindness. They killed to free themselves from a tyranny of love and care." By the time the story ends the Pangbourne children have branched out into political assassination, making an attempt on the life of the female prime minister, the "Mother of her nation." The narrator advances his supposedly-expert opinion that many more violent anarchists will spring from the fertile breeding-grounds of the protected estates of Europe and America.

Unlike *Empire of the Sun*, to which it is a sequel of sorts, *The Kindness of Women* is told in the first person. It deals with the substance of Ballard's life in England, and has to struggle hard to overcome the handicap imposed by the fact his life after leaving the internment camp could easily be seen as a long anticlimax. Because it deals with more recent events and with intimate relationships, it takes care to protect its "characters" by changing all their names, but it is not a *roman à clef* in the conventional sense. Although one could attempt to measure its accuracy by comparing the accounts of the characters with their real-life equivalents—thus, for instance, measuring the extent of the fictionalization of the late Dr Christopher Evans as Richard Sutherland—this would not provide any real indication of the truthfulness of the story. Although the details of Miriam's death in the novel differ considerably from those of Helen Ballard's death, the differences would be insignificant if one could accept that the subsequent account of its effect on the narrator's state of mind were an accurate recapitulation of Ballard's actual experience.

There is, of course, a temptation to read the novel in exactly this way, as if all its differences from history were on a par with changing the names of the characters. It is, however, worth noting that there is a great deal of actuality that has been omitted from the novel, including the central enterprise of Ballard's actual career. Although it is mentioned on occasion that the narrator of *The Kindness of Women* is a writer, there is not a word about what he is writing or how he approaches his vocation. Given that it is so brutally frank in its descriptions of sexual relationships, the text hardly warrants description as "censored", but its careful omission of everything relating to the author's primary activity does not encourage the view that it offers a full picture of his mental life. However careful it might be as an exercise in psychosurgical dissection, its minute attentiveness to matters of urogenital detail cannot make up for the fact that the heart and guts are left to lie almost entirely unexamined.

Like *The Kindness of Women, Rushing to Paradise* (1994) seems at fist glance to be a recapitulation of things surpassed, deftly recombining elements of *The Drowned World*, "The Terminal Beach", *High-Rise* and *Empire of the Sun*. Its teenage protagonist, Neil Dempsey, falls under the spell of the curiously charismatic Dr. Barbara Rafferty, who continually trumpets the slogan "Save the

Albatross" in her attempt to keep the French from using the Pacific island of Saint-Esprit as a nuclear test-site. Using tactics borrowed from Greenpeace (whose *Rainbow Warrior* had been sunk by French agents in 1985) Dr. Barbara leads an ill-assorted crew of eco-warriors to the island, where they establish a sanctuary not merely for albatrosses but for any other endangered species the world cares to send.

Although *Rushing to Paradise* is a literal robinsonade, it is set in a world in which there are no more desert islands. Saint-Esprit receives far more visitors than the apartment block in *High-Rise*, and the passing traffic becomes so intense that Dr. Barbara becomes increasingly paranoid about the sanctity of her sanctuary. It is not isolation from the world that sends her little colony free-falling towards savagery but the desire to secure isolation and to establish a protected enclave where society can begin again from scratch. Neil retains his non-judgmental attitude to Dr. Barbara's tactics long after the reader has seen which way the wind is blowing, but in the end her methods become a little too much for him to stomach, especially when his crucial role in her grand plan seems about to be usurped by an even younger analogue, Nihal. He plays his part in bringing her experiment to an end, although he wonders at the end whether he and she might one day be able to start the whole thing over.

The political allegory at the heart of *Rushing to Paradise* is more conventional than that in *The Day of Creation* or *Running Wild*. Although the story is not a straightforward cautionary tale about the tendencies of charismatic leaders, Dr. Barbara is explicitly compared to the author of the Jonesville massacre, and hers is a story of absolute corruption fostered by near-absolute power. Having been struck off for practicing euthanasia a little too publicly, she proceeds by measured steps to the practice of callous mass murder—not for the sake of the albatross, but for the sake of ill-formed Utopian ideals, which conceive of adult males as a plague without which the world would be far better off. The novel is wryly humorous without being outrightly comic or satirical, and it seems at times to be mocking notions that Ballard had formerly taken in deadly earnest—especially in "The Terminal Beach"—as well as various follies of contemporary history.

Like *Running Wild*, *Cocaine Nights* (1996) is thinly disguised as a murder mystery. The solution to the mystery is by no means as obvious, but it is related to the novel's real theme with similar obliquity. As in the earlier story, what is important is not who did the deed, but why they (or anyone) should do such a thing. Whereas

JAUNTING ON THE SCORIAC TEMPESTS, BY BRIAN STABLEFORD

Running Wild was set in a custom-designed Thames Village, *Cocaine Nights* is set in Estrella de Mar, a retirement village on the Spanish Costa de Sol. The protagonist, Charles Prentice, is a travel writer to whom the idea of settlement is anathema; to him, the whole idea of Estrella de Mar seems strange, and this does not help his quest to understand why his brother Frank, the proprietor of the Club Nautico, has confessed to setting a fire that killed five people.

No one, including the policeman in charge of the case, believes that Frank is guilty, but Charles cannot identify anyone else who had a motive. While he continues his amateur investigation, convinced that Frank will eventually retract his absurd confession, he is continually side-tracked, tantalized and attacked, in the manner of the great tradition of amateur sleuthing, but he quickly becomes aware of the fact that the assumptions of that great tradition are irrelevant to his own situation. It slowly becomes apparent that the key to the mystery is tennis pro and one-man amateur crime wave Bobby Crawford, but the puzzle facing Charles is far deeper and more perverse than any mere matter of breaking Crawford's seemingly cast-iron alibi.

In the later phases of the plot, Charles becomes Crawford's confidant, and actually goes to work for him in applying the lessons learned in Estrella de Mar to the neighboring resort of Residencia Costasol. He hopes that by standing, as it were, in his brother's shoes, he will eventually come to understand how the Estrella de Mar tragedy unfolded. Inevitably, and ironically, he eventually comes to understand it far too well.

Like Pangbourne Village, Estrella de Mar is held up by its observers as a model for an emergent future: a future in which people will retire in their thirties, with half a century of idleness before them, a world no longer prey to wars and ideologies. The text suggests that the most urgent problem facing people in such a world would be a tendency to retreat into inactivity, to detach themselves entirely from society. The one character in *Cocaine Nights* who stands outside the processes of the plot is the psychiatrist Dr Sanger; it is he who poses the rhetorical question of how people in that kind of world can be "energized" and united in a cause. Politics and religion, he suggests, are equally impotent, but there remains one thing that *can* generate a sense of community: crime. Having been told this on page 180, Charles spends the rest of the plot embodying the wisdom, helping Bobby Crawford in his criminal crusade to awaken the inhabitants of the Residencia Costasol from their torpor, progressing in measured steps from petty theft, drug-peddling and triv-

147

ial arson to the human sacrifices that will make the spiritual revivification of the resort irreversible.

* * * * * * *

By the time he wrote *Cocaine Nights*, Ballard's reputation as a writer of literary fiction was secure. When he first broke out of the science fiction ghetto there had seemed to be a possibility that the whole genre might be redeemed from all the prejudices that had accumulated while it was being marketed as the lowliest of the many garish brand of pulp fiction, but that did not happen. In spite of the fact that the actual Space Age was over almost as soon as it had begun, the imagery of popular science fiction remained firmly committed to the imagery of futuristic space travel, which became even more absurd in the TV shows and movies that displaced printed texts at the heart of the genre in the late 1970s. Ballard's escape from genre confinement was correlated with the careful de-emphasizing of the science-fictional elements of his work—a progressive process which ultimately resulted in their extirpation from his longer works. In his short stories, however, he continued to play with science-fictional imagery, albeit in a conscientiously skeptical fashion.

Although Michael Moorcock's several attempts to resurrect *New Worlds* never contrived to establish a viable audience, something of the spirit of that enterprise was inherited by *Interzone*, a magazine that borrowed its title from William Burroughs. Initially edited by a cumbersome collective, *Interzone* eventually came into the sole charge of David Pringle, a long-time Ballard fan and the author of an early monograph on his work, *Earth is the Alien Planet* (1979). Pringle was eager to publish Ballard and Ballard was prepared, on occasion, to oblige him—although when Pringle interviewed him in 1996 for a special issue celebrating is 65th birthday Ballard lamented, somewhat disingenuously, that he had been forced to reduce his output of short stories drastically because there were no suitable markets left.

The longest of Ballard's *Interzone* stories is "Memories of the Space Age" (1982), a story so thoroughly Ballardian as almost to qualify as self-parody, set in a deserted Cape Kennedy where the only survivor of the last space mission—who thus qualifies as the only man to have committed murder in space—pilots an assortment of small planes, teasing and tempting the dream-stricken protagonist and the wife of his victim with his fanciful flights. "The Object of the Attack" (1984), is a more obviously ironic account of an assassination attempt, which turns out not to have been aimed at the politicians and members of the royal family who were present, but at a far more dangerous man: an astronaut-turned-religious-mystic ambitious to become a charismatic leader. "The Man Who Walked on the Moon" (1985) is a reflective account of an impostor who obtains handouts from tourists in return for telling tales of his delusory but mythically-charged career as an astronaut. "The Message from Mars" (1992) is yet another dissection of the hopelessness of dreams of space conquest.

Despite their preoccupation with the Space Age, these stories only qualify marginally as science fiction. Perhaps surprisingly, they are marginal even to Ballard's notion of what science fiction ought to have become. His early insistence that science fiction would do better to devote itself to the exploration of *inner* space had been allowed to slide almost into oblivion. The one *Interzone* story that takes on such a task directly is "The Enormous Space" (1989), a painstaking reprise of a plot he had used several times in the first phase of his career, most notably in "The Overloaded Man" (1961). The formula is an account of a domestic experiment, whose protagonist carefully removes himself from the everpresent world by cultivating an altered state of consciousness. In this version, the central character converts the home from which his ex-wife has fled into a metaphorical desert island, analyzing the necessarily-brief success of his project in exactly those terms:

"In every way I am marooned, but a reductive Crusoe paring away exactly those elements of bourgeois life that the original Robinson so dutifully reconstituted. Crusoe wished to bring the Croydons of his own day to life again on his island. I want to expel them, and find in their place a far richer realm formed from the elements of light, time and space." (*War Fever* p. 120)

Most of Ballard's subsequent contributions to *Interzone* were only qualified for inclusion there by their playful and quirky surrealism, and they fit in perfectly well with the stories he published elsewhere in the same period, which include the Borgesian "Report on an Unidentified Space Station" (1982) and the satires "The Secret History of World War 3" (1988), "Love in a Colder Climate" (1989) and "War Fever" (1989). These were collected, along with most of the *Interzone* stories and one story left over from an earlier phase of his career—the chilling fabular *conte cruel* "The Air Disaster" (1975), one of the few stories Ballard ever equipped with a climactic twist—in *War Fever* (1990).

Jaunting on the Scoriac Tempests, by Brian Stableford

Had he been so inclined, Ballard could have continued his explorations of inner space without risking stigmatization as a science fiction writer, and the fact that he virtually abandoned them, in favor of idiosyncratic analyses of the world as it is, had far more to do with his own personal development as a writer than any determination to maintain the respectability of his reputation. In the end, inner space became almost as uninteresting to him as outer space, and his attention was entrapped by the world between. Although his social critiques remain distinctive, they remain social critiques, adrift in a vast crowd, whereas some of his earlier experiments took his pen into literary territory where, as the old joke has it, the hand of man had not previously set foot.

* * * * * * *

Thanks to the Spielberg film, *Empire of the Sun* now overshadows everything else that Ballard wrote. Not only is it his best-known work, but a case could certainly be made for its being his most engaging, or at least his most reader-friendly. Its autobiographical aspect adds an important extra dimension to the fascination with which the reader follows Jim's responses to the events that envelop him.

One could argue, however, that it is precisely the debt that *Empire of the Sun* owes to memory and actuality which makes the book less striking as an instance of extraordinary creativity than some of its predecessors. Although *The Kindness of Women* slyly implies that *Crash* is a more autobiographical work than anyone without inside knowledge could have guessed, the embroideries of *Crash* are far more elaborate, and at least a little more astonishing, than those of *Empire of the Sun*. Although *The Crystal World* is probably slighter than it was intended to be, if it is considered as part of a collective with the two novels with which it forms a trilogy of sorts, *The Drowned World* and *The Drought*, the whole assemblage is very remarkable indeed. No one had ever written anything like them before, and, in association with "The Voices of Time" and "The Terminal Beach", they were the works that secured the coinage of the adjective "Ballardian" and established its exchange-rate.

There is, therefore, some cause for regret in the fact that, after *Empire of the Sun*, J. G. Ballard's work became gradually less Ballardian, and that the Ballardian elements that it retained became less intense, more studied and decidedly whimsical. On the other hand, there is certainly some cause for celebration in the fact that even

JAUNTING ON THE SCORIAC TEMPESTS, BY BRIAN STABLEFORD

Cocaine Nights is Ballardian enough to guarantee that few readers would misattribute it in a blind testing. Although it is a social critique set in the present, which politely masquerades as a mystery story, its analysis of nascent social problems is highly unusual and its slyly- and wryly-proposed solution to those problems is even more unusual. The present in which it is set stands in for one of the many futures into which we presently seem to be headed, and the mystery within its mystery is the unanswered question that has echoed throughout the disparate parts of Ballard's entire literary corpus. Exactly what, in the light of a scrupulously careful dissection of his actual and potential experience, should a man care about, if he can ever achieve the perversely difficult task of re-setting himself to care at all?

Jaunting on the Scoriac Tempests, by Brian Stableford

LORD, WHAT FOOLS THESE MORTALS BE! CONFRONTATION WITH DEATH IN JAMES MORROW'S *THE ETERNAL FOOTMAN*

One of the most common synonyms for "human being"—derived, like so much else in Western culture, from the ancient Greek—is "mortal." This serves to contrast us with other animals not because we are the only ones that die, but because we are the only ones that *know* that we must die. This awareness is by no means comforting, and it is hardly surprising that the primary task of the human imagination throughout history has been the supplementation of knowledge by the faith—or, at least, the hope—that death is not the end. Psalm 49 goes so far as to suggest that the faithless do not even have a proper awareness of mortality—"Man that is in honor, and understandeth not, is like the beasts that perish"—while those who do can be certain, along with the psalmist, that "God will redeem my soul from the power of the grave." The most common Latin-derived synonym for "human being" is, of course, "individual", meaning "undivided one"—implying that death divides, and that the redemption of the soul from "the power of the grave" is crucial to the definition of humanity.

If we are to enquire, as rational skeptics, into the imaginative power of religion, we can hardly avoid the conclusion that the most fundamental function of religious faith is to provide psychological arms and armor against our awareness that we must die. What differentiates religions one from another at the deepest level is not so much that they conceive of gods and their earthly representatives in different ways but that they adopt different strategies of psychological palliation; it is for this reason that all of the major religions have been subject to schismatic arguments about tactics. If, like Friedrich Nietzsche, we try to discriminate between religions on the grounds of the extent to which they are life-enhancing or life-denying, the principal criterion of preferability is bound to be the effectiveness of the armaments with which they equip their followers for the everyday business of coping with the awareness of mortality; the first hurdle to be cleared in the vexatious vocation of "getting a life" is coming to terms with the fact that it cannot last forever and might end at any time.

Religions do, of course, serve other functions as well as this one; in the past they have obligingly provided explanations for the fact that the world exists at all and how it got to be the way it is now, and scriptural codifications of the moral order at which human society ought to aim. Unfortunately, the one thing that unites all religions is that they all got the explanations completely wrong, and their miscellaneous attempts to impose unchanging and absolutist moral codes have proved something of a handicap to the cause of moral evolution and progress. Their failures in these regards have inevitably rebounded on their fundamental cause, with potentially shattering effect.

Given all this, it is not in the least surprising that the post-theistic trilogy James Morrow began in *Towing Jehovah* and continued in *Blameless in Abaddon*—books that weighed the secondary aspirations of Western Christianity in an exceptionally scrupulous balance and found them severely wanting—should reach its final and most critical phase in *The Eternal Footman*, whose key image is that of mortal redividuals uncomfortably confronted by their *doppelgänger* "fetches": personal mortality made incarnate. *The Eternal Footman* asks the two final questions that need to be asked about the fate of Western Christendom: how good was the psychological armor with which it provided its adherents, and what shall we put in its place now that we are obliged by the pressure of rationalism to set it aside? It does not attempt to provide a firm answer to the second question, and is artfully deft as well as wittily sarcastic in its treatment of the first; the reason why some poets and novelists are better legislators than most prophets and all avatars of Ozymandias is that they know their limitations.

* * * * * * *

The Eternal Footman addresses its key questions in the same satirical fashion as its predecessors. It describes what happens after the suicidal Jehovah, seemingly tired of puerile human attempts to evade consciousness of his extinction, celebrates the Millennium by disintegrating his body and sending his skull into geosynchronous orbit, where it functions as the ultimate *memento mori* of the Western World. Then, beneath the mocking glare of the Cranium Dei, the West is subjected to the last and nastiest of all the plagues that God has seen fit to visit upon it.

The first revelation of this new disease is vouchsafed to Nora Burkhart, a delivery driver for Ray Feldstein's Tower of Flowers, purveyor of funeral wreaths to the proud and humble alike. The body of Nora's beloved son Kevin is confronted and swiftly possessed by his fetch Quincy Azrael. Black "fear syrup"—also known as "Sartre sauce"—comes bubbling from his mouth as his excruciation on the existentialist rack begins. Quincy pops back out occasionally to engage Kevin and Nora in conversations to which his own contribution is divided between weak jokes and sharp philosophical debate, but he always wins his arguments by the simple expedient of repossession.

When the pathology of the new "abulic plague" is fully revealed as the activity of a protein nicknamed Nietzsche-A, those redividuals who have only *seen* their fetches are found to be in a prefatory "Nietzsche-positive" phase, in which they may remain for some considerable time. Only after fusion with their fetches do sufferers move to full-blown "thanocathexis". The first phase, in which the fear syrup begins to flow, is followed by an "aphasic quadriplegia," whose paralyzing effect is followed in its turn by a horrid eruption of boils and abscesses, which eventually fade to pocks and fistulas as the desiccated body finally expires.

While Nora is learning all this, mostly the hard way, the reclusive monumental sculptor Gerald Korty is inspired by his reading of Thomas Ockham's *Parables for a Post-theistic Age* (whose genesis was described in *Towing Jehovah*) to plan an appropriate reliquary for God's remaining bones. The delight he feels when the Vatican accepts his design turns to wrath when he discovers that the Church has bought his work only to pervert it and suppress its intent. He then commits himself to a crusade against the plague led by the psychoanalyst Adrian Lucido (who is "Freudian by training, Jungian by temperament"). Lucido employs the drug hyperion-15 in intimate and essential harness with the new, custom-designed religion of Somatocism. His base of operations is that region of Mexico that once played host to the mysterious civilization of the Olmecs, upriver from the port of Coatzacoalcos, and Korty establishes his own base even further upriver, in a location he renames El Dorado.

The deities of Lucido's synthetic religion mirror quasi-Freudian stages of human development and are named with anagrams of Diagoras, the first identifiable atheist (who lived in the fifth century BC). Idorasag is the goddess of suckling, the "world gland"; Rigosada is the lord of laughter, a cosmic jester; Orgasiad is the goddess of copulation, the incarnation of eroticism; Soaragid is the lord of the dance, a celebration of life itself. Their temples are, respectively, a labyrinth, a hall, a grove and a cave, while their Olmec-inspired and Korty-defined idols are a shaggy female ape, a grinning humanoid crocodile, a lamiaesque serpent-woman and a were-jaguar.

When the civilization of the USA collapses for want of fuel Nora decides to make her laborious way along the plague-devastated east coast to Coatzacoalcos in order that Kevin might take Lucido's cure. She is delayed by the crusade launched against the Jews of America by the Anglo-Saxon Christian Brotherhood, whose battlefields she must cross, but fares better when she hooks up with the Great Sumerian Traveling Circus and Repertory Company. She plays Inanna in its production of *The Epic of Gilgamesh*—the plot of which is, of course, concerned with Gilgamesh's fruitless quest to wrest the secret of immortality from the gods, who have reserved it for themselves at humanity's expense. In the end, it is Anthony Van Horne, the one-time tower of Jehovah, who delivers Nora and Kevin, along with his own stricken child, to Lucido's clinic, crossing the Gulf in a paddle steamer that formerly served as a whorehouse. Kevin's subsequent relief is, alas, only a stay of execution; hyperion-15 and Somatocism are merely instruments of procrastination.

When Lucido's search for a more permanent "antidote" to thanocathexis leads him into the darkest heart of paganism, Korty returns to the quest to create an appropriate object for the veneration of future ages. He decides that it must be hewn in the form of the human brain from the last surviving fragment of "Oswald's rock," the residuum of the asteroid whose impact wiped out the dinosaurs; the hollow of the brain is to be excavated into a series of "temples" celebrating human knowledge, kindness, creativity and doubt, their imagery embodying all the *little* myths recommended by Thomas Ockham as testimony to the proper studies and achievements of humankind.

In the meantime, Nora's own fetch, Goneril, becomes her guide in hallucinogen-aided mock-Dantean dreams which offer her two contrasted visions of post-theistic existence: the city of Deus Absconditus and the ecofreakish village of Holistica. Their realization will depend on the fate of Korty's brain; Nora's attempt to save it from the eruption of Mount Catemaco in order to secure the future of Deus Absconditus and banish Holistica to the mists of what-might-have-been provides the novel with a defiantly melodramatic climax. That climax cannot, however, be the final phase of a novel about mortality; it merely serves as a bridge to a majestically graceful final descent in the general direction of grief-afflicted but fetch-free philosophical sanity.

****

It is not everyone, of course, who finds the awareness of mortality excessively disturbing. Even some of those who have argued for its status as the foundation-stone and paramount fact of human self-awareness have been prepared to argue that it ought to be liberating rather than oppressive. Lucretius takes this view in *De rerum natura*, the summary of Epicurean philosophy that became the substitute Bible of so many Western European skeptics—including Anatole France, who awarded it the central role as inspiration for *The Revolt of the Angels* in the first classic of the anti-Jehovist satirical tradition to which Morrow's trilogy belongs. The fear syrup that is the first explicit symptom of abulic plague is presumably called "Sartre sauce" because the father of existentialism, Martin Heidegger, showed clear Lucretian tendencies in *Being and Time*, suggesting that it was only by conscious acceptance of the fact of mortality that human beings could begin to live "authentically." It was Sartre's Being and Nothingness that put the heavier emphasis on the "absurdity" of mortality, re-demonizing it in no uncertain terms.

Even these careful dissenting voices, however, testify to the fact that the awareness of mortality has long been viewed in Western society as something essentially, deeply and uniquely problematic. It is not only traceable to our oldest myths, but—even more revealingly—to core aspects of those myths, which have been subtly and slyly de-emphasized. "Death awareness doesn't kill people," Quincy Azrael tells Nora Burkhart. "Death kills people. Death awareness merely turns people into quivering blobs of ineffectuality. You know about Prometheus. His transgression, you may recall, lay as much in blessing people with death amnesia as in telling them the recipe for combustion."

Nora does, indeed, recall the relevant mythological detail. "According to Aeschylus," she obligingly thinks, "prior to Prometheus's intervention, everyone on Earth had known the exact date and hour of his or her death, a situation inflicting chronic lethargy on a majority of humankind. When finally unburdened of this awful information, men and women gradually—inevitably—began acting as if they might live forever. They built cities, pursued science, practiced arts, and challenged the gods".

Quincy goes on to observe that in the East—where the pursuit of science and the gods did not progress as far as industrial revolutions and coca-colonization—death denial takes "forms that render my species irrelevant". The message of the orbiting Cranium Dei is therefore addressed to the West alone: the civilization whose roots lie buried in the culture of Aeschylus as modified by St Paul. The latter's crucial role consisted of agreeing with the Jewish apocalyptic writers of the first century BC that the Promethean role had actually been played by angels expelled from Heaven, and taking from the myth of Adam in Eden (into which Christian mythology deftly imported one such fallen angel) the lesson that death is "the wages of sin." Even Islam is exempted from Morrow's analysis, although the Moslems are "people of the book" firmly committed to the notion that the faithful will live after death in paradise.

* * * * * * *

It could be argued that there are significant cultural differences between the various sectors of the West, with respect to "death denial", which are at least as great as the differences between Christianity and Islam. Morrow is an American writer and *The Eternal Footman*—unlike its predecessors—is mostly set in the Americas. A British critic can hardly approach the book without being acutely aware of the fact that America is a foreign country where they do things differently. Jessica Mitford's ultra-English, quasi-anthropological study of *The American Way of Death* followed in the footsteps of one of the most scathing literary twentieth-century satires penned by a westward-staring Englishman, Evelyn Waugh's *The Loved One*. The British reader of Waugh and Mitford is expected to react with both horror and laughter to resounding echoes of the mission of Hubert Eaton, who took over the arid Tropicano cemetery in 1913 and converted it into Forest Lawn by irrigation, distilling his vision into a remarkable hybrid of the Apostle's Creed and a business plan, "The Builder's Creed" (1917). It is not obvious, however, that the rapid spread of British crematoria—equally businesslike and usually denuded of religious symbolism in order that they might supply the needs of a multicultural society—is any less eloquent as testimony to the extent and depth of "death amnesia."

Douglas J. Davies's chronicling of this phenomenon in *Death, Ritual and Belief* calls attention to the fact that the bereaved of Britain often forget to collect the ashes of their loved ones from the crematoria.

If it is the case that the four developmental stages in *Western Attitudes Towards Death* identified by Philippe Ariès are more clearly discernible in his native France than elsewhere, it is nevertheless undeniable that similar shifts in attitude have been manifest throughout Western Christendom. Ariès suggests that a near-universal acceptance of death as an everpresent domestic or "tame" reality was modified after the twelfth century by increased concern with and exaggerated anxiety regarding one's own death. The eighteenth century, he suggests, saw a growing sense of social intimacy with others, which shifted the focus of concern to grieving death of loved ones—but in the twentieth century, he argues, this double burden of fear and grief has resulted in a dramatic renewal and reinforcement of the age-old death amnesia, whereby death has become the "unnamable," carefully isolated from everyday experience and carefully redecorated with falsifying euphemisms. It is this process that provides the historical stem connecting the Promethean root to Morrow's Millennium, and the justification for accepting that his satire is applicable to the whole of Western culture as well as to those American tendencies that invite the best-aimed blows of his sarcasm's heavy hand.

The most surprising element of Ariès' analysis of western attitudes to death is, perhaps, the earliness of the signs that he detects of a growing terror of death. In his earlier essay on "Changing Attitudes Towards Death in the Modern Western World" Arnold Toynbee claims that the fear even of one's own death did not become acute in Christendom until the seventeenth century, when faith first began to dissolve in the acid of reason and science. One of Toynbee's key examples of that post-revolutionary Terror is the sarcastic lexicographer Samuel Johnson, whose exaggerated anxieties were recorded by the loyal but faith-depleted Boswell in the latter part of the eighteenth, when Ariès' Frenchmen had already been caught up in the cult of *sensibilité*. Because Morrow's analysis is less concerned with the phases of the problem than the possibility of its solution, however, he is less interested in the spread of the shadow cast by the Enlightenment than the advent of new light within the shadow. Of all the heroes borrowed from Thomas Ockham by Gerald Korty none stands taller and prouder than the humanist Desiderius Erasmus, whose life spanned the fifteenth and sixteenth centuries and whose career provided a careful counterpoint to Martin Luther's reckless revolutionism.

Erasmus is supposed to be the central figure in Korty's Temple of Doubt, although the Vatican authorities are careful to substitute St Augustine in the reliquary they actually construct on the set of *Ben Hur*. Erasmus's name is subsequently bestowed upon the river that runs through the city of Deus Absconditus—"the purest river this side of the Jordan"—and his modest conservatism is reflected in the post-Christian churches that survive there, including the Assembly of the Turned Cheek, the Assembly of the Gift Cloak and the Assembly of the Beloved Enemy.

Twenty-eight per cent of the churches of Deus Absconditus are said to be based on a humanistic version of the Sermon on the Mount, the rest owing their inspiration to "Judaic and Buddhist roots". In preferring Deus Absconditus to the rival future of Holistica—an extrapolation of modish technological retreatism—Nora Burkhart and her author are consciously attempting to carry forward a well-established tradition: one that has been set against the exaggeration of death awareness throughout modern history, from the Age of Reason through the Age of Enlightenment to the Age of Industry. It may need to be emphasized that this adherence sets Morrow against *both* the main trends of contemporary American ideology. Although the trilogy's most obvious target is the religiosity of Fundamentalism, it also takes care to trash the pretensions of "New Age" neo-paganism. Beneath the carefully-constructed religion of Somatocism, which embraces all the supposed wisdom of Freud and Jung, is a blind brutality, and although the ecologically aware inhabitants of Holistica are resolutely nice they are also utterly dimwitted: paradigmatic examples of "Man that is in honor, and understandeth not" and is therefore "like the beasts that perish."

Deus Absconditus is not Utopia—a point which the text is careful to make explicit as well as obvious. It has much in common with Satirev, the inverted image of the perversely life-denying Veritas in Morrow's novella *City of Truth*, especially in that its citizens are blithely unashamed of the absurdity of their contrivances. Indeed, the very essence of life as it is lived in Deus Absconditus is that institutions are judged by their efficacy rather than their fidelity to truth or principle. The basic philosophy of its design is that faith is not merely stupid but unnecessary; it is built on the proposition that good psychological armor need not be so heavy as to weigh a man down and the hope that—however paradoxical it may seem—levity might actually be a better defense than leaden seriousness.

159

The main problem with Deus Absconditus as an institutional framework for post-theistic society is not that it is a sketchy joke but that it is, like Quincy Azrael's stand-up routine, one that we have heard before. Once the calculated levity is set aside, it must be admitted that what Morrow is tentatively advocating by means of the image of Deus Absconditus—like most of what he is opposing—has already been tried, and so far found wanting. Donald Davies points out that attempts to replace the religious ritualization of death with a more satisfactory secular alternative go back at least as far as Auguste Comte, the inventor of "the law of three stages", which proposed that the evolution of human thought progressed, by necessity, from the theological/fictitious via the metaphysical/abstract to the scientific/positive.

Comte is a forgotten man today, but in the nineteenth century heyday of his influence his followers ardently set about designing and creating human institutions of the third and final kind. Comtean "churches" were established in many places, their native progress being chronicled in D. G. Charlton's *Secular Religions in France 1815-1870*. Davies observes that the last surviving English example, the Liverpool Temple of Humanity, did not close its doors until the Second World War. The British Humanist Association remains ready, willing and able to send officials to conduct secular funeral services—they took part in 3,000 of them in 1995-96—and the American Humanist Association is even more up-to-date, posting its own Humanist Memorial Service (a version written by Larry Reyka) on the Internet for the use of anyone who cares to do so.

Given that Gerald Korty's efforts as a monumental mason are so eerily reminiscent of the endeavors of the Comteans, and given that *The Eternal Footman* is an all-out assault on death amnesia, it is perhaps surprising that one of the things Nora Burkhart's visionary tours of Deus Absconditus miss out on is its cemeteries. She gets to see a ball game, but not a funeral. Even in the novel's coda, when the plot has to practice what it has preached and refuse to let its long-suffering martyrs off the hook, even until the narrative curtain falls, we readers are not allowed to be participants in the ensuing funeral rituals. We are told, in fact, that Anthony Van Horne and his wife cannot attend Nora's funeral because they have to attend a school play in which their grandson, Barry Lawson-Van Horne, has a small part—and it is to this play (a dramatization of the now-historic Annunciation which opened *Towing Jehovah*) that the reader's viewpoint is removed.

This narrative move is, however, by no means out of keeping with the spirit of Comtean secularism and Humanist mourning, whose central tenet is that it is the life of the dead that requires celebration, not their afterlife, and the fact that the dead live on in the hearts and minds of the living that is our best defense against the attrition of grief and the fear of annihilation. Larry Reyka's memorial borrows its summation from the Roman poet Seneca, a devoted follower of Lucretius whose prolific commentary on the subject of mortality insists that "in the presence of death, we must continue to sing the song of life" and that is exactly what the citizens of Deus Absconditus endeavor to do.

Having noted this, though, it is also necessary to note that Nora's visionary odyssey to Deus Absconditus and Holistica is by no means the heart of *The Eternal Footman*'s rhetorical flow, and might easily be regarded as a mere tributary. Morrow is too conscientious a writer to ignore the fact that post-theistic society will require some kind of institutional framework, but he also knows the value of the advice that Satan gave to Arcade when Anatole France's fallen angels were poised for counter-revolution: that the real battlefield is the hearts and souls of human beings, who must be free to find their own idiosyncratic ways to make life worthwhile. *The Eternal Footman* recognizes that each of us has to make his or her own particular peace with the awareness of mortality, and its author is exceedingly careful not to present the fetches as a faceless horde to be met with weapons of mass-destruction.

The fetches' effect is most consistent upon the young and the old; the active adult characters, whose ideas are mature without being hypostasized, find themselves engaged in very different combative confrontations. Significantly, they are not all *destructive* confrontations. Even more significantly, the character who is most definitely enriched by her fetch—thus obtaining, in spite of the ravages of grief, the kind of liberation of which Lucretius wrote in *De rerum natura*—is Nora Burkhart, the deliverer of funeral wreaths.

* * * * * * *

The Eternal Footman is prepared to remind its readers that death, even in the midst of disaster, has its good points. The only one of Quincy's arguments that impresses Kevin is, in fact, that which points out the evolutionary bounty of death. "For well over a billion years, life on this planet knew a kind of immortality. The bacteria, algae, amoebas, and primitive worms enjoyed ceaseless existence: a growing at one end, a sloughing off at the other, but nothing you would call death. Then, half a billion years ago, sexual reproduction came on the scene, along with its faithful handmaiden, death. The invention of death made possible the individual, in all its astonishing variety. Death broke life free of immortality's chains".

It might be worth noting that the Buddhist approach to the problem of death-awareness—of which Morrow seems not to disapprove, given the statistical breakdown of faiths surviving in Deus Absconditus—is a cunningly daring extrapolation of this argument. Buddhism suggests that life is everlasting in spite of death, unless and until one can achieve the final liberation of nirvana. It involves no belief in an unchanging "soul" or any kind of permanent entity underlying the flux of physical and mental states; the "problem" of the indivisible individual is not to gain immortality but to transcend the process of evolution that indefinitely-repeated death facilitates.

It might be worth noting, too, that Quincy Azrael—or perhaps Gerald Korty's fetch, Julius Azrael, who introduces himself to his own victim immediately after Quincy makes this apologetic speech—could have made a further point about the shaping power of death. Although embryological development is still a mysterious process, we do know that the shape of a body is sculpted in much the same way that Korty sculpts the first of his Somatocist idols, by selectively killing off those elements of the developing cell-mass that "are not the [required entity]." The fact that neural tissue does not regenerate is also mysterious, but the fact that the absence of that capacity presumably has some selective advantage suggests that it is the permanent withering of synaptic connections that creates the preferred pathways in the brain which are the electrical foundation of the personality. Bodily and mentally, we are etched by death; death is the lens that focuses the potential ubiquity of DNA into the precise definition of a species, and the potential ubiquity of Everyman into the precise definition of a person. Death may threaten each of us with the prospect of becoming nothing, but without the everpresence and relentless activity of death none of us could ever have become anyone.

It is for this reason that the fetches in *The Eternal Footman* are fundamentally paradoxical. Julius Azrael, in introducing himself to Gerald Korty, refers to himself as "your reliable leveler," and "leveler" is frequently used thereafter in the text as a synonym of "fetch." The confrontation with his fetch does indeed place the great artist on a level with the rest of his kind—but it certainly does not mean that he (or anyone else) cannot try to rise above the level, or that he cannot succeed.

Immediately after *The Eternal Footman*'s definitive summary of the "symptomatology" of abulic plague there is a sidetrack, which consists of a description of a modish dinner party—one of many, it is stated, at which the sole topic of conversation is the circumstances in which the participants first met their fetches and the precise nature of the early verbal and physical exchanges of their combative relationship. Here the emphasis is very firmly on the wide range of manifestations and possible responses, extending as far as sexual opportunism. "We understand each other's needs," Derrick the accountant observes, "but Roderick is cold to the touch, and he never wants to talk afterwards".

Although the consensus at this party is that the fetches are evil—an impression never dispelled by Quincy, even at his most philosophical—it is not entirely surprising thereafter that, when Nora finally finds herself in a situation from which no salvation seems possible, the *deus ex machina* invoked for her benefit by Morrow is her fetch, coiffed like Medusa with cottonmouth snakes.

"Death serves many functions, as I hope you've learned by now," Goneril tells Nora, when she is asked whether she has saved her double only to destroy her. When she returns, not long afterwards, she comes bearing the enlightening gift of a pulque-based psychedelic cocktail, the means by which Nora sees the future: not the future of destiny, which a prophet might have seen, but the future of conflicting and manipulable possibilities, whose foresight is the advantage that ensured that intelligent consciousness would be selectively favored in human evolution in spite of the penalty of death-awareness.

The real poverty of prophecy—and hence of prophecy-based religion—is not its inaccuracy but its failure to appreciate the value of an unknown future. The worst of all worlds would be one in which accurate prophecy were actually possible, and the best thing that can be said of the one in which we actually find ourselves is that we do have the opportunity to influence the future that is not yet hewn from the fog of possibility. Only an idiot would contend that everyone has an equal opportunity to "get a life"—and the fetches whose first and easiest targets are the adolescent and the elderly understand well enough who among us is best-placed to realize that fact—but only an idiot would deny that the quest is devoid of value because all lives must end. *The Eternal Footman* is frank in its admission that there is something fundamentally deceptive about the construction of hope—Kevin is a conjuror, Nora a dreamer and part-time actor, Gerald Korty a maker of little myths, Anthony Van Horne a navigator of Ships of Fools—but the point of the story is that there are deceptions and deceptions, some of which are life-enhancing while others are life-denying, and most of which will still work, even if we admit that we are only pretending.

When Voltaire said that if God did not exist it would be necessary to invent Him he was being sarcastic. He knew that the God of religious faith did not exist and had indeed been invented. His own response to that awareness was to substitute deism for theism, and this is the position finally taken up by Gerald Korty, who asks that his Humanist monument should be set up with a tilt "toward the stars...and mystery...toward the God beyond God". It is an accurate measurement of the extent to which intellectual history has moved on that James Morrow's work examines—seriously as well as satirically—the post-Voltairean proposition that if, it is now necessary, or at least desirable, to un-invent God, then we must figure out ways to live without Him. Deism remains an available refuge even in a post-theistic age, but does not serve to accomplish much in terms of reassurance in the face of mortality. If we are to live authentically, we need better conjuring tricks, better dreams, better scripts and better navigators.

We know already, thanks to the assiduous taxonomic activities of modern academic chroniclers like Toynbee, Ariès and Davies, if not to the efforts of such freelance predecessors as Lucretius and Seneca, what the various secular strategies are by which one might seek to reconcile oneself to the fact of death; they mostly come down to *carpe diem*, although the real problem is not so much to seize the day as to know what to do with it if and when its slippery flanks can actually be grasped. Art works for some, work for others, and there are very few who cannot find temporary solace in at least one of the seven deadly sins (which actually pay no wages, although they routinely exact fines).

We, unlike our children's children, have been born too soon to have any real hope of actually giving T. S. Eliot's eternal Footman the sack, but we really ought to rejoice in the fact that we have been born late enough to know that, even while he holds our coats, we are not forced merely to stand naked before the censorious eye of Jehovah. Like Voltaire's Candide, we have the opportunity to tend our own potentially-Edenic gardens and grow our own funeral wreaths therein. We no longer need books of answers that pretend to offer Truth, but we do need books that demand and insist that we ask the right questions. That is why the trilogy concluded with *The Eternal Footman* is one of the finest and most timely literary products of its day.

DEAN R. KOONTZ

Making a Career

Dean Ray Koontz was born on the 9th July 1945 in Everett, Pennsylvania. From 1946-63 he and his parents—he was an only child—lived in the small town of Bedford. His early life was drastically disturbed by the behavior of his father, Ray—a violent alcoholic with schizophrenic tendencies, whose multitudinous schemes for making a fortune and inability to hold down a job left the family perpetually poor. Dean's mother, Florence, did her best to protect him, but she and the Catholic Church to which they belonged were only partly effective shields. He did well at high school, where he met Gerda Cerra, whom he married in 1966 after he graduated from Shippensburg State College with a degree in English. In the same year he won an *Atlantic Monthly* short story contest with a piece written for the College magazine, "The Kittens," a *conte cruel* about a child's brutal response to parental insensitivity.

Koontz worked in Pennsylvania as a teacher for three years while selling stories to the science fiction magazines and publishing his first novel, *Star Quest* (1968). Disillusioned with teaching, he then took advantage of Gerda's offer to support him while he tried to establish a writing career. He did so with iron discipline and great determination, making the most of the abundant but somewhat underpaid opportunities that the paperback boom of the early 1970s provided. He branched out several into other genres, with mixed results; he disowned three books carrying a joint byline with Gerda, on the grounds that they were mutilated by the publisher. Some of his pseudonymous works were, however, successful—most notably *Chase* (1972 as K. R. Dwyer), whose successor under that pseudonym, *Shattered* (1973), provided his first significant economic breakthrough.

The commercial genre to which *Chase* and *Shattered* belong is usually labeled "thriller," but the label covers a broad spectrum and

JAUNTING ON THE SCORIAC TEMPESTS, BY BRIAN STABLEFORD

Chase is more aptly described as a suspense novel: a story in which dramatic tension is maintained by a seemingly inescapable and gradually escalating threat. At the other end of the thriller spectrum the heroes are the primary characters, their antagonists merely providing challenges to be met; in the suspense novel, it is the antagonist who is looms largest, the protagonist being more victim than hero until the table-turning climax. The thriller genre, unlike science fiction or horror, is one whose ending is unbreakably built into the formula, but the ultimate success of the protagonist in a suspense novel is more a matter of survival against the odds rather than an assertively triumphant flourish. This was the kind of story of which Koontz—well-equipped by his own formative experience—was to become a master.

Although he has done much of his work in a formularized genre, Koontz owes his mastery of it partly to the fact that he has never been a repetitive writer. He always took delight in finding new possibilities within his chosen genre, and always strove for originality even while recognizing and honoring the limits of expectation pertaining to his field. He constrained his larger ambitions for a time while he was building a reputation, but as soon as he was firmly established he began to take advantage of the freedom that came with security. This gave his later work a distinctive quality invaluable to a writer ambitious to stand out within a formularized genre, and secures its interest as a product of idiosyncratic authorship.

Because their careers have run parallel and alphabetical order places them close together on bookshop shelves Koontz is often compared to his fellow bestseller Stephen King, but the differences between them are considerable. Although Koontz's determination to push the envelope of the suspense genre regularly takes his novels across the boundary of the naturalistic, he has always remained a suspense writer, while King—although he frequently uses a sustained element of suspense to carry his plots along—remains essentially a horror writer. When horror fiction flirts with the boundary between the natural and the supernatural it usually does so by heightening a protagonist's anxiety as to what is real and what is not; when it comes down on the latter side the hyper-reality in question is usually flagrantly supernatural, and when the horrific agencies take effect their depredations tend to be physically extravagant.

King rarely excepts himself from these expectations. Koontz, by contrast, rarely tolerates any ambiguity as to what is actually happening; when his plots stray beyond the limits of naturalism they are far more likely to employ "paranormal" effects or science-fictional notions than outrightly supernatural devices, and usually do so in a perfectly forthright manner. In the notes to *Strange Highways* (1995), whose title story is one of his explicitly supernatural stories, he claims that only four of his previous novels—*The Funhouse* (1980), *The Mask* (1981), *Darkfall* (1984) and *Hideaway* (1982)—had been unambiguously supernatural, with *The Servants of Twilight* (1984 as *Twilight*; revised 1988) a borderline case; even in these novels, however, the essence of the threat is not some horrid supernaturally-originated curse but the candid malice of human or not-quite-human antagonists.

It seems probable that Koontz could have established himself as a successful science-fiction writer had he concentrated his efforts on cultivating the awkward artistry of that genre's best work rather than investing his early efforts in literary mass-production. Had the window of opportunity not been opened by the 1970s paperback boom to make steady money by sheer hard labor, his career might have followed a different path. His approach was, however, amply justified by the fact that, when the boom faltered, he not only survived the downturn but used his practiced professionalism to make further progress. He soon established himself, in spite of his earlier profligacy in pseudonymous production, as a "brand name author" immune to economic fluctuations in the lower strata of the literary marketplace.

Koontz marked this progress by putting geographical distance between himself and his troubled roots; in 1975 he and Gerda moved to Nevada, and the following year went on to California. Their escape was temporary; his mother had died in 1969 but his father was still alive. Ray Koontz came to join them in 1977 and remained a near-psychotic presence in their lives until he died in 1991, a year after suffering a stroke. In a 1994 interview in *Locus* Koontz wondered publicly whether Ray Koontz was his biological father at all, referring to an article about the first experiments in artificial insemination carried out by Johns Hopkins University, which used poor women from central Pennsylvania as subjects and donor sperm from famous writers, artists and musicians—but he was content to let the hypothesis go untested.

JAUNTING ON THE SCORIAC TEMPESTS, BY BRIAN STABLEFORD

Methodical Evolution

Several of Koontz's early novels employ science-fictional devices to tackle problems of theodicy, which troubled him as he lapsed from his early faith into a carefully-considered, but seemingly temporary, agnosticism. *Fear That Man* (1969) features a captive God, *A Darkness in my Soul* (1972) an insane God. The majority, however, set such large issues aside in order that their protagonists may take a pragmatic approach to the problems consequent on their being rudely thrust into intolerable circumstances. The hectic flamboyance of such novels as *Hell's Gate* (1970) and *Warlock* (1972) could not be reproduced in more naturalistic fictions, but the attitudes and intellectual methods adopted by their protagonists could be applied to more plausible situations in a far more controlled manner.

Although *Hanging On* (1973), a comedy novel set against the backdrop of World War II, may seem something of a diversion from the main current of Koontz's work, its humor is an extrapolation of the same improvisatory pragmatism that is employed in earnest in so many of his works. Indeed, Koontz often took opportunities when commenting on his work to emphasize the role of humor; the 1994 *Locus* interview is titled "A Comedian in Hell," and his note to the reader in *Ticktock* (1996) points out that he had "blended large measures of humor into the mix" of *Watchers* (1987), *Lightning* (1988), *The Bad Place* (1990), *Hideaway* and *Mr. Murder* (1993) "to name a few."

Another theme prominent in Koontz's early science fiction is genetic engineering, whose possibilities are usually developed in a manner that takes full advantage of their lurid aspects as well as their scope for balancing hope for progress against the hazards of spoliation. To some extent, this was a natural product of the time, but Koontz was one of the first sf writers to become preoccupied with the notion, and his attitude was never as straightforward as the formularistic requirements of mass-production plotting required. Science fiction borrowing the thriller formula tends to fall victim to what Isaac Asimov calls "the Frankenstein syndrome," extrapolating the convenience of the normalizing story-arc into a tacit assumption that all innovation is bad. Koontz's early genetic engineering stories, including *A Darkness in my Soul*, whose short version appeared in 1968, "A Third Hand" (1970) and *Nightmare Journey* (1975), as well as such mutational romances as *The Dark Symphony* (1970), retain the Frankenstein formula but routinely combine it with problematic narrative countercurrents.

Trapped by their format, such countercurrents usually dissipated into mere eddies, but they were carried forward, in a subdued but insistent fashion, into much of Koontz's later work; there too they sometimes manifested themselves explicitly in accounts of biotechnological experiments, but even novels that make no use of literal biological transformation often focus on psychological processes that might lead either to awful spoliation or to some kind of redemption. This underlying pattern was transplanted into Koontz's suspense novels at an early stage, developed with particular fervor in such novels as *Night Chills* (1976), where the transformative force is subliminal advertising, and *The Vision* (1977) where it is a progressive version of the murder-sensitive clairvoyance that also featured in the near-simultaneous *The Face of Fear* (1977 as Brian Coffey). *The Key to Midnight* (1979 as Leigh Nichols) also uses a vision to release repressed memories of participation in a psychotropic experiment. *The Eyes of Darkness* (1981 as Nichols) features a similarly clandestine transformative experiment.

The manifestations of this theme in Koontz's late-1970s work inevitably broadened out to take in other kinds of psychological disturbance, sometimes flirting with the supernatural. *Whispers* (1980)—which cemented the economic breakthrough contrived by *Shattered* and established Koontz's own name as one to conjure sales with—and *Voice of the Night* (1981) substitute mysterious voices for unsummoned visions. It was in this phase of his work that Koontz came closest to producing generic horror fiction, in such novels as *Phantoms* (1983)—which many readers would consider supernatural in spite of the science-fictional gloss laid upon its ancient quasi-demonic adversary—and *Darkfall*, which crosses genres extravagantly in its combination of gangster fiction and supernatural horror. This phase continued in *Twilight* (as Nichols), *Twilight Eyes* (1985) and *Strangers* (1986), but *Shadowfires* (1987 as Nichols) re-emphasized the suspense element, which remained fundamental to his work thereafter in spite of continual experiments combining it with material drawn from other genres.

The most conspicuously successful of these experiments was *Watchers*, which recovered Koontz's early interest in genetic engineering and gave it graphic form by pairing its human protagonist with a dog whose intelligence has been artificially boosted. Similar super-smart animals were to recur in his future deployments of biotechnology, and also in more adventurous texts such as *One Door*

Away from Heaven (2001), providing him with a useful new model of stoical victimhood. In the same year as *Watchers* Koontz published "Twilight of the Dawn" (1987), which he described in the afterword to *Strange Highways* as "my personal favorite of all the short fiction that I have written"; it describes a fervent atheist's reclamation by faith, representing that redemption as the most vital transformation of all.

Lightning also used a science-fictional motif—time travel—to add spice to Koontz's suspense formula, before *Midnight* (1989) attempted to recapture the essence of *Watchers*' success. Further variants followed in some profusion. *The Bad Place* carefully revisits hackneyed devices—a husband-and-wife detective team and an amnesiac client—but among its revitalizing moves is the introduction of another kind of stoical victim; one of the detectives is provided with a mentally-disadvantaged brother—another motif that was to recur, with slight variations, in later novels. *Cold Fire* (1991) reverts to the theme of *The Vision* and *The Face of Fear*, but substitutes a mercurial kind of intuition for straightforward clairvoyance. That kind of intuition was also redeployed and further developed, partly because of its convenience as a plot lever, but also because it fit in very well with notions that Koontz was now developing as to the best way to map the moral battleground providing the context of the skirmishes fought between his protagonists and their various antagonists.

This gradual re-hypothesization of the relationship between good and evil could not answer the problems of theodicy that Koontz had addressed with such slapdash inventiveness in his early sf, but it did provide a philosophical approach to the necessity of living in a morally problematic universe. Dramatically displayed in the conclusion to *Hideaway*, this acute consciousness of the complex interplay between good and evil—whose innate ironies were routinely reflected in the element of humor that Koontz now considered a key component of his work—became the most distinct note in his literary voice in the late 1990s and the early years of the 21st century.

From *Dragon Tears* (1993) onwards, Koontz's books became increasingly dependent on exotic murderers as adversaries and made regular use of science-fictional devices as instruments of mystery. The principal exception is *Ticktock*, which redeploys a motif from *Dragon Tears* in a different context, offering a chimerical combination of supernatural horror and "screwball" comedy. Although Koontz's revisitations of the science fiction field were more obvious attempts to maintain the variety of his work, his development of an extensive company of idiosyncratic homicidal psychopaths was equally intriguing. As with other moves he had made in the course of his career, this one chimed in with the temper of the times, but Koontz's attitude to the phenomenon of serial murder was very different from the fascinated cultivation of dark charisma undertaken by such writers as Thomas Harris. Although Koontz is too various and versatile a writer to be unlocked by a single key, the treatment he meted out to this curious set of adversaries probably offers the best available insight into the particular quality of his work.

The Reconstruction of Paranoia

Suspense stories, viewed *en masse*, cannot help but present a paranoid image of the world. Each individual protagonist who finds himself, or herself, under the pressure of some urgent and nasty threat, can regard it as an anomalous circumstance, but a writer who produces such works on a wholesale basis is bound to see his work as an infinite series of returns to a universe in which paranoia is entirely justified. It is, inevitably, a considerable asset to such a writer if he can readily adopt a paranoid viewpoint—although he must not, of course, be paranoid himself, because literary productivity on an effective scale demands exceptional mental stability and intellectual control.

There is nothing paradoxical about this dual requirement; in much the same way that perfectly sane actors delight in "mad scenes", perfectly sane writers routinely relish the creation of characters at a opposite extreme. The binocular vision does, however, prompt the writer to produce some account of the reasons why the heterocosms within his texts are so uniformly and insistently menacing. An extra dimension is added to the problem by the pressure of melodramatic inflation; within a genre, and within an individual writer's oeuvre, there is an inevitable tendency to raise the stakes continually, always discovering new threats, more deadly than those that have become contemptible through familiarity, and new adversaries, even nastier than those who have already been defeated. By the time Koontz came into the suspense genre many of its traditional adversaries had come to seem common-or-garden scarecrows, devoid of any real power to disturb. Hyping up the threats by means of supernatural or science-fictional devices is a tricky business, because any gain in the magnitude of the threat has to be purchased at the cost of removing its apparent imminence to a world of fancy.

Increasing the exoticism of naturalistic adversaries has a similar effect—plausibility declines as the threat is exaggerated.

Koontz's awareness of this problem and his strategies for coping with it, are elaborated in his two writing guides *Writing Popular Fiction* (1973) and *How to Write Best-Selling Fiction* (1981). He makes brief acknowledgement of the pressure of melodramatic inflation in the early pages of *The Face* (2003), where he observes that "In recent years, influenced by the operatically flamboyant villains in films, every...would-be serial killer...seemed to be obsessed with developing a dramatic persona.... Their sources of inspiration, however, were all hackneyed. They succeeded only in making fearsome acts of cruelty seem as tiresome as the antics of an unfunny clown." Significantly, the adversary featured in this novel is introduced to the reader by the nickname "Corky," although his given names are eventually revealed to be Vladimir Ilyich. His surname, Laputa, is taken from the flying island populated absurd philosophers that Jonathan Swift's Lemuel Gulliver visited in the third part of his travels; the nexus of forenames suggests Lenin in a clown's make-up, but his professed allegiance to the cause of anarchy is as apolitical as it is unfunny.

The main sequence of Koontz's serial killer novels began with a group of three, comprising *Mr. Murder, Intensity* (1995), and the novel-length title-story of *Strange Highways*. The sequence was interrupted by *Dark Rivers of the Heart* (1994), the most politically-controversial of all Koontz's novels and one of the few later novels that remains dutifully within the bounds of everyday possibility, save for marginal symbolic intrusions of a more muted sort than those which abundantly decorate the margins of *Intensity*.

Mr. Murder juxtaposes a writer with his "evil twin"—a clone raised by a soulless corporation to act out literally that which is literary endeavor for the author. The female protagonist of *Intensity*, having suffered abuse as a child, obtains a precious but extremely hazardous opportunity to intervene on behalf of another child threatened with ultimate abuse. The latter novel was represented by its author in interviews as a renunciation of Freudian theories that he had formerly held in some respect, and a defiant assertion of moral responsibility in the face of psychoanalytic excuses for bad behavior. This affirmative mood is carried over into "Strange Highways," which dramatizes elements draws from Koontz's own personal history, exaggerating them luridly by means of a rare excursion into flamboyant supernaturalism. Although it is shorter than any of Koontz other novels of this period—thus necessitating its release as the lead item of a collection—it is certainly not lacking in incident, and its breakneck pace is well suited to its carefully-managed supernatural excess.

"Strange Highways" describes a young man's brief return to the small Pennsylvania town he escaped during his college years, which he flees in panic as old memories reassert themselves. He is, however, diverted in the course of his flight into a seemingly-impossible encounter on the edge of an even smaller town that is in the process of being consumed by subterranean fires eating their way through abandoned coal mines. (The locale is loosely based on Saxton, Pennsylvania, where Koontz worked, unhappily, in connection with the Appalachian Poverty Program in 1966-67.) Like the writer protagonist of *Mr. Murder*—but unlike Koontz himself—the protagonist of the story has an "evil twin": a brother, this time. The protagonist is shunted back in time in order to try to nip his brother's career as a serial killer in the bud, the price of success being that he must reaffirm the fundamentals of his lost Catholic faith. Although he fails to make the most of the opportunity at the first attempt, the agency that has sent him back proves stubborn; like the writer that he is now destined to become, he is allowed to rewrite his script until he gets it right.

Having completed this short sequence, Koontz spent the next few years in other literary territory—although serial killers sometimes crop up there in more peripheral roles, as in *Seize the Night* (1999), which also involves redemptive trips in time. The novels of this interval include some of his most ideatively adventurous, and represent a considerable resurgence of science-fictional themes. *Sole Survivor* (1997) offers a relatively straightforward science-fictional solution to its mystery, while *Fear Nothing* (1998) and *Seize the Night* revisit the territory of *Midnight*, cloning Midnight Cove as Moonlight Bay for what seems to have been intended as a trilogy of biotechnological menace stories (the third, *Ride the Storm*, did not appear on schedule.) *False Memory* (1999), in which phobias begin to transform the reality of their sufferers, and *From the Corner of his Eye* (2000), which plays ingeniously with the uncertainties of quantum mechanics, are more enterprising. Koontz then brought multiple murders back into primary focus in a second quick-fire sequence of novels, this one uninterrupted by any diversion.

This second group comprises *One Door Away from Heaven, By the Light of the Moon* (2002), *The Face* and *Odd Thomas* (2004). Seen as a collective, the quartet is considerably more baroque than the earlier triptych, but it echoes some elements of the pattern that the triptych made up in association with *Dark Rivers of the Heart*: the first and third novels re-examine and re-evaluate the central stereotype, while cultivating considerable narrative intensity; the second explores a broader context, and the fourth cultivates a new kind of intimacy.

The adversary in *One Door Away from Heaven* is Preston Maddoc, who conceals his fondness for killing behind a philosophical mask, having established himself as a famous "bioethicist" and advocate of euthanasia. His next intended victim is his physically-handicapped but precocious stepdaughter Leilani, whose disabilities are the result of her mad mother's sport with all manner of exotic drugs—a continuing habit that now seems likely to produce a further brood. Two of the novel's protagonists are ambitious to save Leilani, but their story runs parallel to another, in which a strange small boy and an adopted dog are on the run from a powerful agency bent on his destruction. That agency turns out to be a company of evil alien shapeshifters, who are anxious to destroy the boy simply because he is a virtuous alien shapeshifter. The two plotlines converge because Maddoc is a UFO-nut convinced that government cover-ups of the existence of alien visitation are concealing the proof that the defiant atheism underlying his amoralism is fully justified. The ultimate confrontation between the would-be killer and the protectors of his victim is more than a matter of hard-won survival; underlying the stakes of the physical struggle is a symbolic jackpot, contested between a champion of moral chaos and a champion of moral order.

The killer in *By the Light of the Moon*, Lincoln Proctor, is also an amoral scientist, although his dead victims are merely the collateral damage of his experiments with transformative nanotechnology. The novel's protagonists—including the hero's quasi-autistic brother—are his final victims, but they are luckier than their predecessors because their transformation is more successful. Their unlooked-for metamorphoses convert them into a mini-league of superheroes, gifted with visions and intuitions of other crimes—and, once they have begun to master their new talents, the ability to do something about them. *By the Light of the Moon* substitutes an evolving technological context for the political context of *Dark Rivers of the Heart*, and it retains the extravagant fantasization of its immediate predecessor instead of the determined naturalism of the earlier novel, but it delves deeper into the fundamental nature of its virtuous characters in much the same way as *Dark Rivers of the*

Heart, exploring the equipment that allows them to be productively rather than destructively transformed.

The Face reverts to the pattern of *One Door Away from Heaven* in devoting its primary fascination to the peculiar insanity of its adversary, Corky Laputa. Like his immediate predecessors, Laputa is a duly certified intellectual, but his field is literary theory; his expertise in deconstructing literary texts is seen as a symptom of his obsession with spreading chaos, whose other manifestations include handing out drugs to schoolchildren, vandalizing suburban lawns, flooding restrooms, torturing his academic rival to death and planning to kidnap the son of a famous movie star. The last scheme, and the attempts by the star's security chief to frustrate it—aided by an old friend who has made a pact with the Devil to extend his time on Earth in order to lend a hand—provide the plot of the story; the essence of the narrative is, however, its furtherance of the rhetoric of *One Door Away from Heaven* in building an image of an archetypal adversary. Like Preston Maddoc, Corky Laputa loves sowing the seeds of destruction—he simply *is* evil, without the possibility of explanation or excuse—but he has constructed an elaborate philosophy to support his evildoing. Significantly, neither man is allied with the actual forces of hell, whose work goes on alongside theirs, ultimately helping in *The Face*—albeit unintentionally—to provide the means of Corky's frustration; like Preston Maddoc and Lincoln Proctor, Corky Laputa is a far cry from the Satan-inspired adversary of "Strange Highways."

As with "Strange Highways," *Odd Thomas* reverts to a more intimate association with its protagonist in the context of a single-threaded narrative. The eponymous first-person narrator, who is gifted with the ability to see the dead, feels a conscientious duty to avenge those who can be avenged, and carefully maintains a false facade in order that he may do this work unobtrusively. His adversaries, unlike those of the previous three novels, *are* active Satanists, albeit of a common-or-garden self-deluding variety, rather than careful intellectuals. Odd is forewarned of the danger they pose because he, unlike them, can see the anticipatory gathering of shadowy observers he calls "bodachs," which routinely flock to scenes of mass mayhem.

Although they do not appear to be active adversaries, the bodachs add a more interesting dimension to the exploits of *Odd Thomas*'s atrocity-planners. As in *One Door Away from Heaven*, Koontz relegates consideration of the nature and origin of these extraordinary entities to the margins of his conclusion, and Odd Thomas has to be much more tentative in his interpretation of their nature and motivation than the alien child who knew whereof he spoke, but their role in the surrounding scheme is crucial. Like the diabolical aliens of the earlier novel, they provide a hypothetical justification for the paranoid attitude that suspense novels are collectively obliged to strike.

Unusually, within Koontz's oeuvre, *Odd Thomas* is framed as a tragedy; although the suspense plot dutifully achieves its built-in conclusion, the extension of the narrator's personal story adds a harrowing coda. If his name were not enough, Odd confesses from the outset that he is an unreliable narrator, although there is an element of double bluff in this, because Koontz makes sure that the reader can see clearly enough that Odd's unreliability is not confined to his supposedly-deliberate distortions of the narrative in the interests of maintaining suspense. Although Odd is by no means mentally handicapped—as the Thomas was who served as one of several viewpoint characters in *The Bad Place*—his innocence extends way beyond the mask he feels obliged to present to the world to hide his gift. These layers of teasing deception impose a tone of macabre humor on his story that is considerably deeper than the wry black comedy of *The Face* or the scathing sarcasm that spices *One Door Away from Heaven* and *By the Light of the Moon*.

The curiously plaintive tone and downbeat culmination of *Odd Thomas* seem a far cry from the stark melodrama and conclusive affirmation of "Strange Highways," but the two books do share a similarly insistent moral fervor, whose essence is the assertion that anyone who finds himself living in a nightmare must do everything possible—no matter what odds or limits confront him—to turn it into a better dream. This is a dictum easily transferable from the world of Koontz's fiction to the world of his readers, whose menacing aspects are less urgent; the ostensible point of his work is not to celebrate the fact that the experienced world has its nightmarish aspects, but to dramatize the necessity of working in the service of a better dream.

The Politics of Popular Fiction

In chapter 46 of *Odd Thomas* the narrator calls in on a teacher of twentieth-century American literature, who has no function within the plot other than to give Odd the opportunity to observe that: "Considering that the modern and contemporary literature taught in most universities is largely bleak, cynical, morbid, pessimistic, misanthropic dogmatism, often written by suicidal types who sooner or later kill themselves with alcohol or drugs, or shot-guns, Professor Takuda was a remarkably cheerful man." Although the text does not say so, Professor Takuda—like Corky Laputa's hated academic rival, Maxwell Dalton—is presumably a traditionalist rather than a deconstructionist: someone who believes in the capacity and the responsibility, of literature not merely to represent life as it is but to adopt a moral stance in respect of that actuality. Unsurprisingly, the Professor would like to give up teaching and become a novelist.

Although it must be remembered that it is a character rather than the author who expresses this harsh judgment of the kinds of contemporary literature taught in universities, the fact that room is deliberately made in the novel for the judgment to be made seems to indicate that a dimension of contrast is being carefully drawn. The claim is being tacitly made for *Odd Thomas*, and for Koontz's work in general, that it is *not* "bleak, cynical, morbid, pessimistic, misanthropic dogmatism" produced by a man likely to do away with himself.

This may seem a slightly suspect declaration, given that the world of Koontz's fiction is extravagantly populated with multiple murderers and even more fearsome agents of absolute evil, who spend their time drawing elaborate nets of violent intent around innocent children and other helpless individuals. That sort of subject-matter, some critics might argue, is intrinsically bleak and morbid; given its best-selling potential, it also tends to attract the suspicion that a certain cynicism might be involved in its continual redeployment. On the other hand, Koontz does take care, in accordance with the norms of popular fiction, to provide heroic counterpoints to this tacitly bleak view of the hazards that the world contains: he is certainly optimistic, and far from misanthropic, in maintaining that evil can always be opposed and almost always defeated. Indeed, the formula that is a necessary, but not sufficient, condition of suspense fiction's popularity is the dogmatic insistence that evil *must* be defeated, however difficult the task may be and whatever the cost.

What the quixotic Odd is really doing, in offering his judgment of Professor Takuda, is striking a blow against the common notion that popular fiction is worthless paraliterary trash by comparison with literary fiction. Criticism of that kind is heaped upon authors like Koontz on a regular basis, by narrators who never doubt their own reliability in spite of the fact that some of them espouse theories that deny the very possibility of "reliability," and it is understandable that he should take advantage of his admittedly-unreliable narrator to voice some resentment against it.

It is not necessary to take sides in this war in order to appreciate the depths of the feelings involved, or to comment on the tactics employed by the contending parties. Koontz has always been an active combatant, not merely in commenting on his works and the responses they evoke, but in organizing the works themselves; *Odd Thomas* the novel is, in part, formulated as a shell-burst amplifying the point made by Odd Thomas the character. Like the great majority of successful practitioners in the various commercial genres, Koontz does not work in a cynical fashion, but takes his work extremely seriously—and he is not a naive reader of his own produce. Speaking for himself rather than putting words into the mouth of a character, Koontz said in the 1994 *Locus* interview that "Literary fiction is not writing about our *lives* anymore. Science fiction has always done that and been concerned about that." Although the fantastic elements of *One Door Away from Heaven, By the Light of the Moon, The Face* and *Odd Thomas* are bound to seem to unsympathetic readers to remove the texts from possible consideration as informative and helpful accounts of the way the world is, that is not their narrative function. What they are supposed to do is to dramatize, symbolically, the greater context in which real lives are—or ought to be—lived.

The world within a text is inescapably morally ordered, by virtue of the fact that it has an author who determines how rewards and penalties are ultimately to be distributed within it; an author who attempts to replicate the experienced world's apparent lack of moral order is only *pretending* to lack godlike omnipotence. Koontz sees no virtue in that kind of pretence; he is prepared to exercise non-mimetic creativity, and determined to sit in ultimate judgment over the characters he moulds. He is conscious in doing this that; although he is a quintessentially modern novelist in terms of the hypothetical lives he describes and the cultural decor that surrounds them, he is also harking back to narrative traditions that reached their height in the nineteenth century.

It was in the nineteenth century that the foundations were first laid for the commercial genres that Koontz likes to fuse with his core suspense story. They were first set out in France, by such *feuilletonists* as Eugène Sue and Paul Féval, whose self-conscious literary methods Koontz echoes, even to the point of reproducing the alchemical combination of humor and horror that became Féval's chief stock-in-trade. These key elements of genre fiction were imported into Britain by such writers as Edward Bulwer-Lytton and W. Harrison Ainsworth, with whom Koontz also has something in common. Bulwer-Lytton, annoyed by criticism that his work was too vulgar and violent, and insufficiently respectful of the bounds of plausibility, complained that no work of fiction could properly be considered "realistic" unless it had some larger, tacitly supernatural, context whose structure could be considered symbolic by those who hesitated to take it seriously. Koontz is working within that tradition, continuing its refinement as he refurbishes its foundations.

It is possible that the suspense story has now reached something of an *impasse*, in which further melodramatic inflation can no longer be achieved without paying some kind of cost in terms of plausibility. The dramatic personas adopted by literary and cinematic serial killers have indeed become unfunnily clownish, and the supernaturalization of menace by modern horror writers may have reached the limits of conceivable grossness. Koontz has reacted to this situation in several different ways, but his primary strategy has foregrounded two main elements. On the one hand, he has been careful to import other elements into his plots, so that they are not "pure" suspense stories, always having some other literary currency on which to draw. Some of his experiments in this vein have worked better than others, and some are bound to test the limitations of individual readers' tolerance, but it has certainly helped to maintain a valuable element of surprise in his work. On the other hand, he has taken care to maintain the moral fervor of his work by refusing to make concessions to contemporary moral relativism.

Although he deploys a range of symbolic systems for representing the fundamental dualism of good and evil, making them actively manifest in his stories in a variety of ways, Koontz remains committed to the notion that all shades of grey can ultimately be sorted into black and white, and that there are, in essence, only two kinds of people in the world: people who try with all their might to do the right thing, and people who don't. The people who don't are, within the world-view of his books, in constant peril of slipping to an opposite extreme. His heroes often have to work hard at doing the right thing, and very often need help—whether from angels, timeslips, smart dogs or the simple generosity of the writer in levering them in the direction of good fortune—but the underlying essence of their success is their determination to *do right*.

It is the absence of such a determination that Koontz, like Odd Thomas, regrets in the work of some other writers, and the absence of a similar commitment that he regrets in some critics. He is not sympathetic to characters or critics who complain that they simply cannot determine what the right thing to do might actually be. The characters have the advantage, or disadvantage, of operating in fictitious worlds that are not merely innately morally ordered but overfull of manifest evil that leaves no room for doubt as to the absolute necessity of its destruction; the critics' situation is far less clear.

Koontz's own situation is, however, also less clear than it might be, and that lack of clarity is reflected in the element of humor that runs insistently through all his work, giving all his adversaries—no matter how deeply steeped in pure evil they might be—a clownish quality. Having renounced psychoanalytic explanations of vicious behavior, he seems to have been forced into a position from which even the nastiest violence seems implicitly absurd. In some of his early twenty-first-century works, *One Door Away from Heaven* and *Odd Thomas* providing the most conspicuous examples, that absurdity communicates itself to at least some of his fighters for right, giving the entire enterprise a pantomime quality. Perhaps that is the inevitable eventual outcome of the relentlessly sane contemplation of an infinite array of paranoid worlds.

TERRY PRATCHETT

The Way to Discworld

Terry Pratchett was born in Beaconsfield, Buckinghamshire, on 28 April 1948. He attended Wycombe Technical High School before working as a journalist, initially on the *Bucks Free Press*, then on the Bristol-based *Western Daily Herald* and the *Bath Chronicle* In 1980 he became the press officer for the Central Electricity Generating Board's Western Region, a position he held until 1987. His first published story, "The Hades Business," written for his school magazine when he was thirteen, was subsequently sold to *Science-Fantasy*, where it appeared in 1963. His first novel, *The Carpet People* (1971), was a children's fantasy set in a world integrated into the weave of a carpet.

In the 1970s, when the commercial fantasy genre had yet to take off—in spite of the crucial precedent provided by the paperback editions of J. R. R. Tolkien's *Lord of the Rings*—fantasy was regarded by publishers as a branch of children's fiction, except for a few works forming a kind of fringe to the science fiction market. Pratchett was one of many writers patiently awaiting a viable exit strategy from this circumstantial trap; in the meantime, he wrote two comedies mocking popular science fiction motifs, and the ludicrousness of the genre's pretensions to rationalism, *The Dark Side of the Sun* (1976) and *Strata* (1981). These early books were issued by a small press based in Gerrards Cross in Pratchett's native Buckinghamshire, operated by Colin Smythe; the conventional editorial wisdom in the commercial sector was that humor did not sell well in any popular genre, science fiction least of all.

This conventional wisdom was already being tested by the massive success of Douglas Adams, but all such ground-breaking successes—that of *The Lord of the Rings* being another cardinal example—are initially regarded as freaks of chance rather than indicators of things to come. Pratchett's next two books, *The Color of Magic*

(1983)—an aggregation of four novelettes rather than a novel—and *The Light Fantastic* (1986), were also issued in hardcover by Colin Smythe; their paperback reprints, however, exposed the folly of the prevailing myth, establishing Pratchett as a potential best-seller. His subsequent works not only fulfilled that potential, at least in Britain, but set new standards for future writers to match.

By the time *The Color of Magic* was published, fantasy had become firmly established as a genre label; the crucial breakthrough had been made in 1977 and change thereafter had been rapid, The new genre was already beginning to dominate the bookshop space previously devoted to sf, so Pratchett's move into comic fantasy was well-timed. It was, however, a natural evolution of his work rather than a response to market conditions. *Strata* had given wry consideration to a favorite theme of 1970s sf, popularized by such novels as Larry Niven's *Ringworld* and Bob Shaw's *Orbitsville*: the notion that the universe might be littered with world-sized artifacts manufactured by advanced alien species. Pratchett suggested that, if the technical capacity to construct such artifacts were assumed, then they might just as easily reproduce mythical structures, such as the Aristotelian system of crystal spheres, as the rings and hollow spheres favored by sf writers, especially if one bore in mind such difficulties as simulating gravity on the inner surface of a sphere.

The Color of Magic extrapolates this notion further by imagining Discworld: a blatantly ridiculous artifact consisting of a vast circular plate supported by four elephants standing on the shell of a great space-swimming turtle, on whose surface various kinds of magic are fully supported by an extremely mercurial natural order. Because planetary romance was the most convenient subgenre of sf for accommodating such tales, distant planets had been used as backgrounds for magical fantasy for many years, but the conventional etiquette of sf had restricted the limits of invention usually applied to such stories. In consequence, they often imagined kinds of magic as parsimoniously rule-bound as the "science" whose alleged extrapolations provided sf with its customary lexicon of motifs. Pratchett, enthusiastic to make more flamboyant use of his imagination, preferred a world so utterly absurd that it could not only contain almost any physical entity he cared to invent but naturally implied an equally generous metaphysical context.

Once he had invented Discworld, Pratchett was equipped with a playground so wonderfully elastic that he needed no other. *The Color of Magic* and *The Light Fantastic* became the founding elements of a series that extended over the next twenty years without showing the slightest evidence of potential exhaustion. The subsequent volumes of the series' main sequence were *Equal Rites* (1987), *Mort* (1987), *Sourcery* (1988), *Wyrd Sisters* (1988), *Pyramids* (1989), *Guards! Guards!* (1989), *Moving Pictures* (1990), *Reaper Man* (1991), *Witches Abroad* (1991), *Small Gods* (1992), *Lords and Ladies* (1992), *Men at Arms* (1993), *Soul Music* (1994), *Interesting Times* (1994), *Maskerade* (1995) *Feet of Clay* (1996), *Hogfather* (1996), *Jingo* (1997), *The Last Continent* (1998), *Carpe Jugulum* (1998), *The Fifth Elephant* (1999), *The Truth* (2000), *Thief of Time* (2001), *Night Watch* (2002) and *Monstrous Regiment* (2003).

Although these books built up a massive following among teenagers, they were not labeled as children's books. Eventually, however, the increasingly dark and sophisticated concerns of the main sequence books led to a fission, by which it was supplemented with a secondary sequence consciously aimed at younger readers. The first items explicitly marketed in this fashion were *The Amazing Maurice and His Educated Rodents* (2001), *The Wee Free Men* (2003) and *A Hat Full of Sky* (2004), but two earlier novellas formulated as picture books are similar in kind. *Eric* (1990) is co-credited to the artist whose covers had given the series a distinctive image, Josh Kirby, and its provision of extra space for him to extend his contribution was a useful augmentation of Discworld's visual dimension. *The Last Hero* (2001) is similarly co-credited to Kirby's successor, Paul Kidby, who took over the role when Kirby died.

One side-effect of the explicit labeling of the secondary series was to attract a flood of awards; while Discworld novels represented as adult fiction had seemed a slightly guilty pleasure even to their most devoted admirers, and had attracted a good deal of vituperative contempt from critics who disapproved of adults reading fantasy on principle, Discworld books represented as children's fare seemed far less problematic. Indeed, once they were carefully pigeonholed as children's books, *The Amazing Maurice and His Educated Rodents*, which won the Carnegie Medal, and *The Wee Free Men*, which won half a dozen more decorations, suddenly seemed highly ingenious, zestfully stylish and insidiously educational. The main sequence books share all these characteristics, but it had somehow never seemed fitting to acknowledge the fact.

In addition to *The Carpet People*, Pratchett had written two short series of novels marketed as children's books alongside the early Discworld novels, but both of them had been more carefully limited in their ambitions. The trilogy consisting of *Truckers* (1989),

Diggers (1990) and *Wings* (1990) follows the odyssey of a company of "nomes" in search of new home following their expulsion from the department store whose underfloor spaces they have long mistaken for their natural habitat. The trilogy comprising *Only You Can Save Mankind* (1992), *Johnny and the Dead* (1993) and *Johnny and the Bomb* (1996) confronts its schoolboy hero with a series of exotic challenges; in the first, enemy spaceships in a Space Invaders game send out a surrender message; in the second, ghosts protest against the "development" of their graveyard; in the third, a bag-lady turns out to be a time traveler with a fondness for the Blitz.

The former series is the purer comedy, drawing a great deal of its humor from the nomes' innocent literal-mindedness, as it moves towards a wry celebration of sf's standardized "cosmic breakout" climax. The second is more conspicuous in its use of humor to introduce more serious ethical issues, but is compelled by its use of the everyday as a basic setting to employ normalizing story-arcs of a stereotyped kind. No such intrinsically-fixed limitation could be applied to Pratchett's principal non-Discworld novel for adults, written in collaboration with Neil Gaiman; *Good Omens: The Nice and Accurate Prophecies of Agnes Nutter, Witch* (1990), offers a satirical account of a prophesied apocalypse going hilariously awry, leading to a chaotic muddle crying out for innovative re-ordering. Even this situation was, however, bounded by its Earthly setting, with all the historical baggage that implied; Discworld always had the advantage of a back-story that could be filled in as its present moment moved on, and a future that could entertain any number of apocalypses.

The fact that Pratchett has written no other adult fiction apart from *Good Omens* and the Discworld novels does not, therefore, reflect any lack of versatility on his part—quite the reverse. As Discworld evolved, the vast spaces of its flat surface being gradually sketched in and its metaphysics being expanded with astonishing elaboration, it became an ideal medium for a greater flexibility than any previously-imagined world, or universe, had ever contrived. Its greatest strength was its manifest absurdity, because absurdity breaks down all preliminary expectation, allowing ideas to be marshaled into any imaginable configuration, and extrapolated in any conceivable direction. There is no paradox in the observation that logic is at its most demanding, its most powerful and its most ingenious when it is required to operate within a framework where it is free from the burden of expectation imposed by the dogmatic familiarities of "common sense."

The Discworld Subseries

Almost as soon as the Discworld series had established its popularity, it began to diversify into a number of parallel subseries with slightly different concerns and narrative methods. Although some books remained defiantly individual and others built bridges between the various subseries, the majority carried forward a set of distinctive trains of thought. This structure ensured that the Discworld remained a dynamic entity, evolving at a pace that could not have been sustained within an invented world of a more "realistic" nature.

This feature of Pratchett's imaginary world brings it into sharp contrast with other "secondary worlds" of fantasy, many of which are changeless, while many others move through measured patterns of change towards some ultimate finality. Commercial genrification favors the development of segmental series, whose formulas are infinitely repeatable, or infinitely elastic series which can expand indefinitely while remaining safely confined within fixed horizons of expectation. The Discworld series seemed to fit this pattern for a while, but its early volumes flattered only to deceive; the series and its setting has changed dramatically as it has grown. The gradual accretion of characters and motifs has not only increased the series' complexity but has imported a hectic historical progress more rapid and bewildering than anything Europe and America have so far contrived to produce.

The Color of Magic and *The Light Fantastic* follow the adventures of a hapless and incompetent wizard named Rincewind, who is forever getting into trouble, usually extracting himself with so little margin to spare that he frequently sees the hooded figure of Death waiting to collect him. The two books are pure comedies. Further novels featuring Rincewind and his wizard peers, the ill-assorted faculty of the Unseen University of Ankh-Morpork, including *Sourcery* and *Interesting Times*, maintained a similar slapstick manner, but added further complexities as they delved deeper into the perverse mechanics of magic and subjected the litany of perilous situations to satirical scrutiny.

Rincewind eventually established a niche as a kind of ultimate fall guy, ideal for deployment—in parallel with rather than in the company of mob-handed analogues—in such amiably satirical texts as the parody of Australian folkways and mores *The Last Continent*. After *The Light Fantastic*, however, he was set aside for a while; *Equal Rites* began the process of diversification by launching a second subseries featuring the wise but irascible witch Granny Weatherwax and her younger associates, who live in the rural enclave of Lancre far away from the sprawling proto-metropolis of Ankh-Morpork.

As its title suggests, *Equal Rites* places the assumptions of sexism at the centre of a comedy in which the long-awaited seventh son of a seventh son—who is, of course, destined to have exceptional magical abilities—turns out to be a girl. In the course of exploring the ramifications of this premise, however, it raises more fundamental questions about the ethics of magic—to which the witches of Lancre, though deeply respectful of time-tested custom, take a fervently pragmatic attitude. Although Granny Weatherwax and her kin returned in *Wyrd Sisters*, which seemed more refined than its predecessor in playing with Shakespearean motifs, her subseries continually harked back to such ethical questions and her down-to-earth responsive strategy.

Witches Abroad, another excursion into pre-mapped literary territory—this time that of traditional fairy tales—placed Granny Weatherwax in a broader context, introducing her evil sister in order to sharpen the ongoing discussion of the morality of witchcraft. *Lords and Ladies* returned to Shakespearean fairies of an ultra-mischievous stripe, while *Maskerade* borrowed the theme of *The Phantom of the Opera*. This pattern of development reached its most urgent pitch in *Carpe Jugulum*, where Lancre is invaded by progressive vampires of a Stokeresque stripe, who are enthusiastic to reduce the region's human population to well-husbanded domestic stock. The subseries then produced a tangential offshoot of its own in *The Wee Free Men*, which began a sequence tracking the education of a young witch isolated in a rather different rural community.

Having discovered from reader feedback that the most popular motif in the first two novels was the hooded figure of Death, whose laconic gallows humor tended to the plaintive as Rincewind continually evaded him, Pratchett gave Death a leading role in *Mort*, which describes his travails in training an apprentice and adopting a daughter. *Reaper Man* examined the consequences of his being pensioned off, and Pratchett removed him from the scene again, in much the same experimental spirit, in *Soul Music*. In both cases, Death's absence generates unanticipated havoc—a line of thought that allowed Pratchett to reconstruct his role in the series so that he became something of a hero rather than a manifestation of macabre irony. Death's heroic status remained highly peculiar—and the relentless pressures of duty obliged him to employ an associate to carry out less orthodox projects—but he nevertheless became the series' most dependable father figure and wise fool. The role of sidekick and legman was amply fulfilled by his grand-daughter-by-adoption, Susan Sto Helit, although *Hogfather* offered him a chance to play a more active part than usual as an emergency stand-in for the Discworld's Santa Claus, while Susan carried out a parallel investigation.

Death's ultimate adversaries in *Hogfather* are the Auditors of Reality, whose metaphysical role is to keep the laws of nature running smoothly, and who therefore have a deep-seated antipathy to such troublesome factors as the human imagination, especially in its whimsically playful mode. In *Hogfather* they merely hire an ingenious assassin to assassinate the eponymous gift-bringer, but in *Thief of Time* they go much further, attempting to rid the universe not merely of fancy but of life itself, thus bringing about an absolute uniformity whose predictability will never again be prejudiced. This menace forces Susan and humankind's other steadfast allies, the Monks of History, to work very hard indeed, while Death—obliged by custom—has to rally the other horsemen of the apocalypse (including the fifth member of the original group, who left to follow a solo career as a milkman before they became famous) for their fateful ride.

It is in the Death sequence that Pratchett's metaphysical extrapolations reach their most absurd consequences. By the same token, it is these books that probe the most basic philosophical issues raised in the series. The plot of *Thief of Time* is enacted with great slapstick flair by bizarre comic characters, but its underlying drama lays bare fundamental issues concerning the nature of life, time, order and humanity. In so doing, it contrasts sharply with the Ricnewind and Granny Weatherwax sequences—and even more sharply with the sequence that began with *Guards! Guards!*

Before launching the last of his principal subseries, Pratchett wrote *Pyramids*, which did not become part of any obvious sequence, although it made its contribution to the gradually-unfolding map of Ankh-Morporkian society by providing an elaborate account of the training establishment of the Assassin's Guild, whose graduates were to feature in numerous subsequent volumes. The novel's more important role was, however, to carry forward a more literal kind of mapping that had begun in a much sketchier fashion accounts of Rincewind's travels. *Pyramids* itself provides a moderately comprehensive introduction the Discworld's version of ancient Egypt, with proper emphasis on its exotic funerary practices. Some of the series' other singletons, including *Small Gods* and *Monstrous Regiment*, serve a similar function; the former describes, and scathingly satirizes, the intolerant theocracy of Omnia, while the latter offers a conscientiously disapproving account of the bombastically militaristic nation of Borogravia. Other detached volumes focus on the impact made in Ankh-Morpork by new inventions: in *Moving Pictures* a film industry is established in Holy Wood, while *The Truth* examines the upheavals caused by the city's first printing press and newspaper.

Although the subseries introduced by *Guards! Guards!* was the last to emerge, it also proved the most substantial, by virtue of providing a crucial opportunity to carry forward the history of Ankh-Morpork and map out the patterns of social and technical progress increasingly inherent therein. *Guards! Guards!* introduces the ramshackle Ankh-Morpork police force, whose Night Watch here consists of only four individuals, headed by the depressed alcoholic Sam Vimes. Like the police procedural thrillers it parodies, the novel describes the redemption and moral renewal of Vimes, who becomes exactly the kind of hero the extremely mean streets of the archetypal city need and deserve: a case-hardened pragmatist who accepts the near-universality of stupidity, cupidity, corruption and treachery but sets out to make things better one step at a time.

Unlike Granny Weatherwax, whose pragmatism is adapted to the preservation of rural stability, Sam Vimes is an agent of civilization, who is always trying to facilitate change, and to tease out a little more of the Utopian potential that seems to exist—albeit deeply buried—in the philosophical ramifications of the idea of "civilization." In uneasy and deeply mistrustful partnership with Ankh-Morpork's Machiavellian patrician, Lord Vetinari, Vimes uses the Watch as an instrument to exemplify and promote racial equality in *Men at Arms*, and assists the advent on an industrial revolution in *Feet of Clay*. He then expanded his operations into the field of inter-regional diplomacy in *Jingo*, which introduces the rival quasi-Arabic city-state of Klatch, and *The Fifth Elephant*, in which he becomes an envoy to the quasi-Teutonic state of Uberwald, where surface-dwelling vampires and werewolves co-exist uneasily with troglodytic dwarfs.

The plots of the Vimes novels are modelled on conventional thrillers, replete with seemingly-impossible crimes and nasty serial-killers, but their comedic elaboration and their fantasy-world setting free them from the constraints of the conventional thriller story-arc, which is inevitably orientated towards the restoration of the *status quo*. Vimes is never content to be a mere solver of mysteries and thwarter of villains; he is fully aware of his role as a key force in promoting the welfare of his fellow citizens, even while he is almost fully occupied in preventing the fragile order of the city and its relations with its neighbors from falling apart.

This is nowhere more evident than in *Night Watch*, a timeslip fantasy in which Vimes and the serial killer he is pursuing across the roofs of the Unseen University are hurled back to the days immediately preceding the city-wide riots associated with the succession of an irredeemably corrupt patrician by Lord Vetinari's only-slightly-preferable predecessor. Vimes is forced to become his own personal mentor, and to save as much of the city as he can from wanton destruction, by applying his own case-hardened brand of *realpolitik*. By taking on this kind of role, Vimes soon became a substantial background presence in novels outside his own subseries. In *The Truth* he is the first person to recognize the implications of William de Worde's newspaper, and in *Monstrous Regiment* he exploits that invention ruthlessly to assist a tiny company of Borogravian soldiers—all of whom are young women in disguise—to bring the best possible peace-settlement out of a bloodily destructive war.

The politicization of the Discworld series in the Vimes subseries was one of the main factors in making it much darker as it went along. The makeshift improvisations by which Rincewind continually preserves himself from disaster and the homely practicality with which Granny Weatherwax settles small-scale disputes do not stand in any stark contrast to Vimes' hard-nosed commitment to maintaining exactly as much of the rule of law as is practicable, by whatever means are allowable within it, but Vimes' actions are contained within a very different kind of bigger picture—a picture almost, but not quite, as big as the one within which Death and Susan Sto Helit are operative. Granny Weatherwax has her work cut out sorting out vicious elves and sophisticated vampires, but her problems are limited to particular situations and the preservation of the routines of agrarian Lancre. There is much more than that at stake in Vimes' adventures, where every setback threatens a pattern of progress so fragile that the Discworld could easily slip back into a Dark Age—an eventuality to which Death himself is steadfastly opposed, although it is devoutly desired by the Auditors of Reality.

Vimes' adventures do stand in stark contrast to Death's, but the two are fighting the same fight on different fronts, against the same forces of destruction. Vimes, a fervent protector of life whenever such protection is feasible, would doubtless be surprised to discover that the Watch's heroic counterparts within the latter phases of the Discworld series are Death and his adoptive grand-daughter, but the logic of that situation is a key feature in the inexorable maturation of the series, and hence of the fission that spun off the calculatedly adolescent subsequence begun with *The Amazing Maurice and His Educated Rodents.*

To some extent, *The Amazing Maurice* is, as might be expected, a return to the purer comedy of the early volumes in the series. When a cat and a company of rats who have been foraging on the Unseen University's rubbish tip ingest enough magic to become intelligent and articulate, Maurice the cat immediately takes charge of their future prospects, recruiting a boy with a penny whistle to help them run a Pied Piper scam in a series of small towns. When they reach Uberwald, however, they find themselves in a town where the local rat catchers have a scam of their own in operation, which has got seriously out of hand. Despite its careful mode of address, *The Amazing Maurice* duplicates the pragmatic politics of the Vimes series in the negotiations that ultimately take place between the rats and the town mayor, and it also duplicates the philosophical concerns of the Death subseries in its deft but remarkably ingenious description of the existential implications that self-conscious intelligence has for rats and cats, and in tracking their painstaking development of moral codes suited to their new condition.

The Wee Free Men models its setting on Lancre, and obtains its plot from the same arena of inspiration as *Witches Abroad* and *Lords and Ladies*. Like its predecessor, it retains the moral and philosophical depth of its parent subseries in spite of its calculated orientation to the concerns of younger readers. The members of the eponymous band of tiny ruffians represent themselves as rebels against all authority and morality, but that only brings the heroine's innocent contemplation of her duty, and the ethics of witchcraft in general, into clearer focus. She must also learn to cope with the seductions of fantasy; there, too, the hard-headedness of the renegade "pictsies" provides a useful exemplary counterpoint, and a lesson that she carries forward into the direct sequel, *A Hat Full of Sky*. The extension of the series in this new dimension is, therefore, in no way inconsistent with its overarching ambitions and methods.

The Construction and Navigation of Secondary Worlds

In order to understand the full measure of the Discworld series' achievement it is necessary to look more closely at the evolution of genre fantasy that took place while it was being written, and to which it made a substantial exemplary contribution. The fact that the core of the nascent genre has so far consisted of rigidly-formularized works, whose rapidly-acquired stereotypes immediately lent themselves to parody in such volumes as Diana Wynne Jones's *Tough Guide to Fantasyland* (1996), has generated considerable contempt among disapproving critics, but this was a necessary phase in a process of development that has considerable potential for future elaboration.

One of the reasons why fantasy of a Tolkienian stripe took so long to establish itself as a popular genre, in spite of reader-pleasing potential that can no longer be doubted, was the problem posed—for writers and readers alike—by setting stories entirely within worlds unlike our own. Writers and readers have long become used to colluding in the illusion that the world in which a story is set is the one with which the reader is already familiar, which allows ready-made stocks of knowledge to function an asset on which writer and reader can draw in making their way through the story. It requires only a slight adjustment to navigate a course through stories set in our world, upon which fantasy elements merely *intrude*, as menacing or humorous anomalies, but introducing an entire new world to a reader is a more challenging task, requiring heavier narrative labor.

Until recently, the great majority of works attempting this task had to begin by setting the "primary world" in place within the text and then moving into the secondary world by means of a journey or a portal of some kind. This narrative method has the advantage that the story's protagonist can carry the reader into the secondary world as an innocent and wondering viewpoint, so that both of them may learn about it together. Writing a story set *entirely* in a secondary world, employing a native protagonist—to whom everything that is strange to the reader must be perfectly familiar—is more difficult still.

Traditionally, the problem of writing stories entirely set in a secondary world was solved by the use of such formulas as "Once upon a time." Such signals inform the reader that the world within the text is *not* a simulacrum of the experienced world, and that a "reserve set" of assumptions must be engaged in order to become comfortable within it. That reserve set of assumptions related to a standardized image of an imaginary past, when animals might have talked, various supernatural entities might have appeared among humans, and various kinds of magic might have worked. One restriction of this literary method was that it only provided access to *one* ready-made secondary world, whose elasticity was by no means infinite. Another problem, which became apparent during the so-called Age of Enlightenment, was that the imagined past in question was gradually losing its claim to imaginative plausibility as progress in natural and human sciences built a very different image of the past. It was partly for this reason that fantasy came to be regarded as a kind of fiction only fit for children, whose sense of the past had not yet been fully refined.

Modern genre fantasy could not become easily readable—and hence widely popular—until it had a secondary set of assumptions of its own to call upon. The imaginary past having been reduced to the status of a childish fancy, some other mode of displacement from the known world was necessary. Cardinal examples were also required that could re-establish at least one reserve set of fundamental assumptions in the minds of a large population of readers.

An early response to the first requirement was made by science fiction writers, sf being the subgenre of fantasy most urgently in need of a solution to the problem of writing immersive fantasies set entirely within secondary worlds. Sf writers had to develop ways of setting stories in a plethora of possible futures and a multitude of other worlds, without the inconvenience of having to lead the reader by the hand from a simulacrum of the primary world in every story. Contributors to the sf pulp magazines of the 1930s soon developed a series of techniques for building such exotic constructs in the minds of a few skilled readers, but the difficulties involved meant that sf remained an essentially esoteric form of literature; even so, the establishment of sf as a popular genre made it possible for at least some readers to dive straight into fantasies set on other planets, distant futures and "parallel worlds" displaced from ours in a fourth spatial dimension.

The development of immersive fantasy by sf writers opened up the vast estates of the future and alien planets to literary development, making planetary romance and far-futuristic fantasy available as magical milieux and facilitating the growth of "sword and sorcery" fiction of the kind pioneered alongside the sf pulps by Robert E. Howard and other writers for *Weird Tales*. It also facilitated the development by writers for *Unknown*, most notably L. Sprague de Camp and Fletcher Pratt, of a distinctive kind of portal fantasy, in which scientifically clued-up protagonists were displaced into secondary worlds whose native inhabitants, though magically talented, were stuck in obsolete ways of thinking that made them vulnerable—usually with humorous consequences.

The second requirement was filled by the commercial success of paperback editions of *The Lord of the Rings*, which provided an exemplary model that other writers could imitate and vary. Parallel worlds modelled on Tolkien's Middle-Earth began to appear in slowly-increasing profusion in the 1970s and 1980s. The early imitations had to be slavish to be readily construed, so the new genre writers quickly produced a syncretic "fantasyland" of their own, similar to but more robust than the traditional fantasyland of fairy tales. As a steadily-increasing population of readers developed the ability to accommodate and orientate themselves in such worlds without undue difficulty, however, the scope for variation inevitably increased, and practiced writers became more skilful at managing the process.

Discworld was, at its inception, a comic reflection of genre fantasy's newly-hatched fantasyland, gleefully juxtaposing the newly-minted clichés with ideas drawn from elsewhere, contriving all manner of absurdly chimerical combinations. To some extent, Pratchett was drawing upon the same collisions of modern attitudes of mind and obsolete ways of thought that the *Unknown* writers had pioneered, but his ability to work in the medium of immersive fantasy rather than portal fantasy liberated him from the limitations of the normalizing story-arcs that portal fantasies almost invariably followed. Discworld was entirely disconnected from the primary world, free to develop as it might—and it had abundant potential to do exactly that, as it drew upon the rapidly-increasing expertise of fantasy readers to become much more elaborate.

Pratchett's Discworld-set plots extrapolate, with acute precision as well as considerable inventiveness, the consequences of the premises he establishes, which are usually versions of fanciful notions familiar to the reader, made concrete in characters who take them for granted. At the same time, his narrative voice colludes with the reader in constructing a commentary that not only exposes the logical problems arising from the extrapolation of the premises but draws definite philosophical lessons from their swift but sustained reduction to absurdity. There is a sense in which the early Discworld books can be viewed as mere compendia of jokes, which mostly work by adding witty twists to conventional fantasy motifs, but there is also a sense in which—when the series is seen as a whole—they are much more sophisticated.

Discworld had to be introduced to its readers as one more version of a conventional fantasyland (with added silliness in the form of the four elephants and the great turtle) but once its readers were accustomed to its basic geography and apparatus, the scope was there for its gradual complication and transformation. More importantly, the establishment of an active commentary, delivered from a viewpoint outside the minds of the protagonists—while simultaneously making the most of the narrative opportunities granted by access to those minds—established a kind of narrative binocular vision that allowed the reader to take a uniquely privileged view of events and actions taking place in Discworld.

That kind of binocular vision is a difficult narrative situation to establish and maintain, let alone put to constructive use, and the fact that Pratchett set it up so cleverly and employed it so productively is eloquent testimony to his literary ability. The series may have begun with all sorts of dependencies on the reader's prior acquaintance and skill, but within a few years Discworld had become an archetypal fantasyland in its own right, perhaps as powerful as Tolkien's and infinitely more flexible. More importantly, the Discworld novels became a school, not merely for the general skills required to read immersive fantasy but the specific skills required by the reader to enter wholeheartedly into a fantasy while retaining the capacity to stand back from it: to read it inside *and* out, as both humorous adventure and insidious satire.

The Utility of Nonsense

Seen in this light, the Discworld series has imaginative roots that go far deeper than the immediately-precedent apparatus that opened up the scope for it to operate. Its dependence on the establishment of Tolkienian genre fantasy and its echoes of *Unknown*-style comic fantasy were transitory and superficial; when it emerged from their shadow it could more easily be seen for what it really is: a dramatic revitalization of the tradition of "nonsense" fantasy that flourished in the Victorian era in the works of Edward Lear, Lewis Carroll, W. S. Gilbert and F. Anstey but became much weaker after the turn of the century.

To some extent, the weakening of the nonsense tradition was a consequence of the withering of the Victorian dogmas it sought to undermine; as the rigidity of Victorian dogmas and mores declined, opposition to them became more reasoned. The ambitions of the Prohibition movement in America briefly called forth a similar response in the works of writers like Thorne Smith and James Branch Cabell, but that dialectical opposition was less strident and even shorter-lived. There was, however, another factor involved in the fading of the nonsense tradition, and that was the limitation of its formats. Those favored by Lear and Gilbert were highly artificial while the novelists were forced to use proto-portal fantasy constructions that strongly resembled dreams, even when they were not explicitly represented as such, and intrusive fantasies that led inexorably to normalizing conclusions. Extreme nonsense cannot take full anarchic effect when it is confined to story-forms that must, in the end, return protagonists and readers to the all-too-sensible primary world. The advent of immersive genre fantasy eliminated that necessity, and opened up new scope for nonsense—whose most extravagant, ingenious and skilful exploiter Pratchett rapidly became.

"Nonsense," in this literary meaning, is no mere *absence* of sense; it is, instead, a kind of radical anti-sense. It sets out to challenge, mock and contradict that which passes for "common sense" but is, in fact, merely common. Lear and Carroll had no opportunity to familiarize themselves with the theory of ideology, which holds that those who exercise political power and moral authority always try to pass off as "obviously" or "naturally" true ideas that actually serve their own limited interests, but they understood the logic of the process well enough. Satirists had, of course, been assaulting particular ideological constructions for centuries, on a piecemeal basis; what nonsense aspires to do is attack the entire root-systems of ideologies rather than their individual manifestations—but while nonsense fantasies always had to use story-arcs doomed to return to the ideologically-polluted primary world, they could only work against ideological systems that became extraordinarily conspicuous and manifestly controversial.

Discworld, by establishing itself at the outset on the furthest fringe of absurdity—being not merely flat but mounted upon a giant turtle by means of elephantine adhesion—set itself firmly beyond all common sense. On Discworld, none of the assumptions we make about the physical and metaphysical context of the experienced world is "obviously" or "naturally" true; everything is questionable, challengeable and risible. The purpose of setting up that situation is not to render the world within the text incoherent, but rather to establish every aspect of its coherency as a topic for investigation. Here, absurdity is a precondition of analysis, and the construction of jokes becomes a method of experimental testing.

Much attempted nonsense of this kind does decay into mere silliness, flailing for the sake of flailing rather than winnowing wheat from chaff, but Pratchett goes further than that. His most important protagonists, Granny Weatherwax, Sam Vimes and Susan Sto Helit (as guided by Death), are all constructive agents, anxious to make what progress they can within the breaches that nonsense creates all around them. They find themselves in a world where nothing can be taken for granted, whose very existence challenges everything that their readers might take for granted, and they do the best they can—without the aid of dogmatic ideologies—to make it a better place. Pratchett's minor characters usually start from a position of extreme ignorance, having only just begun to doubt the ridiculous verities thrust upon them by their upbringing, and they are sometimes painfully slow learners, but in the end, the only true enlightenment usually begins to dawn on them—which is, as Polly the barmaid-turned-soldier realizes during her epiphanic breakthrough in *The Monstrous Regiment*, that "The presence of those seeking the truth is infinitely preferable to those who think they've found it."

A more elaborate manifesto for the series and it method is laid out in *Thief of Time* when Lobsang, the recently-revivified son of personified Time, tries to explain to Susan why the world has just fallen apart and what will be involved in fitting it all back together again. "Can you grasp all that?" he asks, when he has contrived a plausible analogy. "Yes," she says. "I think so." "Good," he replied. "Everything I have just said is nonsense. It bears no resemblance to the truth of the matter in any way at all. But it is a lie that you can...understand, I think. And then, afterwards—"

At that point, the speech breaks off, because all that remains is to get on with the story.

PRIMARY BIBLIOGRAPHY

Bacon, Francis. *New Atlantis. A Worke Unfinished, bound with Sylva Sylvarum, or a Naturall Historie.* London: J. H. for W. Lee, 1626 (actually 1627).
Ballard, J. G. *The Atrocity Exhibition.* London: Jonathan Cape, 1970. As *Love and Napalm: Export USA.* New York: Grove Press, 1972.
___. *Billennium.* New York: Berkley Medallion, 1962.
___. *The Burning World.* New York: Berkley Medallion, 1964. Revised and expanded as *The Drought.* London: Jonathan Cape, 1965.
___. *Chronopolis and Other Stories.* New York: Putnam's, 1971.
___. *Cocaine Nights.* London: Flamingo, 1996.
___. *Concrete Island.* London: Jonathan Cape, 1974.
___. *Crash.* London: Jonathan Cape, 1973.
___. *The Crystal World.* London: Jonathan Cape, 1966.
___. *The Day of Creation.* London: Gollancz, 1987.
___. *The Disaster Area.* London: Jonathan Cape, 1967.
___. *The Drowned World.* New York: Berkley Medallion, 1962.
___. *Empire of the Sun.* London: Gollancz, 1984.
___. *The Four-Dimensional Nightmare.* London: Victor Gollancz, 1963.
___. *Hello America.* London: Jonathan Cape, 1981.
___. *High-Rise.* London: Jonathan Cape, 1975.
___. *The Impossible Man.* New York: Berkley Medallion, 1966.
___. *The Kindness of Women.* London: HarperCollins, 1991.
___. *Low-Flying Aircraft.* London: Jonathan Cape, 1976.
___. *Memories of the Space Age.* Sauk City, Wisconsin: Arkham House, 1988.
___. *Myths of the Near Future.* London: Jonathan Cape, 1982.
___. *Passport to Eternity.* New York: Berkley Medallion, 1963.
___. *Running Wild.* London: Hutchinson, 1988.
___. *Rushing to Paradise.* London: Flamingo, 1994.
___. *The Terminal Beach.* London: Victor Gollancz, 1964.
___. *The Unlimited Dream Company.* London: Jonathan Cape, 1979.
___. *A User's Guide to the New Millennium.* London: HarperCollins, 1996.
___. *Vermilion Sands.* London: Jonathan Cape, 1971.
___. *The Voices of Time.* New York: Berkley Medallion, 1962.

___. *War Fever*. London: Collins, 1990.
___. *The Wind from Nowhere*. New York: Berkley Medallion, 1962.
Balzac, Honoré de. "Jésu Christ en Flandre" in vol. III of *Romans et contes philosophiques*. Paris: Gosselin, 1831; expanded version in vol. XIV of *La comédie humaine*. Paris: Furne, 1846.
Barbey d'Aurevilly, Jules-Amadée. *Du dandyisme et de G. Brummel*. Paris: Poulet-Malassis, 1843.
Beardsley, Aubrey. *Under the Hill*. 1897. London: John Lane, 1904.
Bray, Mrs. *Traditions, Legends and Superstitions of Devonshire*. 1838. London: John Murry, 1838.
Bulwer-Lytton, Edward. *Asmodeus at Large*. Philadelphia: Carey, Lea & Blanchard, 1833.
___. *The Coming Race*. Edinburgh & London: Blackwood, 1871.
___. *Falkland*. London: Henry Colburn, 1827.
___. *Godolphin*. London: Bentley, 1833.
___. *The Last Days of Pompeii*. 1834. London: Richard Bentley, 1834.
___. *The Life, Letters and Literary Remains of Edward Bulwer, Lord Lytton by His Son*. Kegan Paul, Trench & Co, 1883.
___. *Pelham*. London: Henry Colburn, 1828.
___. *Zanoni*. London: Saunders & Otley, 1842.
Byatt, A. S. *Possession*. London: Chatto and Windus, 1990.
Conrad, Joseph. "Heart of Darkness" in *Youth, and Two Other Stories*. Edinburgh: Blackwood, 1902.
Davy, Humphry. *Consolations in Travel*. London: John Murray, 1830.
___. *Elements of Agricultural Chemistry*. London: Longman, 1813.
___. *Elements of Chemical Philosophy*. London: J. Johnson, 1812.
___. *Researches, Chemical and Philosophical*. London: J. Johnson, 1800.
___. *Salmonia, or Days of Fly-Fishing*. 1827. London: John Murray, 1828.
Doyle, Arthur Conan. *A Study in Scarlet*. London: Ward Lock, 1888.
du Maurier, Daphne. *Jamaica Inn*. London: Gollancz, 1936.
Flammarion, Camille, *Lumen*, Paris: Marpon et Flammarion, 1887; expanded edition, 1906.
___. *Récits de l'infini: Lumen; Histoire d'une comète; Dans l'infini*. Paris: Didier et cie, 1872; tr. by S. R. Crocker as *Stories of Infinity: Lumen; The History of a Comet; In Infinity*. Boston: Roberts Bros, 1873.
France, Anatole. *The Revolt of the Angels*. London: John Lane, 1914.
Gautier, Théophile. *Charles Baudelaire: His Life* tr. by Guy Thorne. New York: Brentano's, 1915.
Godwin, William. *Things as They Are; or, The Adventures of Caleb Williams*. London: G. G. & J. Johnson, 1796.
___. *St Leon: A Tale of the Sixteenth Century*. London: Robinson, 1799.
Haldane, J. B. S. *Daedalus; or, Science and the Future*. London: Kegan Paul, Trench & Trübner, 1924.
Harris, W. S. *Life in a Thousand Worlds*. Cleona, Penn.: Holzapfel, 1905.
Hodgson, William Hope. *The House on the Borderland*. London: Chapman and Hall, 1908.

___. *The Night Land.* London: Eveleigh Nash, 1912.
Horne, Richard Henry. *The Poor Artist; or, seven eye-sights and one object.* London: John Van Voorst, 1850.
Hunt, Robert. *Elementary Physics: An Introduction to the Study of Natural Philosophy.* London: Reeve & Benham, 1851.
___. *The Mount's Bay: a descriptive poem...and other pieces.* Penzance: J. Downing & T. Matthews, 1829.
___. *Panthea, the Spirit of Nature.* London: Reeve, Bentham & Reeve, 1849.
___. *Photography: A Treatise on the Chemical Changes Produced by Solar Radiation, and the Production of Pictures from Nature by Daguerreotype, Calotype or Other Photographic Processes.* London: John Joseph Griffin & Co, 1851 (part of the *Encyclopedia Metropolitana*; a revised and expanded edition of *A Popular Treatise on Photography*, London, 1841.)
___. *The Poetry of Science, or Studies of the Physical Phenomena of Nature.* London: Reeve, Bentham & Reeve, 1848.
___. *Popular Romances of the West of England; or, The Drolls, Traditions and Superstitions of Old Cornwall.* 2nd ed. London: Chatto & Windus, 1881 (expanded edition of a text first published in 2 vols. in 1865 by John Camden Hotton).
___. *Researches on Light in its Chemical Relations.* London: Longman, Brown, Green, 1844. (2nd ed., revised and expanded, 1854.)
Huysmans, Joris-Karl. *À rebours.* Paris: Charpentier, 1884.
James, Henry. *Partial Portraits.* New York: Macmillan, 1888.
[Kepler, John]. *Joh. Keppler Mathematici Olim Imperatorii. Somnium se opus posthumus de astronomia lunare.* Frankfurt, 1634; tr. & annotated by Edward Rosen as *Kepler's Somnium. The Dream, or Posthumous Work on Lunar Astronomy.* Madison, WI: University of Wisconsin Press, 1967.
Kircher, Athanasius. *Itinerarium Exstaticum quo mundi opificium, etc.* Rome: V. Mascardi, 1656.
———. *Mundus Subterraneus.* Amsterdam: J. Jansson, 3rd ed. 1678.
Koontz, Dean R. *The Bad Place.* New York: Putnam, 1990.
___. *By the Light of the Moon.* New York: Bantam, 2002.
___. *Chase* (as K. R. Dwyer). New York: Random House, 1972.
___. *Cold Fire.* New York: Putnam, 1991.
___. *Darkfall.* New York: Berkley, 1984; as *Darkness Comes,* London: W. H. Allen, 1984.
___. *A Darkness in my Soul.* New York: DAW, 1972.
___. *Dark Rivers of the Heart.* New York: Knopf, 1994.
___. *The Dark Symphony.* New York: Lancer, 1970.
___. *Dragon Tears.* New York: Putnam, 1993.
___. *The Eyes of Darkness*(as Leigh Nichols). New York: Pocket, 1981. [Reprinted as by DRK, 1991.]
___. *The Face* New York: Bantam, 2003.

___. *The Face of Fear* (as Brian Coffey). Indianapolis: Bobbs-Merrill, 1977. [Reprinted as by K. R. Dwyer, 1978, and as by DRK, 1989]
___. *False Memory.* New York: Bantam, 1999.
___. *Fear Nothing.* New York: Bantam, 1998.
___. *Fear That Man.* New York: Ace, 1969.
___. *From the Corner of his Eye* New York: Bantam, 2000.
___. *The Funhouse: Carnival of Terror* (as Owen West). New York: Jove, 1980.
___. *Hanging On.* New York: Evans, 1973.
___. *Hell's Gate.* New York: Lancer, 1970.
___. *Hideaway.* New York: Putnam, 1992.
___. *How to Write Best-Selling Fiction.* Cincinnati: Writer's Digest, 1981.
___. *Intensity.* London: Headline, 1995.
___. *The Key to Midnight* (as Leigh Nichols). New York: Berkley, 1979. [Reprinted as by DRK, 1992.]
___. *Lightning.* New York: Putnam, 1988.
___. *The Mask* (as Owen West). New York: Jove, 1981. [Reprinted as by DRK, 1988.]
___. *Midnight.* New York: Putnam, 1989.
___. *Mr. Murder.* New York: Putnam, 1993.
___. *Night Chills.* New York: Atheneum, 1976.
___. *Nightmare Journey.* New York: Putnam, 1975.
___. *Odd Thomas* Bantam, 2004.
___. One Door Away from Heaven. Bantam, 2001.
___. *Phantoms.* New York: Putnam, 1983.
___. *Seize the Night* New York: Bantam, 1999.
___. *Shadowfires* (as Leigh Nichols). New York: Avon, 1987. [Reprinted as by DRK, 1991]
___. *Shattered* (as K. R. Dwyer). New York: Random House, 1973.
___. *Sole Survivor.* New York: Ballantine, 1997.
___. *Star Quest.* New York: Ace, 1968.
___. *Strange Highways.* New York: Warner, 1995.
___. *Strangers.* New York: Putnam, 1986.
___. *Ticktock.* New York: Ballantine, 1995.
___. *Twilight* (as Leigh Nichols). New York: Pocket, 1984. [Revised as *The Servants of Twilight* by DRK, 1988.]
___. *Twilight Eyes.* Westland, Mich.: Land of Enchantment, 1985. [Revised ed. 1987.]
___. *The Vision.* New York: Putnam, 1977.
___. *Voice of the Night* (as Brian Coffey). New York: Doubleday, 1980. [Reprinted as by DRK, 1990.]
___. *Warlock.* New York: Lancer, 1972.
___. *Watchers.* New York: Putnam, 1987.
___. *A Werewolf Among Us.* New York: Ballantine, 1973.
___. *Whispers.* New York: Putnam, 1980.
___. *Writing Popular Fiction.* Cincinnati: Writer's Digest, 1973.

Lach-Szyrma. W. S. *Aleriel; or, A Voyage to Other Worlds*. London: Wyman, 1886.
Lee, Vernon. *Ariadne in Mantua: A Romance in Five Acts*. Oxford: Blackwell, 1903.
___. *The Ballet of the Nations: A Present-Day Morality*. London: Chatto and Windus, 1915.
___. *Belcaro, Being Essays on Sundry Aesthetical Questions*. London: Satchell, 1883.
___. *For Maurice: Five Unlikely Stories*. London: John Lane, 1927.
___. *Genius Loci: Notes on Places*. London: Grant Richards, 1899.
___. *Gospels of Anarchy and Other Contemporary Studies*. London: Unwin, 1908.
___. *Hauntings: Fantastic Stories*. London: Heinemann, 1890.
___. *Limbo and Other Essays*. London: Grant Richards, 1897.
___. *Louis Norbert: A Two-fold Romance*. London: John Lane, 1914.
___. *Miss Brown*. Edinburgh: Blackwood, 1884
___. *Ottilie: An Eighteenth-Century Idyl*. London: Unwin, 1883.
___. *Penelope Brandling: A Tale of the Welsh Coast in the Eighteenth Century*. London: Unwin, 1903.
___. *A Phantom Lover: A Fantastic Story*. Edinburgh: Blackwood, 1886.
___. *Pope Jacynth and Other Fantastic Tales*. London: Grant Richards, 1904.
___. *The Prince of the Hundred Soups: A Puppet Show in Narrative*. London: Unwin, 1883.
___. *Proteus; or, The Future of Intelligence*. London: Kegan Paul, Trench & Trübner, 1925.
___. *Renaissance Fancies and Studies*. London: Smith Elder, 1895.
___. *Satan the Waster: A Philosophic War Trilogy*. London: John Lane, 1920.
___. *Sister Benevenuta and the Christ Child*. London: Grant Richards, 1906.
___. *The Snake Lady and Other Stories*. New York: Grove Press, 1954.
___. *Studies of the Eighteenth Century in Italy*. London: Satchell, 1880,
___. *Tuscan Fairy Tales*. London: Satchell, 1880.
___. *Vanitas: Polite Stories*. London: Heinemann, 1892.
___. *Vital Lies: Studies of Some Varieties of Recent Obscurantism*. London: John Lane, 1912.
Lee-Hamilton, Eugene. *The Lord of the Dark Red Star*. London: Scott, 1903.
___. *Poems and Transcripts*. Edinburgh: Blackwood, 1878.
Lévi, Éliphas. *Dogme et rituel de la haute magie*. Paris: Germer Ballière, 1856. Tr. by A. E. Waite as *Transcendental Magic: Its Doctrine and Ritual*. London: Rider, 1896.
___. *Histoire de la magie*. Paris: Germer Ballière, 1860. Tr. by A. E. Waite as *The History of Magic*. London: Rider, 1913.

Maturin, Charles. *Melmoth the Wanderer*. London: Hurst and Robinson, 1820.
Mérimée, Prosper. *Carmen*. Paris: Michel Lévy, 1846.
Michelet, Jules. *La Sorcière*. Paris: Dentu, 1862. Tr. by A. R. Allinson as *Satanism and Witchcraft*. New York: Citadel, 1939.
Mudford, William. *The Five Nights of St Albans*. Edinburgh: Blackwood, 1829.
Morrow, James. *Blameless in Abaddon*, New York: Harcourt Brace, 1996.
___. *City of Truth*. London: Century, 1990.
___. *The Eternal Footman*. New York: Harcourt Brace, 1999.
___. *Only Begotten Daughter*. New York: Morrow, 1990.
___. *Towing Jehovah*. New York: Harcourt Brace, 1994.
Pater, Walter. *Marius the Epicurean*. 1885. London: Macmillan, 1892.
———. *Studies in the History of the Renaissance*. London: Macmillan, 1873.
Poe, Edgar Allan. *Eureka, a prose poem*. New York: G. P. Putnam, 1848.
___. "The Murders in the Rue Morgue". *Graham's Magazine* April 1841.
___. "The Mystery of Marie Roget". *Snowden's Ladies' Companion* November 1842-January 1843.
Pollock, Walter Herries. *The Picture's Secret*. London: Henry, 1883.
Pratchett, Terry. *The Amazing Maurice and His Educated Rodents*. London: Doubleday, 2001.
___. *Carpe Jugulum*. London: Doubleday, 1998.
___. *The Carpet People*. Gerrards Cross, Bucks.: Colin Smythe, 1971.
___. *The Color of Magic*. Gerrards Cross, Bucks.: Colin Smythe, 1983.
___. *The Dark Side of the Sun*. Gerrards Cross, Bucks.: Colin Smythe, 1976.
___. *Diggers*. London: Doubleday, 1990.
___. *Equal Rites*. London: Gollancz, 1987.
___. *Eric* (with Josh Kirby). London: Gollancz, 1990.
___. *Feet of Clay*. London: Gollancz, 1996.
___. *The Fifth Elephant*. London: Doubleday, 1999.
___. *Good Omens: The Nice and Accurate Prophecies of Anges Nutter, Witch* (with Neil Gaiman). London: Gollancz, 1990.
___. *Guards! Guards!*. London: Gollancz, 1989.
___. *A Hat Full of Sky*. London: Doubleday, 2004.
___. *Hogfather*. London: Gollancz, 1996.
___. *Interesting Times*. London: Gollancz, 1994.
___. *Jingo*. London: Gollancz, 1997.
___. *Johnny and the Bomb*. London: Doubleday, 1996.
___. *Johnny and the Dead*. London: Doubleday, 1993.
___. *The Last Continent*. London: Doubleday, 1998.
___. *The Last Hero* (with Paul Kidby), London: Doubleday, 2001.
___. *The Light Fantastic*. Gerrards Cross, Bucks.: Colin Smythe, 1986.
___. *Lords and Ladies*. London: Gollancz, 1992.
___. *Maskerade*. London: Gollancz, 1995.

___. *Men at Arms*. London: Gollancz, 1993.
___. *Monstrous Regiment*. London: Doubleday, 2003.
___. *Mort*. London: Gollancz, 1987.
___. *Moving Pictures*. London: Gollancz, 1990.
___. *Night Watch*. London: Doubleday, 2002.
___. *Only You Can Save Mankind*. London: Doubleday, 1992.
___. *Pyramids*. London: Gollancz, 1989.
___. *Reaper Man*. London: Gollancz, 1991.
___. *Small Gods*. London: Gollancz, 1992.
___. *Soul Music*. London: Gollancz, 1994.
___. *Sourcery*. London: Gollancz, 1988.
___. *Strata*. Gerrards Cross, Bucks.: Colin Smythe, 1981
___. *Thief of Time*. London: Doubleday, 2001.
___. *Truckers*. London: Doubleday, 1989.
___. *The Truth*. London: Doubleday, 2000.
___. *The Wee Free Men*. London: Doubleday, 2003.
___. *Wings*. London: Doubleday, 1990.
___. *Witches Abroad*. London: Gollancz, 1991.
___. *Wyrd Sisters*. London: Gollancz, 1988.
Restif de la Bretonne, Nicolas-Edmé. *Les Posthumes*. Paris: Duchêne, 1802.
Scott, Walter. *Tales of the Crusaders: The Betrothed*. Edinburgh: Constable, 1825.
Shelley, Mary. *Frankenstein; or, The Modern Prometheus*. London: Lackington, Hughes, Harding, Mayor & Jones, 1818.
___. *The Last Man*. London: Henry Colburn, 1826.
Shelley, Percy Bysshe. "A Defence of Poetry" in *Shelley's Poetry and Prose* ed. Mary Shelley. London: Edward Moxon, 1840.
Shiel, M. P. *The Last Miracle*. London: Werner Laurie, 1906.
___. *The Lord of the Sea*. London: Grant Richards, 1901.
___. *The Pale Ape and Other Pulses*. London: Werner Laurie, 1911.
___. *Prince Zaleski*. London: John Lane, 1895.
___. *The Purple Cloud*. London: Chatto & Windus, 1901.
___. *The Rajah's Sapphire*. 1896 (with W. T. Stead).
___. *Science, Life and Literature*. London: Williams and Norgate, 1950.
___. *Shapes in the Fire*. London: John Lane, 1896.
___. *This Knot of Life*. London: Everett, 1909.
___. *The Yellow Danger*. London: Grant Richards, 1898.
___. *The Young Men are Coming!* London: Allen and Unwin, 1937.
Stevenson, Robert Louis. *Strange Case of Dr. Jekyll and Mr. Hyde*. New York: Munro, 1886.
Swedenborg, Emanuel. *Arcana coelestia quae in Scriptura sacra seu verbo Domini sunt detecta, etc* [first published 1749-56]; tr. as *Arcana Coelestia; or, Heavenly Mysteries contained in the Sacred Scriptures, etc.*, vols. 1-3 London: R, Hindmarsh, 1784-88; vols. 4-8, London: J. & E. Hodgson, 1802-3; vols. 9-12, London, 1807-34.

Voltaire. *Le Micromégas de mr. de Voltaire*. Londres (so advertised, but probably Berlin), 1752; tr. as *Micromegas, A Comic Romance. Being a Severe Satire upon the Philosophy, Ignorance, and Self-Conceit of Mankind*. London: Wilson & Durham, 1753.
Waugh, Evelyn. *The Loved One*. New York: Dell, 1948.
Wilde, Oscar. "The Decay of Lying" in *Intentions*. London: Osgood McIlvaine, 1891.

SECONDARY BIBLIOGRAPHY

Anderson, R. E., "Robert Hunt" in *Dictionary of National Biography* vol. XXVIII, ed. Stanley Lee, London: Smith, Elder & Co, 1891.
Ariès, Philippe. *The Hour of Our Death: Western Attitudes to Death from the Middle Ages t the Present*. London: Marion Boyars, 1976.
Bleiler, E. F. *Checklist of Science-Fiction & Supernatural Fiction* (2nd ed.). Glen Rock NJ: Firebell, 1979.
Boase, Frederic. *Modern English Biography*. London: Frank Cass, 1965 (originally published privately in Cornwall in 1892).
Brewer, E. Cobham. *The Dictionary of Phrase and Fable*. London: Galley Press, 1988 (facsimile of the "new and enlarged" 1894 edition; the first edition had been issued in 1870).
Brigg, Peter. *J. G. Ballard*. San Bernardino, California: Borgo Press, 1985.
Brown, Charles N. "Dean Koontz: A Comedian in Hell." Interview, *Locus* 406 (November 1994): 4-5, 81-82.
Butler, Andrew M. *The Pocket Essential Terry Pratchett*. Harpenden, U.K.: Pocket Essentials, 2001.
Butler, Andrew M., Edward James, and Farah Mendlesohn, eds. *Terry Pratchett: Guilty of Literature*. Reading, U.K.: Science Fiction Foundation, 2000.
Charlton, D. G. *Secular Religions in France 1815-1870*. Oxford: Oxford University Press for the University of Hull, 1963.
Davies, Douglas J. *Death, Ritual and Belief: The Rhetoric of Funerary Rites*. London: Cassell, 1997.
Fraser, Antonia, ed. *The Pleasure of Reading*. London: Bloomsbury, 1992,
Goddard, James. and David Pringle, eds. *J. G. Ballard: The First Twenty Years*. Hayes, Middlesex, UK: Bran's Head Books, 1976.
Gunn, Peter. *Vernon Lee: Violet Paget, 1856-1935*. Oxford: Oxford University Press, 1964.
Heidegger, Martin. *Being and Time*. New York: Harper & Row, 1962. (Tr. of *Sein und Zeit*, 1927.)
Jones, Diana Wynne. *The Tough Guide to Fantasyland*. London: Vista, 1996.
Kotker, Joan G. *Dean Koontz: A Critical Companion*. Westport, Conn.: Greenwood, 1996.
Locke, George. *A Spectrum of Fantasy*. London: Ferret, 1980.

Lucretius. *On the Nature of the Universe*. Harmondsworth: Penguin, 1951. (Tr. of De rerum natura, c60 BC)
Mercer, Mick, *The Hex Files: The Bible of Goth*. London: Batsford, 1996.
Mitford, Jessica. *The American Way of Death*. New York: Simon & Schuster, 1963.
Moskowitz, Sam. *Explorers of the Infinite*. 1963. Cleveland, Oh.: World, 1963.
Munster, Bill, ed. *Sudden Fear: The Horror and Dark Suspense Fiction of Dean R. Koontz*. Mercer Island, Wash.: Starmont House, 1988.
Nordau, Max Simon. *Degeneration*. London: Heinemann, 1895.
Pringle, David. *Earth is the Alien Planet: J. G. Ballard's Four-Dimensional Nightmare*. San Bernardino, CA: Borgo Press, 1979.
Ramsland, Katharine. *Dean Koontz: A Writer's Biography*. New York: Harper Prism, 1997.
Sadleir, Michael. *Bulwer; A Panorama: Edward and Rosina, 1803-1836*. Constable, 1931.
Sartre, Jean-Paul. *Being and Nothingness*. London: Methuen, 1957. (Tr. of *L'être et le néant*, 1943.)
Smith, William. *A Classical Dictionary of Biography, Mythology, and Geography*. 21st edition. London: John Murray, 1891.
Stableford, Brian. "William Wilson's Prospectus for Science-Fiction, 1851". *Foundation* 10 (June 1976); reprinted in *Opening Minds* San Bernardino, CA: Borgo Press, 1995.
Suvin, Darko. *Victorian Science Fiction in the UK*. Boston: G. K. Hall, 1983.
Symons, Arthur. *The Symbolist Movement in Literature*. London: Constable, 1899.
Toynbee, Arnold. "Changing Attitudes Towards Death in the Modern Western World" in *Man's Concern with Death* by Arnold Toynbee, A. Keith Mant, Ninian Smart, John Hinton, Simon Yudkin, Eric Rhode, Rosalind Heywood & H. H. Price. London: Hodder & Stoughton, 1968.
Wilson, William. *A Little Earnest Book Upon a Great Old Subject*. London: Darton & Co, 1851.

INDEX

"About Myself" 22-23
Adams, Douglas 182
Adams, Matilda 108
"Adonais" 89, 95
The Adventures of Engelbrecht 125
Aeschylus 156-157
Aesop 28, 30
The Aesthetic Movement 110, 114-115
Ainsworth, W. Harrison 180
"The Air Disaster" 149
Aldiss, Brian 128, 131
Aleriel 72
Allen, Grant 107
The Amazing Maurice and His Educated Rodents 184, 191
Ambit 133
The American Way of Death 157
Amis, Kingsley 130-131
"Amour Dure" 112-113, 122
Anderson, R. E. 81
Andreae, Johann Valentin 96
Anstey, F. 195
Anstruther-Thomson, Clementina 120-121
Aphrodite 20-21
Apollinaire, Guillaume 126
Apollo 21
Apollonius of Tyana 115
À rebours 44
Arcana of Heaven 72
Ariadne in Mantua 118
Ariès, Philippe 158, 164
Aristophanes 23
"Arria Marcella" 115
"The Art of Fiction" 115
Ash-Tree Press 10
Asimov, Isaac 169
Asmodeus at Large 58, 97-98
"The Assassination of John F. Kennedy Considered as a Downhill Motor Race" 126

Astronomie Populaire 85
The Athenaeum 83
The Atlantic Monthly 166
The Atrocity Exhibition 126, 135-137, 140, 142
"Les Aventures d'une pièce de monnaie" 108
Bacon, Francis 64
The Bad Place 169, 171, 177
The Baker 125
Ballard, Helen see Matthews, Helen Mary
Ballard, J. G. 11, 123-151
Ballard, Margaret 123
The Ballet of the Nations 120
Balzac, Honoré de 117
Bananas 133
Barbey d'Aurevilly, Jules Amadée 52
Baring, Maurice 119
Bath Chronicle 182
Baudelaire, Charles 8, 13, 25
Bax, Martin 133
Beardsley, August 22, 119
Beckford, William 51
Being and Nothingness 156
Being and Time 156
Belcaro, Being Notes on Sundry Aesthetical Questions 112
Ben Hur 159
Berkley 128-130, 132
Berne, Eric 137
The Betrothed 101
Blackwood, William 113
Blake, William 52
Blameless in Abaddon 153
Bleiler, Everett F. 80
Boase, Frederick 81
Boehme, Jacob 95
Bohn, H. G. 85
Borges, Jorge Luis 149
The Borgo Press 8-9
Boswell, James 158
Bradbury, Ray 127
Bray, Mrs. 82
Breton, André 126
Brewer, E. Cobham 101
"The Bride" 46-48
British Writers 11
Brooke, Keith 11
Brookes, Joshua 81
Brunner, John 131
Brummell, George "Beau" 25, 52-53, 57
Bucks Free Press 182
Buddhism 162
"The Builder's Creed" 157

"Build-Up" 126
Bulmer, Kenneth 131
Bulwer-Lytton, Edward (Baron Lytton of Knebworth) 8-9, 51-63, 84-85, 94-95, 97, 105, 180
Bunch, David R. 129
"A Bundle of Letters" 46, 48
The Burning World 132-133
Burroughs, William S. 136-137
Butler, Samuel 107
Byatt, A. S. 118
Byron, Lord 8, 16, 51-53, 55
By the Light of the Moon 174-175, 177, 179
Cabell, James Branch 195
"Cage of Sand" 132
Caleb Williams 57
Callander, Alice 115
The Camborne School of Mines 84
Campbell, John W. Jr. 130
Cannabis indica 101
Cannabis sativa 101
Cape, Jonathan 133, 138
"Capo Serpente" 115
Carmen 17
Carnell, E. John 125, 127-129
Carpe Jugulum 184, 187
The Carpet People 182, 184
Carroll, Lewis 195-196
"The Case of Euphemiah Raphash" 43, 46, 50
Cassell's Magazine 43
Cazotte, Jacques 60
Cerra, Gerda (Gerda Koontz) 166, 168
"Changing Attitudes Towards Death in the Modern Western World" 158
Chant de l'amour triomphant 113
Chapman's Magazine 43
Charcot, Jean-Martin 109
Charlton, D. G. 159
Chase 166-167
Chatto and Windus 32, 84
The Checklist of Science-Fiction and Supernatural Fiction 80
The Chemical Wedding of Christian Rosenkreutz 96
Chemistry and Industry 125
Chirico, Giorgio de 125
Chivers, Cedric 22
"Christ in Flanders" 117
Christensen, Alan 9
Christopher, John 128-129
"Chronopolis" 128
City of Truth 159
Clarke, Arthur C. 132
Classical Dictionary 21
Cloud-Cuckoo Land 23, 25

"Cloud-Sculptors of Coral-D" 135
Cobbett, William 82
Cobbold, David (Lord Cobbold of Knebworth) 8
Cobbold, Henry 8
Cocaine Nights 146-148, 151
Coffey, Brian (Dean R. Koontz) 170
Cold Fire 171
Coleridge, Samuel Taylor 15, 66, 82, 87
The Color of Magic 182-183, 186
"A Comedian in Hell" 169
The Coming Race 105
Comte, Auguste 160
"The Concentration City" 126
Concrete Island 138-139
Conrad, Joseph 143
Consolations in Travel; or, The Last Days of a Philosopher 9, 65-79, 86, 105
Constant, Alphonse-Louis 61-63
Cornhill Magazine, The 112
Crash 137-139, 142, 150
Cronenberg, David 138
Crowley, Aleister 62
"The Crucifixion of Christ Considered as an Uphill Bicycle Race" 126
Cruikshank, George 84
"Cry Hope, Cry Fury!" 135
The Crystal World 132, 134-135, 140, 143, 150
"A Culture-Ghost; or, Winthrop's Adventure" 110, 112
Daedalus; or, Science and the Future 122
Dali, Salvador 125, 134, 136, 141
Dandyism 25, 52
Darkfall 168-170
A Darkness in My Soul 169
Dark Rivers of the Heart 173, 175-176
The Dark Side of the Sun 182
The Dark Symphony 169
Darmsteter, James 120
Darwin, Charles 69, 73, 77-78, 106-107
Darwin, Erasmus 57, 86
Davidson, John 28-29
Davies, Douglas J. 158, 160, 164
Davy, Humphry 9, 64-79, 86, 107
The Day of Creation 143-144, 146
"The Day of Forever" 135
De'Ath, Wilfred 131
Death, Ritual and Belief 158
Decadence and the Decadent Movements 7-8, 10, 13-17, 19, 21-27, 30-32, 41-48, 114-115, 119
de Camp, L. Sprague 193
"The Decay of Lying" 13-14, 51
Dedalus 8
A Defence of Poetry 52
Degeneration 17

Delphi 21
De rerum natura 156
Des Esseintes, Jean 15, 26, 44-45
The Dictionary of National Biography 81, 84, 104
The Dictionary of Phrase and Fable 101
Diggers 185
"Dionea" 112-113, 116
Discworld series 183-197
Dogme et ritual de la haute magie 61-62
"The Doll" 117
Doubleday 137
Douglas, Lord Alfred 22, 43
Dowson, Ernest 25, 29
Doyle, Sir Arthur Conan 45
Dragon Tears 171
Drive 137
The Drought 133-134, 150
"The Drowned Giant" 131
The Drowned World 129-131, 133-134, 145, 150
Drumlanrig, Lord 22, 43
Du Maurier, Daphne 118
Dupin, C. Auguste 15, 23-24, 26, 45, 52
Dutton, E. P. 137
Dwyer, K. R. (Dean R. Koontz) 166
"The Eagle's Crag" 42
Earth Is the Alien Planet 148
Eaton, Hubert 157
Ecclesiastes 35, 37-38
Eggeling, John 9
Elementary Physics 83, 86
Elements of Agriculture 66
Elements of Chemical Philosophy 66, 79
Eliot, T. S. 164
Empire of the Sun 141-143, 145, 150
"The Empress of the Earth" 15
Encyclopedia Britannica 84
Encyclopedia Metropolitana 83
The English Illustrated Magazine 47
"The Enormous Space" 149
Equal Rites 184, 186-187
Erasmus, Desiderius 158-159
Eric 184
Ernst, Max 125
The Eternal Footman 152-165
Eugene Aram 58
Eureka—An Essay on the Material and Spiritual Universe 73, 86
Explorers of the Infinite 27
The Eyes of Darkness 170
The Face 173-174, 176-177, 179
The Face of Fear 170-171
Falkland 53-58, 60

"The Fall of the House of Usher" 17, 48-49
False Memory 174
Fama Fraternitatis 96
"Faustus and Helena: Notes on the Supernatural in Art" 112-113
Fear Nothing 174
Fear That Man 169
"The Featureless Wisdom" 117
Feet of Clay 184, 189
Fenton, Elijah 100
Féval, Paul 179
The Fifth Elephant 184, 189
Finnegans Wake 125
The Five Nights of St Albans 55
Flammarion, Camille 9, 73, 77-78, 85
Les Fleurs du Mal 13, 25
For Maurice: Five Unlikely Stories 113-115, 117, 119
Fortnightly Review 115
Foundation 9, 80
The Four-Dimensional Nightmare 130
France, Anatole 117, 156, 161
Frankenstein 35-36
Fraser, Antonia 124
Fraser's Magazine 109-110
Freud, Sigmund 112, 159
From the Corner of His Eye 174
The Funhouse 168
Gaiman, Neil 185
Gale Research 11-12
"The Garden of Time" 129
Garnett, Richard 117
Gautier, Théophile 13-14, 25, 114-115
Genesis 35-37, 69, 73-74, 78
Genius Loci: Notes on Places 117
George, Henry 28
Gernsback, Hugo 9
Gilbert, W. S. 195-196
Gilchrist, R. Murray 13, 114
Gilgamesh, The Epic of 155
Gladstone, Mrs. 22, 28
Gladstone, William Ewart 14, 22
Godolphin 54, 58-60, 84, 94, 104
"The Gods and Ritter Tanhuser" 119, 122
Godwin, William 57, 104
Goethe, J. W. 112
The Golden Legend 116
Golding, William 139
Goldsmith, Cele 129
Gollancz, Victor 32, 130
Good Omens: The Nice and Accurate Prophecies of Agnes Nutter, Witch 185
Google 12
Gospels of Anarchy and Other Contemporary Studies 119

Gothic fantasy 51-57, 62-63
Gould, Kendall and Lincoln 85
Gourmont, Rémy de 114
"The Greatest TV Show on Earth" 140
Great Exhibition of 1851 83
"The Great King" 43, 48, 50
Greene, Graham 135
Grey, Earl 22
Griffith, George 35
Grimm, The Brothers 110
Grove Press 116, 137
The Guardian 142
Guards! Guards! 184, 188-189
Gunn, Peter 118, 120-121
"Guy Harkaway's Substitute" 42
"The Hades Business" 182
Haldane, J. B. S. 121-122
Hanging On 169
Harris, Sir Alexander 22
Harris, Thomas 172
Harris, W. S. 72
A Hat Full of Sky 184, 191
Hauntings 112-114, 121
Head, Christine 121
Heart of Darkness 143
"He Defines 'Greatness of Mind'" 44
Heidegger, Martin 156
Helen of Troy 112
Hello America 141
Hell's Gate 169
"He Meddles with Women" 46
Herschel, John 86
"He Wakes and Echo" 46, 50
The Hex Files: The Bible of Goth 52
Hideaway 168-169, 171
High-Rise 138-139, 145-146
Histoire de la magie 61
Hodgson, William Hope 49-50, 73
Hogfather 184, 188
Hoffmann, E. T. A. 112
Holdsworth, Annie E. 109
Holmes, Sherlock 16, 23-24, 27-28, 45
Horne, Richard Henry 80
"The House of Sounds" 17, 48-50
The House on the Borderland 49-50, 73
Howard, Robert E. 193
How to Write Best-Selling Fiction 173
"Huguenin's Wife" 42, 46-48, 50
Hunt, Henry "Radical" 81-82, 84, 104, 106
Hunt, Leigh 81-82, 104
Hunt, Richard William 81-82

Hunt, Robert 9-10, 80-107
Hutton, James 86
Huysmans, Joris-Karl 15, 26, 44
"The Illuminated Man" 132
"Impotence of Human Wisdom" 100
infinity Plus 11
Intensity 173
"The Intensive Care Unit" 140
Interesting Times 184, 186
Interzone 148-149
itinerarium exstaticum 72
Jamaica Inn 118
James, Henry 111-112, 115
James, William 115-116
Jarry, Alfred 126
Jesus 45
Jingo 184, 189
Job 23, 29, 35, 37, 39-40, 46
Johnny and the Bomb 185
Johnny and the Dead 185
Johnson, Samuel 158
Jones, Diana Wynne 192
Joyce, James 125
Jung, Carl 159
Keats, John 82, 107, 115
Kennedy, Jackie 136
Kent, William 57
Kepler, John 65
The Key to Midnight 170
The Kindness of Women 132, 139-140, 144-145, 150
King Alfred's College, Winchester 10
King, Stephen 167
Kircher, Athanasius 72
"The Kittens" 166
Koontz, Dean 11, 166-181
Koontz, Gerda, see Cerra, Gerda
Koontz, Ray 166, 168
Lach-Szyrma, W. S. 72
"The Lady and Death" 117
"Lady Tal" 115
La Harpe, Jean-François de 60
Lamb, Lady Caroline 51, 54-55
"Lamia" 115
Lane, John 13, 16, 22, 114-115
The Last Continent 184, 186
The Last Days of Pompeii 8, 58-60
The Last Hero 184
The Last Man 35
The Last Miracle 34-35, 38, 40, 45
Laurie, T. Werner 42
Lear, Edward 195-196

Lee, Vernon (Violet Paget) 10-11, 108-122
Lee-Hamilton, Captain 108
Lee-Hamilton, Eugene 108-109, 120
"The Legend of Madame Krasinska" 115-117
Leiber, Fritz 129
Lévi, Éliphas 61-62
Ley, Willy 132
"The Life and Death of God" 140
Life in a Thousand Worlds 72
Life, Letters and Literary Remains (of Lord Lytton) 53-54, 57-58
The Light Fantastic 183, 186
Lightning 169, 171
"Lilith" 112
Limbo and Other Essays 117
Lincoln, Lord 57
Literary Satanism 52
A Little Earnest Book Upon a Great Old Subject 9, 80
Locke, George 80-81
Locus 168-169, 179
Lombroso, Cesare 17
The London Library 10
The Lord of the Dark Red Star 120
The Lord of the Flies 139
The Lord of the Rings 182, 194
The Lord of the Sea 28, 32-35, 38
Lords and Ladies 184, 187, 191
Lorrain, Jean 10-11
Louis Norbert 115, 118-119
Love and Napalm: Export U.S.A. 137
The Loved One 157
"Love in a Colder Climate" 149
Lucretius 156, 161, 164
Lumen 73, 78
Lyell, Charles 86
Lytton, Earl of 53
Machen, Arthur 13, 114
The Magazine of Fantasy & Science Fiction 129, 132
"Manhole 69" 126
"The Man Who Walked on the Moon" 149
"Many a Tear" 47
"Maria in the Rose-Bush" 17
Marius the Epicurean 110
Marlowe, Christopher 112
"Marsyas in Flanders" 117
The Mask 168
Maskerade 184, 187
Matthews, Helen Mary (Helen Ballard) 125, 132
Maturin, Charles 55
Medea di Carpi 113
Melmoth the Wanderer 55
Memories of the Space Age 132

"Memories of the Space Age" 148
Men at Arms 184, 189
Mendès, Catulle 26
The Men of the Time 107
Mercer, Mick 52
Mérimée, Prosper 17
"The Message from Mars" 149
Meyer, Annie 120
Michelet, Jules 62
Micromégas 65
Midnight 171, 174
Million: The Magazine of Popular Fiction 8
Milton, John 52
Miss Brown 111, 115
Mitford, Jessica 157
Modern English Biography 81
Monk, Cummings King 28, 44-46, 49
Monroe, Marilyn 136
Monsieur de Phocas 26
Monstrous Regiment 184, 189-190, 197
Moorcock, Michael 128, 131, 133, 148
Moreau de Tours, Joseph 17
Morrow, James 11-12, 152-165
Mort 184, 187
Moskowitz, Sam 27
The Mount's Bay 82, 84
Moving Pictures 184, 189
Mr. Murder 169, 173-174
Mudford, William 55
Mundus Subterraneus 72
"The Murders in the Rue Morgue" 16, 24, 52
"The Mystery of Marie Roget" 24
Nader, Ralph 137
The National Library of Scotland 9
New Atlantis 65
Newman, Cardinal John Henry 44-45
The New Testament 34, 45
New Worlds 125-128, 131, 133-134, 142, 148
The New York Review of Science Fiction 9
Nichols, Leigh (Dean R. Koontz) 170
Nietzsche, Friedrich 28, 152
Night Chills 170
Nightmare Journey 169
Night Watch 184, 190
Niven, Larry 183
Nordau, Max 17
"Now, Zero" 127
"The Object of the Attack" 148-149
Odd Thomas 174, 176-181
"Ode on a Grecian Urn" 107
"Oke of Okehurst" 112-113, 119

The Old Testament 34, 40, 45, 73-74
Olga Romanoff 25
Oliphant, Mrs. 112
One Door Away from Heaven 170-171, 174-177, 179-181
Only You Can Save Mankind 185
Opening Minds 9
Orbitsville 183
The Origin of Species 73, 107
O'Sullivan, Vincent 13
Ottilie: An Eighteenth Century Idyl 110-111, 116, 118
"The Overloaded Man" 149
Paget, Henry Ferguson 108
"The Pale Ape" 46, 50
The Pale Ape and Other Pulses 7, 42-50
The Pall Mall Magazine 42
Panthea, the Spirit of Nature 10, 80-89, 94-107
Paradoxa: Studies in World Literary Genres 11
Partial Portraits 115
"Passport to Eternity" 124
Pasteur, Louis 78
Pater, Walter 15, 110-111, 116
Pathetic fallacy 18
Pearson, C. Arthur 15, 35
Pearson's Magazine 47
Peitho 20-21
Péladan, Joséphin 62
Pelham 53-54, 57-58
Pelham, Henry 57
Penelope Brandling 118
A Phantom Lover 112-113
The Phantom of the Opera 187
Phantoms 170
Philostratus 115
"Phorfor" 20-21
The Picture's Secret 112
Plato 139
Playboy 131
The Pleasure of Reading 124
Poe, Edgar Allan 8, 16-18, 23, 30, 45-47, 52, 73, 86
Poems and Transcripts 109
The Poetry of Science 10, 80-83, 85-94, 96, 98-100, 103, 105-106
Polidori, John 51
Pollock, Walter Herries 112
The Poor Artist 80
Pope Jacynth and Other Fantastic Tales 114, 117
Popular Romances of the West of England 81-84, 87, 101, 104-105
Popular Treatise on the Art of Photography 83
Possession 118
Les Posthumes 72
Pratchett, Terry 11, 182-197
Pratt, Fletcher 193

"Premier and Maker" 17, 19, 22, 43-44
"Prima Belladonna" 126
"Prince Alberic and the Snake Lady" 114-115, 119
The Prince of the Hundred Soups 110-111, 119
Prince Zaleski 7, 16, 22-32, 36, 42, 44-46
Pringle, David 148
"Project for a New Novel" 126
"Prometheus Unbound" 82, 105
Proteus; or, The Future of Intelligence 122
The Purple Cloud 7, 15, 21, 23, 32-41, 46
Pyramids 184, 188
Pytho 21
Python 21, 26
"Queen Mab" 92, 99, 105
Queensberry, Marquess of 13, 22, 43
The Rajah's Sapphire 22
"Ravenna and Her Ghosts" 117
Reading Gaol 13
Reaper Man 184, 187
The Redondan Cultural Foundation Newsletter 7
Renaissance Fancies and Studies 116
"Report on an Unidentified Space Station" 149
Researches, Chemical and Philosophical 66
Researches on Light and its Chemical Relations 83
Restif de la Bretonne, Nicholas 72
The Revolt of the Angels 156, 161
Reyka, Larry 160-161
Richards, Grant 114
Ride the Storm 174
Ringworld 183
Robert Hunt Memorial Museum 84
Robinson, Mary 120
Robinson Crusoe 139
Roden, Barbara & Christopher 10-11
Romanticism 8-10, 25, 52, 66, 82, 85-87, 114
Rosebery, Lord (Arthur Philip Primrose) 14-15, 22, 28, 43-44
Royal Cornwall Polytechnic Society 83
Royal Institution 66
The Royal Magazine 32
Royal School of Mines 83
Royal Society 66
Running Wild 144-147
Rushing to Paradise 145-146
Ruskin, John 116
Russell, Ray 7, 10
Sade, Marquis de 137
Sadleir, Michael 55, 62-63
St. Augustine 159
"St Eudaemon and His Orange Tree" 117
St. Leon 104
St. Paul 157

JAUNTING ON THE SCORIAC TEMPESTS, BY BRIAN STABLEFORD

Salem Press 7
Salisbury, Lord 14
Salmonia; or, Days of Fly-Fishing 66
Salome 113
Saranyu 19
Sargent, John Singer 113
Sartre, Jean-Paul 156
Satan the Waster: A Philosophic War Trilogy 120
Science-Fantasy 125-126, 182
Science, Life and Literature 13
Scientific Romance in Britain, 1890-1950 9
Scott, Sir Walter 101
Scribner's 11
"The Secret History of World War Three" 149
Secular Religions in France 1815-1870 160
"A Seeker of Pagan Perfection" 116
Seize the Night 174
Seneca 161, 164
"The Serpent-Ship" 20
Servants of the Twilight 168
Shadowfires 170
Shapes in the Fire 7, 13-22, 32, 42-44, 46, 48
Shattered 166, 170
Shaw, Bob 183
Shaw, George Bernard 45
Shelley, Mary 35
Shelley, Percy Bysshe 52, 82, 87, 89, 92, 99
Shiel, Matthew Phipps 7-8, 10, 13-50, 114
Sister Benevenuta and the Christ Child 117
Small Gods 184, 189
Smith, Thorne 195
Smith, William 21
Smythe, Colin 182
The Snake Lady and Other Stories 116
Socrates 45
Sole Survivor 174
Somnium 65
La Sorcière 62
Soul Music 184, 187
Sourcery 184, 186
Southey, Robert 66
"The Spectre-Ship" 43, 47-48
A Spectrum of Fantasy 80
Spencer, Stanley 140
Spielberg, Steven 142, 150
Spiritualism 73, 77
"The S.S." (The Society of Sparta) 27-30, 45
Star Quest 166
Stead, W. T. 22
Stenbock, Count Eric 13
Stevenson, Robert Louis 47

219

"Storm Bird, Storm Dreamer" 135
"Storm-Wind" 128-129
The Strand Magazine 24
The Strange Case of Dr Jekyll and Mr Hyde 47
Strange Highways 167, 171, 173
"Strange Highways" 173-174, 176-177
Strangers 170
Strange Story, A 62
Strata 182-183
Studies in the Eighteenth Century in Italy 109
Studies in the History of the Renaissance 110
"Studio 5, the Stars" 135
A Study in Scarlet 16, 23-24
Sue, Eugène 179
Sutherland, John 8
Suvin, Darko, 80
Swanson, Harriet (Harriet Hunt) 82, 84, 105
Swanson, Jane (Jane Hunt) 82
Swedenborg, Emanuel 72
Swift, Jonathan 173
Swinburne, Algernon 25, 53
The Symbolist Movement in Literature 13
Symons, Arthur 13, 25
Syphilis 17
"The Tale of Kosem Kesamim" 58-59
Tartarus Press 7, 10-11
Tennant, Emma 133
The Terminal Beach 130-131
"The Terminal Beach" 134, 142, 145-146, 150
Thief of Time 184, 188, 197
"A Third Hand" 169
This Knot of Life 13
Ticktock 169, 171
"The Time-Tombs" 127
"Today & Tomorrow" series 121-122
Todorov, Tzvetan 112
Tolkien, J. R. R. 182, 192, 194
"Tomorrow Is a Million Years" 135
Tonkin, John 65-66
The Tough Guide to Fantasyland 192
Towing Jehovah 153, 160
Toynbee, Arnold 158, 164
"Track 12" 127
Traditions, Legends and Superstitions of Devonshire 82
Truckers 184-185
The Truth 184, 189-190
"Tulsah" 19-20, 46
Turgenev, Ivan 113
 "Tuscan Peasant Plays" 108-109
Tuscan Fairy Tales 110
Twilight 168, 170

Twilight Eyes 170
"Twilight of the Dawn" 171
Ulysses 125
Under the Hill 119
University College, London 9
University of Reading 10
Unknown 193-195
The Unlimited Dream Company 140-141
"Vaila" 17-20, 48-49
Vanguard 32
Vanitas: Polite Stories 115
Varsity 124
"Venus Smiles" 135
Vermilion Sands 126, 135-136
Vernon Lee: Violet Paget 1856-1935 118
Victorian Science Fiction in the UK 80
Villiers de l'Isle Adam, Comte de 47
"The Violent Noon" 124
"The Virgin of the Seven Daggers" 114-116, 119
The Vision 170-171
Vital Lies 119
Voice of the Night 170
"The Voices of Time" 128, 131, 142, 150
Voltaire 65, 164
Waite. A. E. 62
"The Waiting Grounds" 127-128
Walford, Edward 107
Walpole, Horace 51, 57
War Fever 149
"War Fever" 149
Warlock 169
Watchers 169-171
Watson, Dr. John 16
Waugh, Evelyn 157
"Wayward Love" 46
"A Wedding Chest" 117
The Wee Free Men 184, 187, 191
Weird Tales 193
Wells, H. G. 45, 106-107, 119
Western Attitudes Towards Death 158
Western Daily Herald 182
Wharton, Edith 112
Wheeler, Rosina 55, 60
Whispers 170
"Why I Want to Fuck Ronald Reagan" 137
"A Wicked Voice" 112-114
Wilde, Oscar 7, 13-14, 18-19, 22, 25, 29, 42-44, 51, 53, 110, 113-116
Wilson, William 9, 80, 85, 89, 107
The Wind from Nowhere 128-129
Wings 185
"Winthrop's Adventure" 113, 122

Witches Abroad 184, 187, 191
Wollheim, Donald A. 130
Wormwood Scrubs 13
Writing Popular Fiction 173
Wyndham, John 128-129
Wyrd Sisters 184, 187
"Xélucha" 17, 19-20, 46
Yama 19
The Yellow Book 113-114
The Yellow Danger 14-15, 32
Yesterday's Bestsellers 8
You and Me and the Continuum 126
The Young Men are Coming 38, 45
Zanoni 54, 58, 60-61, 85
Zicci 58